REACHING THE RURAL POOR

A RENEWED STRATEGY FOR RURAL DEVELOPMENT

THE WORLD BANK

CONTENTS

FOREWORD

Today three out of every four of the world's poor live in rural areas. There will be no success in the war on poverty unless we take the fight to where those people live. Yet, over the last decade lending to rural development, and especially to agriculture, has been in unprecedented decline – both at the World Bank and among our development partners. This situation cannot continue. We must renew our focus on agriculture and rural development. The new rural development strategy presented in this document outlines our 'battle-plan' for such a renewed focus, and our commitment to reverse the downward trend in rural lending.

The core of our new rural development strategy consists of a commitment to: a) focus on those that are the most disadvantaged – the rural poor; b) address rural areas in their entirety and promote broad-based rural growth and service provision both on- and off-farm; c) forge alliances with all stakeholders – with the rural poor, with governments, civil society, academics, international organizations and leaders, and with the business community; and d) refine our approach to respond to changes in the ever-evolving global arena that have a direct impact upon our clients – including changes in trade policies, climate, agricultural science, and technology.

The World Bank's new strategy draws upon the lessons of our past experience and on From Vision to Action, our previous strategy published in 1997. Preparation for the new strategy began with the very people we hope to reach – the rural poor. We developed regional action plans and engaged in extensive dialogue with our clients, civil society organizations, the business community, academics, other international agencies and policy leaders. We identified much that has changed in the global arena as a result of the ongoing process of globalization. What we have learned from our development partners in this process has been distilled into this strategy. We are pleased that during the development of this strategy we have witnessed the beginnings of a new commitment to rural and agricultural development in the international community as a whole. This revitalized commitment was amplified when more than 100 world leaders met at the World Summit for Sustainable Development in September 2002 and pledged to make rural development a priority. We share in this commitment.

In addition to highlighting the need for our client countries to continue their reform agendas and give greater emphasis to rural development, we also recognize the need for policy change within the developed world. The livelihood of most rural inhabitants in our client countries is connected to agriculture, directly through farming, or indirectly through activities such agro-processing, marketing, and providing services or inputs. Thus, increasing agricultural productivity in those countries is critical to achieving rural economic growth and poverty reduction. Protection of the agricultural sector in OECD countries creates significant barriers to agricultural exports from our client countries, and hampers their ability to grow their way out of poverty through increased agricultural production.

We recognize that success in rural development will require agreement among, and active support by, governments, civil society, and the private sector in both developed and developing countries. We must work together. We will assist our clients to develop their own national rural development strategies. These will be built from the ground up, enabling the rural poor to identify their own priorities and action plans. These strategies will provide critical input to the articulation of the country's poverty reduction strategy, and inform the broader policy dialogue between the Bank and our clients in terms of country assistance strategies.

Among our development partners, the Bank will promote a Global Forum for Rural Development to ensure renewed attention to agriculture and rural development. The forum will serve as a focal point for action and advocacy, for analytical and policy work, for coordination, and co-financing. The goal will be to keep agriculture and rural development at the heart of the development agenda until we have won the war against rural poverty.

James D. Wolfensohn
President
The World Bank

ACKNOWLEDGMENTS

Preparation of Reaching the Rural Poor was overseen by the Rural Sector Board of the World Bank, chaired by Robert L. Thompson, followed by Kevin M. Cleaver, Directors of Agriculture and Rural Development Department (ARD). Messrs. Thompson and Cleaver, together with Ms. Sushma Ganguly (ARD Sector Manager) provided guidance throughout the preparation process. All members of the Agriculture and Rural Development Sector Board actively contributed: Joseph Baah-Dwomoh (Africa Region), Mark D. Wilson (East Asia and Pacific Region), Laura Tuck (Europe and Central Asia Region), Mark E. Cackler (Latin America and Caribbean Region), Petros Aklilu (Middle East and North Africa Region), Ridwan Ali (South Asia Region), Jean-Paul Pinard, (International Finance Corporation), Francisco J. Reifschneider (Consultative Group on International Agricultural Research), Gershon Feder (Development Economics), Ridley Nelson (Operations Evaluation Department), Michele E. de Nevers (World Bank Institute).

Csaba Csaki (ARD) managed the Bank-wide rural strategy update process and the preparation of Reaching the Rural Poor. He is the principal author of this document, with significant input from Cornelis de Haan (ARD). The Core Strategy Drafting Group also included Jock Anderson (ARD), Harold Alderman (ARD), Malcolm Bale (EAP), Shawki Barghouti (ARD), Derek Byerlee (ARD), Gershon Feder (DEC), Antonio Nucifora (ARD), Eija Pehu (ARD), Felicity Proctor (ARD), Mona Sur (ARD), Eugene Terry (ARD), Wallace Tyner (Purdue University), Cornelis van der Meer (ARD), and Alan Zuschlag (ARD). Material for specific sections of the strategy document was received from Sanjiva Cooke (ARD), Louise Cord (PREMPO), Abdel-Dayem Safwat (ARD), Ariel Dinar (ARD), Merlinda Ingco (ARD), Christina Malmberg-Calvo (TUD), John Nash (ARD), Nwanze Okidegbe (ARD), Andrea Pape-Christiansen (ARD), Patrick Verissimo (WBI), Melissa Williams (ARD), and Jacob Yaron (ARD).

Regional Teams which organized the strategy update process at the regional level and prepared the regional strategies and action plans included: Karen Brooks, Ernst Lutz (AFR); Laura Tuck, Marjorie-Anne Bromhead (ECA); Malcolm Bale, Angela Chen (EAP); Mark Cackler, Luis Coirolo, Isabelle Tsakok, Adolfo Brizzi (LCR); Petros Aklilu, M. Salah Darghouth, Douglas W. Lister (MNA); and Ridwan Ali, Dina Umali-Deininger, Jeeva Perumalpillai, Manish Bapna (SAR).

Technical coordination of the rural strategy update process was undertaken by a Steering Committee composed of the ARD Core Team members as well as the members of the Regional Teams listed above. Additional members of the Steering Committee include: Odin Knudsen (ESSDVP); John Heath (OED); Lynn Brown, Christin Cogley, Fernando Gonzales, Jason Jacques Paiement, Roland Schurmann (ARD); and Philippe Dongier (SD).

General guidance was provided by the ESSD Council, chaired by ESSD Vice President Ian Johnson, and included: Richard Ackerman (SAR); Hans Binswanger, Roger Sullivan (AFR); Kevin Cleaver, Jane Holt (ECA); Zafer Ecevit (EAP); Doris Koehn, Salah Dargouth (MNA); John Redwood, and Teresa Serra (LCR). Of the Council members, Kevin Cleaver (prior to his appointment as Director of ARD) and Hans Binswanger provided direct input in the strategy formulation.

Internal and external peer reviewers provided valuable comments at several stages in the drafting process. They include: Alain de Janvry (University of California - Berkeley), Geoffrey Fox (Consultant), Stanley Johnson (Iowa State University), Joachim von Braun (University of Bonn), Simon Maxwell (ODI), and Bruno Vindel (Ministre des Affaires Etrangers, France).

Marisela Montoliu-Munoz, (OPCS); John Todd, (SRM); Ridley Nelson, John Heath (OED); Odin

Knudsen, Rita Hilton (ESDVP); Steen Jorgensen (SD); Jim Douglas (ARD); Magda Lovei (ENV); Keith Oblitas (SAR); David Forbes-Watt, Andrew McMillan, Maximiliano Cox (FAO), Manfred Shultze (Free University of Berlin), Holger Kray (Consultant), Derek Poate, Doug Smith (ITAD); all provided thoughtful comments, advice, and input to the strategy.

Editorial support in the drafting of this document was coordinated by Alan Zuschlag with assistance from Wallace Tyner, Antonio Nucifora, Andrea Pape-Christiansen, Andrew Goodland, and Nadine Hasevoets-Tarwater. Administrative support for the strategy update was provided by Christin Cogley and Joyce Sabaya. The graphic design, layout, and typesetting of this volume was done by Patricia Hord Graphik Design.

A series of consultations held in 2001-2002 in all six Bank regions provided an opportunity for local organizations and individuals from national governments, the private sector, NGOs, and academia to contribute the revised corporate strategy, and ensured that the Bank, its clients, and fellow donor agencies were in agreement on the focus of the regional strategies. Many other organizations and individuals outside the Bank contributed to the organization of the regional consultations, and provided constructive oral and written comments. Because of space constraints it is not possible to acknowledge all of them individually, but their contributions were invaluable.

A detailed portfolio analysis, and background studies on global and regional issues, were completed to support the strategy update process. The titles of these studies and their authors are listed in the bibliography of this strategy. The FAO has undertaken a study to provide an agricultural focus to Reaching the Rural Poor. The overall results are summarized in a joint FAO-World Bank book Farming Systems and Poverty: Improving Farmers' Livelihoods in a Changing World by John Dixon, Aidan Gulliver, and David Gibbon.

The Bank would also like to thank the governments of the Netherlands (Bank Netherlands Partnership Program), the United Kingdom (DFID), France, Germany, and Greece for their financial support for the preparation of the strategy and which made the regional consultations possible.

ACRONYMS AND DEFINITIONS

AAA	Analytical and Advisory Activities
AfDB	African Development Bank
ADB	Asian Development Bank
AFR	Africa Region
AI	Agricultural Irrigation
AIDS	Acquired Immunodeficiency Syndrome
APL	Adaptable Program Loans
ARD	Agriculture and Rural Development Department
AusAID	Australian Aid Agency
BB	Bank Budget
BNPP	Bank-Netherlands Partnership Program
CAS	Country Assistance Strategy
CBO	Community Based Organizations
CEM	Country Economic Memorandum
CDD	Community Driven Development
CDF	Comprehensive Development Framework
CGA	Country Gender Assessment
CGIAR	Consultative Group on International Agricultural Research
CSO	Civil Society Organization
DEC	Development Economics and Chief Economist
DFID	Department for International Development
EAP	East Asia and Pacific Region
EBRD	European Bank for Reconstruction and Development
EC	European Commission
ECA	Eastern Europe and Central Asia Region
ESSD	Environmentally and Socially Sustainable Development
ESW	Economic and Sector Work
EU	European Union
FAO	Food and Agriculture Organization
FAO/CP	Food and Agriculture Organization Cooperative Program (with the World Bank)
FDI	Foreign Direct Investment
FPSI	Finance and Private Sector Infrastructure
FY	Financial Year
GDP	Gross Domestic Product
GEF	Global Environment Facility
GTZ	Gesellschaft fuer Technische Zusammenarbeit (German Aid Agency)
HACCP	Hazard Analysis Critical Control Point
HD	Human Development
HDI	Human Development Index
HIPC	Highly Indebted Poor Countries
HIV	Human Immunodeficiency Virus
IADB	Inter-American Development Bank
IBRD	International Bank for Reconstruction and Development
ICSID	International Center for Settlement of Investment Disputes
ICR	Implementation Completion Report

ICT	Information and Communications Technology
IDA	International Development Agency
IFAD	International Fund for Agricultural Development
IFC	International Finance Corporation
IFI	International Financial Institution
IFPRI	International Food Policy Research Institute
IITA	International Institute for Tropical Agriculture
IMF	International Monetary Fund
IPM	Integrated Pest Management
LIL	Learning and Innovation Loans
LCR	Latin America and Caribbean Region
MDG	Millennium Development Goals
MIGA	Multilateral Investment Guarantee Agency
MIS	Management Information System
MNA	Middle East and North Africa Region
NARS	National Agricultural Research System
NGO	Non-Governmental Organization
NRM	Natural Resource Management
ODA	Overseas Development Assistance
OECD	Organization for Economic Cooperation and Development
OED	Operation Evaluation Department
OP	Operational Policy
OPC	Operations Policy and Country Services
OPCS	Operations Policy and Care Services
PA	Poverty Assessment
PAD	Project Appraisal Document
PAL	Programmatic Adjustment Lending
PCD	Project Concept Document
PER	Public Expenditure Review
PPF	Project Preparation Facility
PREM	Poverty Reduction and Economic Management
PRSC	Poverty Reduction Support Credit
PRSP	Poverty Reduction Strategy Paper
PTI	Program of Targeted Interventions
QAG	Quality Assurance Group
QER	Quality Enhancement Review
R&D	Research and Development
RFI	Rural Financial Institution
RNFE	Rural Non-Farm Economy
RPO	Rural Producers' Organization
S&T	Science and Technology
SAC	Structural Adjustment Credit
SAL	Structural Adjustment Lending
SAP	Software Administration Program
SAR	South Asia Region
SDP	Strategic Direction Paper
SDV	Social Development Department
SECAL	Sectoral Adjustment Loan
SFP	Strategic Framework Paper

SIL	Sector Investment Loan
SME	Small/Medium Sized Enterprise
SPS	Sanitary and Phytosanitary
SSA	Sub-Saharan Africa
TF	Trust Funds
VtoA	From Vision to Action
VPU	Vice-Presidential Unit
UNAIDS	Joint United Nations Programme on HIV/AIDS
URAA	Uruguay Round Agreement on Agriculture
USAID	United States Agency for International Development
WBG	World Bank Group
WBI	World Bank Institute
WDR	World Development Report
WIRPI	World Bank – IFAD Rural Partnership Initiative
WTO	World Trade Organization
WUA	Water Users' Association

Throughout this report, except where otherwise noted, the term "agriculture" includes all agriculturally related Bank activities (including agricultural adjustment, agricultural research and extension, agricultural credit, agro-industry and marketing, community based rural development, livestock, fisheries and aquaculture, forestry, agency reform, and perennial and annual crops). "Rural development" includes agriculture plus all other investment activities in the rural space, including natural resource management, rural transport, water and sanitation, telecommunications, education, health and other social services. "Rural space" refers to the geographic area, including small towns designated by each country as rural.

xi

EXECUTIVE SUMMARY

More than a half century of persistent efforts by the World Bank and others have not altered the stubborn reality of rural poverty, and the gap between rich and poor is widening. Most of the world's poorest people still live in rural areas and this will continue for the foreseeable future. The day when the goals for international development will be met is still far off in many parts of the world.

What is more, with globalization, the "poverty challenge is getting bigger and harder," according to World Bank President James D. Wolfensohn. "Many of the benefits of an increasingly interconnected and interdependent global economy have bypassed the least developed countries, while some of the risks—of financial instability, communicable disease, and environmental degradation—have extracted a great price."

FROM VISION TO PRACTICE: THE CASE FOR A REVITALIZED STRATEGY

From Vision to Action, the Bank's previous rural development strategy launched in 1997, had a decisive influence on global thinking—but disappointing results on the ground. In 2001 lending for agricultural projects was the lowest in the World Bank's history (box 1).

The new strategy is results oriented. *Reaching the Rural Poor* stresses practice, implementation, monitoring, and empowerment of the people it is designed to help. The strategy responds to changes in:

- **The global environment** – changes brought about by the forces of globalization and persistent trade distortions

- **Client countries** – challenges of unfinished policy reforms, decentralization, institutional development, poor governance, the expanding roles of the private sector and civil society, and proliferating national and regional conflicts

- **The World Bank** – to apply the lessons learned in the past four to five years while implementing *From Vision to Action*. Work on *Reaching the Rural Poor* began in mid 2000. Starting with the development of regional action plans and extensive consultations at the regional level, the new strategy was designed to respond to the local circumstances and needs of the people who have the greatest stake in its implementation (box 2). Regionally drafted strategies became the framework for the new corporate strategy. This process was followed by intensive dialogs with individuals and with international, national, and local organizations.

Reaching the Rural Poor also reflects and reinforces the Bank's commitment to the UN Millennium Development Goals (www.developmentgoals.org), which will be met only through increases in rural incomes and broadened opportunities for rural inhabitants. The strategy assigns great weight to developing, establishing, and supporting appropriate implementation and monitoring mechanisms and processes at the national, regional and international levels.

Recent Bank Operations in Rural Areas

Rural investment is under-represented in the World Bank's lending. The Bank's lending to rural areas in Fiscal Years 1999–2001 amounted to a total of US$15 billion (about $5 billion annually). This represents around 25 percent of the Bank's total lending and therefore is not congruent with the greater incidence of poverty in rural areas. Figures from Fiscal Year 2002 (FY02) show that this situation has not changed. The situation is particularly acute for agricultural lending, which has declined markedly over the past 20 years, both absolutely and as a proportion of total Bank lending. Of the US$5 billion lending to rural areas in FY02, total investment in the agriculture sector (including agro-industry and markets) was US$1.5 billion. This equates to just 7.9 percent of total Bank lending, whereas in the early 1980s it accounted for more than 30 percent.

a. The term "rural areas" as used throughout this publication includes small and medium sized towns, according to the national definitions. Investment in rural areas covers investments in all sectors (agriculture, natural resource management, rural transport, water and sanitation, telecommunications, education, health, and other social services).

THE KEY FEATURES OF *REACHING THE RURAL POOR*

Reaching the Rural Poor will revitalize World Bank activities in rural areas by adjusting the strategic framework and formulating a program of concrete and attainable actions. The strategy calls for raising the profile of rural development efforts and extending Bank endeavors to reach the rural poor. The strategy:

- Focuses on the rural poor
- Fosters broad-based economic growth
- Addresses rural areas comprehensively
- Forges alliances of all stakeholders
- Addresses the impact of global developments on client countries

Focusing on the Rural Poor

Who are the rural poor? Where do they live? What challenges does poverty pose in their respective localities? Answers to these questions are the basis for an effective rural development strategy. The rural poor include the landless, individuals and households with few assets, smallholders, pastoralists, rural women (especially women-headed households); ethnic minorities, and indigenous populations. The rural poor are not a homogeneous group. Understanding the needs of such different groups is central to the success of the Bank's new strategy.

Fostering Broad-Based Economic Growth

Reaching the Rural Poor makes broad-based economic growth its primary objective. Rural poverty is as diverse as are the rural poor in their livelihood strategies, but in most of the poorest developing countries agriculture is the main source of rural economic growth. That is why improved agricultural productivity and growth are central to the Bank's strategy for reducing poverty. At the same time, the Bank recognizes the importance of nonfarm economic activities in rural development, so their promotion is another key feature.

Addressing Rural Areas in Their Entirety

To reduce rural poverty, the Bank must work with clients to address rural areas in their entirety—all of rural society and every economic, social, and environmental aspect of rural development. Past approaches identified most pieces of the puzzle but failed to put them together in a way that attained objectives. Sustainable rural development requires multidisciplinary and pluralistic approaches to poverty reduction, social and gender equity, local economic development, natural resource management, and good governance. The Bank is moving away from short-term, sector-by-sector approaches and toward coherent cross-sectoral approaches for the sustained reduction of rural poverty.

While the poor have much in common with each other wherever they live, rural areas are distinctly different from urban ones. For this reason, the approaches in addressing the needs of the rural and the urban poor must be tailored specifically to each group. However, the Bank's rural strategy recognizes that urban and rural areas are inextricably linked in the process of development and that the strategy must take into account the diverse range of interactions between urban and rural economies

Reaching the Rural Poor: The Consultative Process — 2

More than 2,000 people (government officials, civil society, nongovernmental organizations, academics, private sector, and donor agencies) were involved in the consultations for the rural strategy. Consultations involved four major stages:

- Consultations on the regional strategies and the initial framework of the corporate strategy. Eleven regional consultations were held in early 2001 (Nepal, Philippines, China, Lebanon, France, Kenya, Senegal, Russia, Panama, Belgium, and Japan).

- Consultations and seminars focused on the corporate strategy and its implementation. In 2002 a series of consultations and seminars on implementation were held in countries including Vietnam, Nigeria, and Ethiopia and at regional development banks.

- Presentations, seminars and panel discussions at major international gatherings with broad-based stakeholder participation. These venues included the International Food Policy Research Institute 2020 Conference in 2001, and in 2002, the Food and Agriculture Organization Council Meeting, the United Nations Conference on Financing for Development, the United Nations PrepComm for the World Summit on Sustainable Development, the European Sustainable Development Conference, the 35th World Farmer Congress, the World Food Summit—Five Years Later, and the European Rural Development Forum.

- Rural strategy website and internet consultations on the final draft of the strategy. A website was created early in the strategy-development process with drafts and all relevant material posted for comment. Numerous comments were received from academics, civil society groups, donors, governments, nongovernmental organizations, and private individuals.

xv

when crafting future development efforts. As development progresses, all countries undergo a transition from a predominantly rural to a more heavily urban economy. Urban and rural areas are a continuum, but they are also internally heterogeneous.

Forging Alliances of All Stakeholders

To broaden stakeholder participation in project and program design and implementation, the Bank is working with clients to overcome the shortcomings of earlier top-down, non-inclusive approaches. The Bank will work with others (governments, development agencies, civil society, private sector, academia) in a broad-based global coalition to make the reduction of rural poverty a major thrust for the coming decade. Through enhanced partnerships and other linkages, the development community will increase advocacy for rural development and share experiences in best practices and innovation.

Addressing the Impact of Global Developments on Client Countries

The process of globalization has brought about a "shrinkage" of spatial distance and a lowering of transaction costs that has resulted in growing interdependence of the world's economies, markets, and people. Globalization encompasses more open international trade in goods and financial services, growth of multinational companies, more uniform labor and environmental standards, and growing global sourcing in supply chains. This expanded market in goods, services, and information provides new opportunities for rural development and poverty reduction. But globalization and economic liberalization carry risks as well as opportunities and create losers as well as winners. Finding ways to harness the growth opportunities while managing risks and compensating losers is a challenge for policymakers everywhere. *Reaching the Rural Poor* reflects the World Bank's increased emphasis on helping countries meet these challenges, addressing global issues such as international trade policy, subsidization of agriculture, and global climate change.

THE STRATEGIC OBJECTIVES OF *REACHING THE RURAL POOR*

The Bank's objectives in rural poverty reduction, and for rural development in general, are geared to helping clients accelerate economic growth so that it is shared by the poor. The strategy therefore focuses on:

- Fostering an enabling environment for broad-based and sustainable rural growth
- Enhancing agricultural productivity and competitiveness

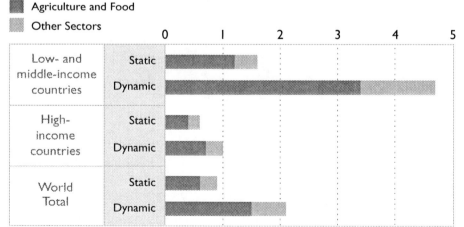

Figure 1: Potential Gains from Full Multilateral Trade Liberalization (percentage of income)

Note: Static gains refer to results holding productivity constant. Dynamic gains allow productivity to respond to sector-specific export-to-output ratios.
Source: World Bank, 2001f.

- Fostering nonfarm economic growth
- Improving social well-being, managing and mitigating risk, and reducing vulnerability
- Enhancing the sustainability of natural resource management.

Fostering an Enabling Environment for Broad-Based and Sustainable Rural Growth

An appropriate macroeconomic policy environment and a supportive institutional framework are essential to growth and poverty reduction and for the success of World Bank supported activities in the rural sector.

World-wide trade policy reform. Because so many of the poor derive their livelihood directly or indirectly from agriculture, developing countries have a huge stake in the full integration of agriculture under multilateral trade rules. A major reason both for the limited growth of agricultural trade and for the inability of developing countries to enlarge their share of this trade is high protection in the large markets of the industrial world. High subsidies and other forms of trade protection impair developing countries' ability to compete in global markets with farmers from the industrial world. They also encourage surpluses that have been sold on world markets, depressing world prices and undermining the potential contribution of agriculture to global prosperity.

The potential economic welfare benefits of global agricultural trade reform for the developing world are estimated at US$140 billion annually. For the developing countries, the impact of agricultural trade liberalization by the industrial countries alone amounted to more than 50 percent of the official development assistance given to developing countries in 2001 (figure 1). These countries are the developing world's largest potential market for agricultural products. Considering the potential for significant increases in income in developing countries from agricultural trade, it is crucial that the industrial countries liberalize their agricultural markets by removing trade barriers to open market access for developing countries' products and by phasing out subsidies.

Bulgaria: Agricultural Sector Adjustment Loans I and II

3

Bulgaria elected a new government in 1997 with a strong commitment to market reform. The government eliminated export bans and controls on profit margins on agriculture and food products, eliminated most import quotas and duties on cereals, and liberalized markets. The Bulgarian adjustment program had the full support of the elected government and Parliament.

World Bank provided sector adjustment loans were designed to promote efficiency in the agricultural sector, generate rural jobs, raise living standards, and enlarge consumer choice by:

- Promoting a land market, including restitution of 80 percent of the designated land area and enactment of several administrative measures to facilitate land transactions

- Developing a private grain market by privatizing the grain marketing agency and limiting the state grain reserves to agreed amounts

- Privatizing state agricultural enterprises, including agreed numbers of grain mills, seed, and food industries

- Privatizing irrigation systems through decentralization by transferring management of operation and maintenance to water user associations on at least 100,000 hectares

- Improving agricultural financing according to agreed criteria

- Liberalizing trade in most agricultural products

- Improving forest legislation and increasing community-based participation in forest management.

The World Bank will continue to assist its clients in improving their own trade policies using the system of multilateral trade rules to expand their trade, thereby enhancing their development prospects. The Bank's comparative advantage is that it can combine trade policy analyses with significant expertise for a comprehensive view of the ways agricultural trade liberalization, globalization, and market integration can promote growth and rural development. This capacity can be used to support better agricultural and trade policies through:

- Increased advocacy for trade liberalization in both industrial and developing countries

- Mainstreaming agricultural trade liberalization and trade-capacity development in the Bank's country assistance and operations
- Facilitating capacity building through technical assistance and training on trade-related issues
- Increased assistance in the area of standards and sanitary and phytosanitary regulations
- Conducting analytical work at both global and country levels to identify key areas for future policy reform.

---

4 Latvia: Agricultural Development Project and Rural Development Project

Latvia's emerging private rural economy has received support from the Agricultural Development Project (ADP) and the Rural Development Project (RDP).

No commercial banks in Latvia were interested in serving small private farmers when ADP was launched in Fiscal Year (FY) 1994. The Agricultural Finance Company (AFC) was set up with a squad of mobile credit officers who took financial services to the farmers instead of waiting for them to come to a site, often far away. The idea of "taking the bank to the clients" eased farmers' transportation problems. In four years, with only 42 staff members, AFC approved US$43 million for 2,860 subloans, with high repayment rates at around 93 percent. The loans were offered at market interest rates in the local currency, Lat, and U.S. dollars. The AFC, now merged with a commercial bank in Latvia, continues to serve the rural population.

The RDP supports a wide variety of rural entrepreneurs. Approved in FY98, the project was directed at helping the government build its rural policymaking capacity in preparation for membership in the European Union. One of the RDP's innovations was the "special credit line" with a government bonus of a matching grant for small farmers and rural entrepreneurs borrowing for the first time. First-time borrowers received a small portion of the loan as a bonus after they had fully repaid their loan. Some 1,300 of these small loans have been made, each for a maximum of US$4,000 equivalent. Most of these loans went to rural, nonfarm entrepreneurs—tourist services, hairdressers, tailors, doctors, and other service providers—and only 20 percent to farmers. Repayment performance is outstanding at around 98 percent. The RDP also successfully introduced participatory approaches to rural development by creating Local Action Groups. Two group leaders received a United Nations Award of Excellence for community-led development.

Sound policy environment in developing countries. The developing countries, too, have work to do if they want to gain long-run benefits from trade liberalization. Their domestic policies must allow domestic producers to respond to changing domestic and foreign conditions. The World Bank will continue to assist its clients in their efforts to improve their own policy environment for rural development and thereby enhance their development prospects (box 3). The nature and degree of the reforms will be influenced by the extent of agricultural trade and subsidy reform in the industrial countries. The Bank's policy agenda will focus on:

- Improving the macroeconomic framework for agricultural and rural growth by correcting remaining biases in the macroeconomic environment
- Espousing the principles of nondiscriminatory taxation and reform credibility in both theory and practice
- Supporting an enabling policy environment for agricultural trade and market access by reducing trade barriers and anti-export bias in order to promote growth in agricultural trade, by widening access to foreign markets, by reducing protection for nonagricultural goods, and by developing policies to minimize the effects of declines in world commodity prices on farmers
- Introducing sound food and agricultural policies; supporting the development of effective markets for agricultural inputs, outputs, and services; removing obstacles to effective market operations
- Designing and targeting safety nets that directly protect the poor, particularly rural dwellers
- Assisting in the establishment of complementary legal and regulatory frameworks that support private enterprises
- Improving the operation of land markets and land administration, promoting land reform for countries with inequitable land distribution, and promoting equal access to secure land holding, especially by women.

Good governance and institutions. Good governance and institutions are indispensable for sound rural development; poor governance inhibits development. Overcentralized institutional structures characteristic of many government administrative systems also sap the effectiveness of development investments and policies. That is why, based on empirical evidence, the Bank has made institutional reform central to its new strategy.

In the decentralization process, local governments must be given sufficient fiscal resources to discharge their new responsibilities. Political decentralization is also necessary, as it promotes accountability and governance reforms at the local level. This is especially important for rural areas because most rural people have had a weak political voice at the national level.

The Bank will encourage governments to concentrate on: providing public goods; establishing legal, administrative, and regulatory systems that correct for market failures; facilitating efficient operation of the private sector; and protecting the interests of the disadvantaged. Decentralization offers great scope for improving delivery of public sector functions. Facilitating further decentralization in rural areas is an important part of the policy agenda outlined in the strategy. To promote the development of effective institutions for rural development, the Bank will support:

- Strengthening of local administrative capacity
- Transfer of responsibility for services to the administrative level closest to the users
- Enhanced accountability for public administration at every level
- Participatory approaches, including increased political space and participation in decision-making bodies for women
- Economies of scale in government functions
- Appropriate private sector involvement in the delivery of public services, with public accountability.

Rural financial services. To achieve broad-based economic growth and reduce vulnerability, people and enterprises in rural areas need access to financial services. Many developing countries have no formal financial institutions to provide services. Supply-driven agricultural credit has proven unsustainable and unsuccessful and is no longer supported by the Bank, although many countries still use it.

To ensure new and innovative approaches, the Bank will strengthen its support for the development of financial products and institutions that fill the special needs of poor rural clients. This will include financial instruments for income generation and reduction of financial risk and recognize the multiplicity of potential delivery mechanisms, suppliers, and users of rural financial services (box 4). To this end, the Bank will:

- Continue to expand its menu of instruments in rural finance and test them for effectiveness, replicability, and sustainability
- Continue to support provision of credit to farm and rural nonfarm enterprises where market failures inhibit the flow of liquidity, while observing sound market development approaches and discipline in financial intermediation
- Work to narrow gaps in knowledge about the relation between financial services and poverty.

The Agricultural Growth – Poverty Reduction Connection 5

- A 1 percent increase in agricultural GDP per capita led to a 1.6 percent gain in the per capita incomes of the poorest one fifth of the population in 35 countries analyzed.[a]

- A 10 percent increase in crop yields led to a reduction of between 6 percent and 10 percent in the number of people living on less than US$1 a day.[b] In Africa, a 10 percent increase in yields resulted in a 9 percent decrease in the same income group.

- Wheat prices would have risen 34 percent, and rice prices 41 percent, more between 1970 and 1995 in the absence of international agricultural research.

- The average real income of small farmers in southern India rose by 90 percent and that of landless laborers by 125 percent in 1973–1984, as a result of the "Green Revolution."[c]

Sources: a. C.P. Timmer, 1997. How Well Do the Poor Connect to the Growth Process, Consulting Assistance on Economic Reform Discussion Paper 178 (Cambridge, Mass.: Harvard Institute for International Development); b. Irz , L. Lin, C. Thirtle, and S. Wiggins, "Agricultural Productivity Growth and Poverty Alleviation," Development Policy Review 19(4): (2001); c. P. Hazell and C. Ramasamy, 1991. The Green Revolution Reconsidered: The Impact of High-Yielding Rice Varieties in South India (Baltimore, Md.: Johns Hopkins University Press).

xix

Enhancing Agricultural Productivity and Competitiveness

With so many poor rural residents and changes in the agricultural sector—compounded by the deteriorating natural resource base—agriculture has never been more important than it is today in achieving Bank goals. International experience has demonstrated the direct relation between agricultural growth and rural poverty reduction (box 5). Agricultural development also induces economic growth in other rural sectors by generating demand for inputs and providing materials for processing and marketing industries. Future Bank activities will therefore focus on:

- Providing an enabling policy and institutional environment to foster agricultural growth
- Supporting sustainable intensification of production through the use of new technologies
- Enhancing the quality of food produced
- Encouraging, partly through demand-driven extension services, more efficient use of farm inputs and reduction of post-harvest losses

- Increasing the productivity of water use
- Supporting agricultural diversification, especially into high-value products
- Strengthening farmer-to-market linkages
- Enhancing food safety and addressing competitiveness through quality control and supply chain management
- Applying differentiated strategies to fit various farm types
- Supporting the development of physical and services infrastructure.

A Refocused Agenda for Agriculture

The new agenda set by this strategy expands and refocuses the Bank's existing support program for agriculture with a number of important new features. These include shifting the emphasis from:

- a narrow agricultural focus to a broader policy context—including global factors;
- a focus on crop and livestock yields to market demands and incomes;
- staples to high value crops;
- primary production to the entire food chain;
- a single farm type approach to heterogeneity;
- public to public-private partnerships, including community driven development;
- avoidance of issues to a head on approach (biotechnology, forestry, water).

Policy and institutions. *Reaching the Rural Poor* treats agriculture as the leading productive sector within the rural economy and closely linked to nonfarm activities. The strategy recognizes that the production of staple foods is the main source of income for many poor rural households, but that—to get out of the poverty trap—they must diversify into livestock, higher value crops, and nonfarm activities. The Bank's experience has shown that agricultural investments are more effective if set within appropriate policy and institutional environments with adequate infrastructure and market development. In their design, future Bank–supported activities in agriculture will incorporate successful aspects of the lessons learned (box 6).

Agricultural science and new technology. Beyond providing an enabling policy and institutional environment, Bank support for agriculture

---

6 Underlying Factors of Success in Agricultural Development

- Policies must neither discriminate against agriculture nor give it special privileges. This means, for example, that agriculture should be taxed lightly, using the same progressivity and instruments as for other sectors.
- The economy should be open, employment-sensitive, and oriented toward smallholders.
- The importance of external markets, including specialty and niche markets, should be fully recognized and exploited.
- Foreign direct investment should be recognized as an integral part of the agricultural development process.
- Land reform is essential where land is very unequally distributed.
- Rapid technological progress is needed, and both the private and public sectors have important roles in research, extension, and financing.
- Rural areas need substantial investment in education, health, and infrastructure, such as roads.
- The needs of women——a neglected group of farmers and farm laborers——must be built into programs.

will stress sustainable intensification through the application of science. Since most high potential agricultural areas have reached the limits of their exploitable land and water resources, much of their future growth in productivity depends on inputs of knowledge. Public and private investments in science and technology will receive continued Bank support. The Bank will also invite global policy dialog to ensure fair access to new technologies and will continue to provide leadership and financing to the system operated by the Consultative Group on International Agricultural Research (CGIAR), a major provider of international public goods in agriculture. The Bank remains committed to helping developing countries assess, explore, and safely use biotechnology and other new technologies and to promote environmentally sustainable pest management systems (box 7).

Agricultural extension services. To bring new technology to farmers, agricultural extension services are crucial and can also play an important role in delivering information on rural development, business development, and marketing. In the poorest countries, government will have a role in financing extension. Elsewhere, the private sector, nongovernmental organizations, and universities can compete to provide extension services subject to periodic review by local institutions.

Water productivity. Water is becoming a scarce and precious commodity, and agriculture is a major user. Getting "more crop per drop" is therefore essential. Future investment priorities for agricultural water use will concentrate on making existing systems more productive, because irrigation management is often poor and the potential for constructing new irrigation systems is limited. This will require: ensuring the integrity of infrastructure, for example, repairing leaks in irrigation canals; addressing adverse environmental impacts; providing demand-driven irrigation to improve the livelihoods of poor producers; and improving management and cost-effectiveness. Irrigation and drainage development and improvements will be viewed in the context of integrated watershed and catchment systems. Bank–supported investments in irrigation will be on a smaller scale than in the past, with the emphasis on water use on farms,

rehabilitation of existing irrigation systems, and participation by farmers and other private investors in management.

Market expansion and diversification. Markets are now the driver for agricultural growth. Food retailers and processors today source from around the world. Consumer demands and market and trade liberalization are opening new niches and specialized markets for agricultural produce, offering farmers an opportunity to diversify into high-value, high-quality items such as fresh fruit and vegetables, fish, and flowers. Therefore, the Bank will focus on strengthening farmers' connections to markets through supply-chain management structures, improving product quality, establishing appropriate post-harvest systems, and assisting clients in refining methods of product certification and improving food safety.

Farm-type tailored strategies. Better technology, access to inputs, and product markets improve poor farmers' income-earning capacity. But they do it in different ways, depending on farm types, production systems, and market opportunities. Future

---

Mali: IPM Special Initiative-Capacity Building and Policy Reform

7

Cotton is a basic higher value crop and a main source of export revenues for Mali. About 90 percent of Mali's pesticide imports are used on cotton. In the 1990s, due to pesticide resistance and inappropriate use, pesticide costs crept up steadily while yields stayed flat or declined. Evidence of occupational health problems and pesticide residues in food mounted. Based on a comprehensive status report produced by a local research institution and a stakeholder policy workshop, an Integrated Pest Management (IPM) Special Initiative was developed. The Initiative takes a problem-focused view, cutting across project components.

Policy reform elements include expanding participatory farmer training for IPM, strengthening regulatory controls, building capacity for monitoring environmental and human health impacts, and adjusting fiscal and economic incentives (eliminating hidden subsidies for cotton and food crop pesticides, providing sustainable funding for regulatory and training activities by eliminating import duty exemptions for pesticides).

productivity increases therefore depend on tailoring technologies to specific groups of farmers in

more narrowly defined production and market environments. Accordingly, the Bank is committed to using a different strategy for each major farm type: commercial, family, and subsistence. Extension and advisory services will be strengthened and broadened to address the knowledge and management services needed by farmers and other rural households. To link farmers to input and technology providers, strong producer organizations and community-driven groups should work toward and increasingly function in an inviting environment for private investment.

Physical and services infrastructure. Farms, households, and other components of rural systems need a minimum bundle of rural infrastructure services to function efficiently. These basics include:

- An adequate supply of safe drinking water. Unsafe water is a major contributor to diarrhea, a frequent cause of death among children in rural areas.
- Health and education infrastructure. Clinics and schools are needed to ensure quality health care and education.
- Transportation infrastructure and services. Without roads and railroads, farmers cannot send their produce to markets outside their localities, and trade cannot expand.
- Information systems. Marketing today depends on adequate information about what people want, at what price, and who can supply it.
- Adequate and dependable energy supplies. Energy is essential for virtually all activities in rural areas.

Adequate infrastructure of every type is imperative for agricultural and rural development. The Bank thus intends to enhance its support to clients' efforts to put in place the basic physical and social infrastructure for rural economic growth (box 8).

Fostering Nonfarm Economic Growth

If poverty is to be reduced, a flourishing agricultural sector is essential in most developing countries, but agriculture alone cannot do the whole job. Rural communities also need nonfarm

---

8   Peru: Roads Bring Markets to the Rural Poor

New roads in the Sierra countryside, built under the Peru Rural Roads project, have made the outside world and its markets more accessible for the area's 3 million poor.

The program's design was innovative with a strong poverty focus, grassroots participation, and collaboration among key players— the Ministry of Transport and Communications, the Inter-American Development Bank, the World Bank, and more than 20 nongovernmental organizations. An institutional collaborative framework was set up to make the most of each stakeholder's best talents.

The program reduced the isolation and facilitated the integration of the beneficiary communities, enhanced economic opportunities, and spurred local entrepreneurship. More than 11,000 km of rural roads were rehabilitated, and 32,300 seasonal unskilled, and 4,700 permanent, jobs were created in 410 local road maintenance enterprises. This innovative partnership program received a 2001 World Bank President's Award for Excellence.

---

9   Madagascar: Rural Nonfarm Investment Benefits the Poor

Aqualma, a shrimp-processing and export company in a remote corner of Madagascar has become one of the country's top private enterprises, with exports of US$26 million in 2000.

Established in 1992 with support from the International Finance Corporation, the company has had a profound impact on the local economy and living conditions. Of Aqualma's 1,200 employees in 2001, 80 percent had never previously held a wage-paying job.

Employees and local villagers gained access to education and health services through the primary school and clinic established by the company. The project generated many connections with small local enterprises during the construction and operational phases.

Future plans include expanding production on a new site, for which a community development plan and a conservation management plan to protect biodiverse habitats are being developed.

---

income-producing activities. Nonfarm activities, often with linkages to agriculture and natural resources, have important multiplier effects (box 9). They are also an important source of employment for rural women. Developing effective support to the rural nonfarm economy is therefore an essential part of the Bank's rural strategy. The Bank will work with clients and others to exploit current opportunities, seek new ones, and tackle the removal of barriers that exclude rural people from diversified employment and business activities. Its interventions will address the institutional support needed by a diversified rural economy at the national, subnational, community, and local levels.

Strengthening skills and organization capital.
The Bank will support future labor market and enterprise development in rural communities. Skills needed range from functional literacy and numeracy, to specific labor-market skills, to managerial and administrative skills for enterprise development, including market assessments and detection of business opportunities. Close attention will be paid to women's demands and needs. Research links growth in nonfarm activities to declining poverty for both male- and female-headed households, but the drop is faster for woman-headed households. Trade, professional, and other common interest associations, and cooperatives will also be promoted.

Promote local economic development and intersectoral linkages.
Recognizing that many ministries and private players share sectoral responsibility for the rural economy, the Bank will support formation of cross-ministerial and other working groups nationally and locally, with both public and private participation. Such groups at the subnational and local levels should address local-level competitiveness and the wider enabling environment of both the farm and nonfarm sectors and identify and seek means to remove barriers (legislative, regulatory, taxation, infrastructure, and financial).

Strengthening the supply chain and product linkages.
Trends in consumer markets, quality requirements, and competition require better planning and coordination of supply chains from input suppliers, primary producers, traders, and processors, to retailers. Competitiveness depends on effective and flexible logistics and low transaction costs within the chain. The public sector's role is to create adequate conditions for the development of efficient private sector supply chains, promote investment in physical infrastructure, and support effective subcontracting systems and quality inspections through appropriate legal frameworks and enforcement systems.

Support micro-, small, and medium enterprises.
The development of small rural enterprises requires first and foremost a good investment climate. This will be promoted through assessment and policy dialog. Especially in rural areas, the development of small and medium enterprises (SMEs) is inhibited by lack of a skilled labor force and public and private financial, technological, and other services. The Bank will promote SME development by supporting commercial business development services (box 10), and, through small and medium enterprises, efficient service delivery, especially in rural infrastructure services.

Kenya: Entrepreneurs Build Market for Business Services · 10

The Kenya Micro and Small Enterprise Training and Technology Project, an innovative World Bank project with a rural component, has been using vouchers since 1998 to enable small, local rural entrepreneurs to purchase skills and management training. As a demand-side instrument, the voucher project departs from the old approach of supporting public training institutions. Now, diverse suppliers are packaging their services for rural entrepreneurial clients. Skilled craft workers have emerged as the leading providers of training. Local private agencies handle voucher allocation.

More than 25,000 vouchers have been issued, 60 percent of them to women entrepreneurs. Among training recipients, employment and income have increased 50 percent. The project subsidizes up to 90 percent of the cost of each voucher, but cost-sharing percentages rise with second and third vouchers. Rural entrepreneurs now frequently purchase training without vouchers from providers who have demonstrated the value of their services.

Recognize and support labor mobility. Migration and labor mobility are essential aspects of economic development, job creation, and poverty reduction. Therefore the Bank will support policies that increase mobility through information on, for example, labor legislation, communications, and skills development as well as on welfare and entitlements. Particular attention will go to policies that minimize the potential for social tensions and environmental damage.

Improving Social Well-Being, Managing and Mitigating Risk, and Reducing Vulnerability

To improve social well-being and minimize the vulnerability of the rural poor, the Bank will endeavor to improve access to nutrition and health services, help mitigate the effects of HIV/AIDS, increase access to rural education and improve its quality, and help improve food security for the rural poor. To achieve these objectives and foster broad-based growth and sustainable management of natural resources, the Bank will also promote inclusiveness and removal of barriers that exclude individuals on the basis of gender or ethnicity from economic and social opportunities.

Health and nutrition. The Bank will stress governments' obligations to ensure that resources for health care reach the rural poor. The Bank will also emphasize the importance of improving dietary quality and micronutrient status. Supplementation and fortification, including biofortification through purposeful plant breeding, are important strategies to combat micronutrient deficiencies.

HIV/AIDS. HIV/AIDS is threatening the progress made in agricultural and rural development in the past 40 years, particularly in developing countries where 95 percent of the infected population live. Combating the disease is therefore a core element of the Bank's strategy to support rural development, especially in Africa. The Bank gives high priority to stopping the spread of HIV/AIDS, helping communities cope with its impacts, and mainstreaming HIV/AIDS issues in Bank operations.

Rural education. Universal primary education with gender equality and quality improvements will be the Bank's top priority in education. In addition, the Bank will promote literacy and training opportunities for unschooled rural youth and adults and ensure that investments in agricultural and vocational training programs are in line with current needs. It will also support development of curricula appropriate to the needs of rural and agricultural populations and piloting of new approaches to private education.

Food security and risk. As articulated in the World Development Report 2001 on poverty, a workable strategy for reducing poverty must enhance security by reducing the risk of natural, financial, and health shocks and by enabling households to mitigate their consequences. But policies, institutions, and investments still have to be designed and adapted to directly manage, reduce, or counteract the special risks of rural residents, particularly the poor. In addition to deepening the understanding of household and community risk and vulnerability, the Bank is promoting new policies and instruments for managing and coping with risk (box 11). In doing so, it will seek to avoid potential market distortions and disincentives from risk management. Instruments that can play a role in this strategy include new types of insurance based on weather rather than yield outcomes and novel mechanisms for commodity price insurance. New instruments being assessed for their effectiveness include market-based financial products not yet readily accessible to many of the poor—such as forward contracting, hedging, and pool pricing. The Bank is also exploring ways to help poor people learn about and use insurance and to reduce costs for primary insurers and reinsurers.

Targeted transfers are one way of reducing income and health uncertainties for the poor and vulnerable. However, such programs face special challenges in rural areas due to difficulties in defining targeting criteria, collecting beneficiary contributions, and administering programs in sparsely populated communities with undeveloped infrastructure. The poorest countries, the ones that need poverty programs the most, also have the greatest need to be selective to avoid compromising macroeconomic stability or reducing investment in human and physical capital.

World Bank–supported programs and policy advice are based on the experience that many targeted food security programs are more cost-effective than generalized food subsidies. Today, food insecurity for most households boils down to lack of access or purchasing power for an adequate diet and lack of complementary inputs such as safe water to maximize the nutritional impact of the food eaten. Food assistance may be given to families (rather than individuals), but any food assistance should be a part of a comprehensive nutrition program for vulnerable children or health programs for pregnant women. The Bank is also emphasizing strengthening informal support programs building upon traditional rural community structures. Although these informal safety nets frequently fail in times of shared hardship, this risk may be reduced with support from government.

Social inclusion. An important priority of the rural strategy is to help make institutions more responsive to the rural poor, thereby improving social well-being and reducing vulnerability. Bank activities in this area focus on institutional reform to establish minority rights and opportunities and to strengthen the political voice of women, refugees, ethnic minorities, the landless, and the disabled. It is now widely acknowledged that one of the most critical factors in revitalizing rural development is to raise the productivity of women farmers. In most of the developing world, women do most of the agricultural work. Women are usually in charge of household food security, yet in some areas they are constrained in their access to, and ownership and control of productive resources such as land and finances. Decentralized development efforts such as community driven development (CDD) offer the potential for increased community participation in all aspects of rural developent as well as offering greater inclusion of all social groups in rural decision making.

Enhancing Sustainability of Natural Resource Management

Agriculture, as a heavy consumer of natural resources—especially water and soil nutrients—has an obligation to play a commensurate role in their conservation. Many producers are already concerned about the deteriorating land and water base in their areas, and public awareness of environmental issues adds urgency to the search for solutions to conservation issues—many of them global in nature. Increasing the efficiency and sustainability of water use in agriculture and improving irrigation system performance are key strategic conservation goals. Ensuring sustainability of intensive agricultural production systems will take, as a priority, careful management of natural resources, especially in fragile production environments. To promote conservation and restoration of natural

xxv

assets in rural areas, the Bank has developed guidelines and strategies for the environment, forestry, and water. Devoted entirely to sustainable development, The World Development Report—2003 was released at the World Summit on that topic in August 2002. The Bank will link rural development, especially in agriculture, to effective sustainable resource management. The Bank's objectives in this regard include:

- Reducing desertification and other types of land degradation
- Improving water management
- Enhancing sustainable fisheries management
- Sustaining production of forest products while protecting the environment
- Protecting biodiversity
- Incorporating knowledge about climate change into rural development planning.

The strategy promotes innovative approaches to using natural resources most efficiently to meet agricultural productivity goals while protecting the long-term productivity and resilience of natural resources. Such approaches take into account the interactions among soil, water, solar energy, plants, and animals as well as the social and economic well-being of the people who use these resources.

STRATEGY IMPLEMENTATION

The new strategy provides guidelines and focal points for maximizing the results of World Bank support to clients' rural development efforts. The approach is flexible, action oriented, and client driven. The goal is to transform rural development activities in the Bank from compartments of sector departments and divisions into a coherent, multisectoral effort, supported by internal budgetary and planning frameworks conducive to efficient implementation.

Key Thrusts in Implementation

Raising the profile of rural development in national policy. The Bank will support the development of locally organized national rural development strategies and capable client-country institutions that articulate and work to fulfill the needs of rural inhabitants, specifically the rural poor. To have

an impact, such efforts must be aligned with national development strategy processes and supported by high-quality and focused analytical work by client countries, the Bank, and other development partners. The main thrust of this joint effort will be to strengthen the voice of the rural poor in national planning processes. The Bank will recommend the participation of all stakeholders in rural areas and foster a holistic approach reflecting the multisectoral dimensions of a sustained drive to reduce poverty. The Bank will provide analytical work to deepen and expand the understanding of rural areas in client countries. The improved analytical platform will be a foundation for better decision-making on resource allocation—and more effective advocacy by rural representatives in client countries, members of the Bank's rural development staff, and other development partners.

Scaling-up innovations and successful investments in rural development *Reaching the Rural Poor* pays close attention to identifying and scaling-up good-practice investments both within countries from pilot initiatives and from one country to other countries or continents (Box 12).

Scaling-up good practices must become an integral part of national rural development strategies. Good practices are acquired after years of development experience and often gained through pilot projects. Innovation through pilot projects will therefore also be supported. Effective intervention—with its socioeconomic and gender impacts—must be locally validated and adapted. Scaling-up does not mean the Bank will apply the same approach everywhere. Innovative methods of learning and information sharing among countries and development partners need support. Mechanisms for capturing, validating, disseminating, and adapting good practices have to be developed concurrently. Key lessons learned from this process and good and innovative practices will be shared with development partners as an essential part of this effort.

Improving the impact of bank operations in rural areas. To improve the impact of projects at completion and the quality of project and program preparation, major attention will be given to identifying and sharing improved procedures to sharpen the focus on poverty and the long-term development impact of Bank–supported rural operations. This will include reviewing both the quality enhancement and assessment of projects for their pro-poor features, as well as supporting new and innovative work addressing both poverty impacts and sustainability of interventions. The Bank has established a task force to improve the guidelines on the different aspects of project sustainability now being applied throughout the Bank and their application. The task force will work closely with ongoing Bank-wide initiatives to enhance poverty impacts and the alignment of rural interventions with the Millennium Development Goals.

Pursuing the bank's global and corporate priorities. High-quality, high-impact operations to reduce rural poverty will require continuing international commitment to key global public goods and a constant awareness of their connections to rural poverty. This can be done by ensuring that: the interests of the rural poor are safeguarded in an increasingly global world; new and appropriate technology for poor farmers and rural communities is readily accessible; and the poor countries can deal with the challenges of global climate change. The Bank will help build the capacity of client countries so they can take full advantage of opportunities in the ongoing Doha Round of trade negotiations of the World Trade Organization. The Consultative Group on International Agricultural Research complements the Bank's efforts to enable developing countries to realize their full agricultural technology and production potential. The Bank's current support for the CGIAR will be broadened to programs to meet the new challenges in science and technology for the benefit of poor farmers in developing countries.

Operational Levels for Implementation
Reaching the Rural Poor outlines the framework for action at three different levels of current Bank operations.

- The corporate strategy provides the conceptual underpinnings and macroeconomic foundation as well as the overall implementation thrusts. Based on the Bank's track record and analysis of best practice, the corporate strategy identifies a

---

Possible Areas for Scaling-Up and Innovation ⎰2⎱

Policy and institutions
- Agricultural policy reform
- Development of rural strategies
- Institutional reform and capacity building
- Participatory planning

Agricultural productivity and competitiveness
- Land reform and administration
- Research and extension
- Information technology—marketing and knowledge
- Irrigation and drainage
- Support for producer organizations and user groups
- Food safety and agribusiness

Nonfarm rural economy
- Rural finance, including microfinance
- Development of the rural nonfarm economy including businesses
- Private sector role in service delivery
- Infrastructure and local economic redevelopment, including small towns

Strengthening social services and reducing risk and vulnerability
- Rural health and education service provisions
- Community-driven development and district programs
- Social inclusion with focus on women and girls
- Commodity, climate, and disaster risk management
- Emergency reconstruction

Sustainable natural resource management
- Soil fertility
- Watershed development
- Community natural resource management
- Community forests
- Fisheries

xxvi

menu of interventions and instruments that may work under different country conditions and performance indicators that the Bank can use to gauge its progress in aligning its resources and promoting rural development. The corporate

13 Regional Priorities

The six regional action plans reflect rural development agendas fully consistent with the overall Bank rural development strategy. Each has a poverty reduction focus and a multi-sectoral approach with increased emphasis on the private sector, yet they all maintain a region-specific character. The diversity in these plans is a major strength of this undertaking. The **Africa** action plan places major emphasis on the institutional foundation for reducing rural poverty. It advocates support for government efforts to decentralize, and enhance the participation of rural communities. The **East Asia and Pacific** regional plan calls for financing programs that directly attack poverty through targeted productivity enhancing investments in very poor areas. The **Europe and Central Asia** region focuses on sustainable rural productivity growth and the completion of the transition process in the rural areas. In the **Latin America and Caribbean** region, the action plan puts special emphasis on rural and urban dynamics, and adopts a Local Economic Development approach to addressing rural development built around increased participation of local actors including local and sub-national governments, private sector and organizations of civil society. The **Middle East and North Africa** action plan places a high priority on rationalizing water management and policies. The focus of the **South Asia** regional action plan is the enhancement of human and social capital development in rural areas, as well as decentralization. Major gender concerns across the regions are women's illiteracy, lack of access to social services, economic infrastructure and resources.

For further details, see: From Action to Impact: the Africa Region's Rural Strategy 2002; Reaching the Rural Poor in East Asia and the Pacific Region 2002; Reaching the Rural Poor in Europe and Central Asia 2002; Reaching the Rural Poor in the Latin America and the Caribbean Region 2002; Reaching the Rural Poor in the Middle East and North Africa 2002; South Asia Strategy and Action Plan for Rural Development 2002.

ated framework for actions at the individual country and subregional levels. At the country-program level, the strategy emphasizes strengthening of the analytical underpinnings for country dialog and a framework and incentives for improving cross-sectoral support to poverty reduction interventions in the context of the Country Assistance Strategies (CASs).

- Within countries, the national rural development strategies will be locally developed and driven, reflecting national priorities for rural areas and agriculture. The process of national dialog, together with these national strategies, will guide the rural development aspects of the CASs, as well as the Poverty Reduction Strategies, and provide the specific demand for further Bank operations.

Strategy implementation relies heavily on stimulating the demand for rural development from the two main groups of decisionmakers, the clients and the Bank-country teams. At the client level, the Bank will support the preparation of national rural strategies that integrate the needs of the rural poor in national policy dialogs. At the level of the country teams and other decisionmakers, it will seek to improve the quality and the impact of Bank operations in rural areas by sharpening the focus on poverty, using the most appropriate instruments, seeking economies of scale, and scaling-up investments that have proven effective in reducing rural poverty. Several donors have indicated their interest in cooperating with the Bank. Though probably slower to materialize, an approach that relies on stimulating demand and monitoring lending trends closely is more appropriate to the country-driven nature of Bank programs, and more sustainable in the long term, than relying on preset lending targets.

What the Bank Needs to Change

Enhancing bank-wide multi-sectoral cooperation in the rural space. One of the greatest challenges will be to ensure that rural poverty is truly reflected in Bank-supported programs and operations in the manner and form envisaged in this strategy. Each level of the Bank decision making structure must become an integrated part of the implementation process. This will entail new and innovative relations

strategy also provides a vehicle to convey the Bank's message on rural development to external partners and audiences and garner interest and collaboration of partners around rural poverty reduction efforts.

- The regional action plans, built upon local consultations, differentiate region-specific needs in line with the overall message of the corporate strategy (box 13). The plans provide a differenti-

between all Bank units active in rural areas. The implementation of this strategy also requires that operations in rural space are designed in a multi-sectoral fashion and that self-standing sectoral operations are coordinated within an overall strategy. Specific regional organizational arrangements are proposed to improve coordination of activities in the rural space and to achieve the strategy's objectives. These arrangements would operate within the framework of existing management structures.

Improving the application of instruments. Addressing rural poverty in a comprehensive fashion requires that an evolving set of instruments, with the right focus, are applied to Bank operations in rural areas. The balance between the different instruments is a complex implementation issue. There is clearly no one "golden rule" as to the optimal distribution between different Bank instruments of programmatic, adjustment or investment lending, or between economic, social or natural resource outcomes. Nevertheless, some general directions for Bank operations in rural areas are:

- The diversity of needs within rural areas between regions, countries, and sub-country regions requires the use of a broad set of instruments supporting a number of sectoral interventions, within the framework of the Country Assistance Strategies.

- Traditional investment projects will continue to play an important role, however they should be blended with the new type of operations such as the Learning and Innovation Loans, the Adaptable Program Loans, and the Poverty Reduction Support Credits, etc., according to country requests and new conditions;

- The broader use of new instrument modalities, such as programmatic lending, should be pursued after careful assessment of lessons from field experience and assurance of an adequate rural focus.

Improving linkages to development partners. There is growing consensus among international development partners—including the Bank, FAO, IFAD, EC, regional development banks, and major

bilateral agencies—that national and global poverty reduction targets will not be met unless poverty in rural areas is reduced. Understanding what it takes to meet the needs of the rural poor has never been closer, as many agencies have recently taken stock of their experiences and redefined their approaches and commitments to poverty reduction in rural areas. The further development of relations with international partners aimed at improving the distribution of labor among the various partners is based on the Bank's and the partner's specific comparative advantages. Coordinated support to client countries for the development of national rural development strategies, in conjunction with Poverty Reduction Strategies and Country Assistance Strategies, will be a major focus of the Bank's interactions with international partners.

Improving linkages to the private sector and civil society. Increasing links and improving relationships with the private sector and civil society within a country framework are among the top priorities for the Bank in each region. The Bank's links to representatives of civil society and nongovernmental organizations have increased dramatically over the past ten years. Internet websites and information sharing now provide the opportunity for increased direct dialogue and interaction between the Bank and NGOs. The consultation process on regional action plans and the new corporate framework for the rural strategy proved to be a valuable and productive means of enhancing relationships with both large numbers of NGOs as well as with the private sector across all regions. In a rapidly globalizing world, links with multinational companies that have an impact on rural development are also essential.

Monitoring Implementation Progress and Managing Risks.
This strategy presents a program for revitalizing Bank activities in rural areas and increasing the effectiveness of the Bank's work in reducing rural poverty. *Reaching the Rural Poor* pays close attention to monitoring and evaluation of strategy implementation. The targets and benchmarks will be used against the current baseline for evaluating progress over a five-year period. The Implementation Monitoring framework is designed

xxix

around results-based management principles, expressed as inputs, outputs, outcomes, and impacts. The Bank's Agriculture and Rural Development Sector Board will work closely with senior Bank management to ensure alignment of the rural strategy implementation framework with emerging Bank work on results-based management.

Several risks are inherent in implementing the strategy. Some of these depend on events that are beyond the control of the Bank and of the countries concerned. The main risks perceived are:

- Not all sectors operating in rural areas take up the challenge of rural poverty reduction.
- The necessary institutional arrangements, incentives framework, and appropriate staff skills mix are not addressed.
- The opportunities do not materialize for the institutional learning and innovation that are expected to emerge in the context of a sharpened focus on programmatic lending operations.
- The Bank, its country partners, and other stakeholders cannot mobilize country buy-in to intensifying emphasis on attacking rural poverty.
- The client countries do not achieve long-term growth and do not address issues related to enhanced and more equitable access to assets for all.

The successful implementation of the new strategy is a challenge for both the Bank and for its clients and partners. The Bank recognizes that it cannot work alone. It will deepen relationships with client countries, strengthen existing alliances and forge new ones with other development partners, the private sector and organizations of civil society to broaden the understanding of rural development issues, share experiences, build capacity, and mobilize the necessary resources to overcome rural poverty.

INTRODUCTION

I n 1996 the World Bank began developing a comprehensive rural development strategy entitled *From Vision to Action* (World Bank, 1997). Approved by the Board in March 1997, this strategy identified rural poverty reduction, improvement in the well-being of rural people, and the elimination of hunger as the main strategic objectives in the Bank's rural development activities. *From Vision to Action,* provided a solid conceptual foundation for the Bank's rural development activities and resulted in a new generation of rural development programs. In general, however, implementation of *From Vision to Action* has not brought about the anticipated results.

Bank lending for projects in the rural space during FY99-01 was approximately 25% of total Bank lending. This includes lending to agriculture, which in FY01 was the lowest in the Bank's history, both in absolute and percentage terms. A similar trend can be seen in most other international agencies. This is particularly disconcerting when 75% of the people who live on less than one dollar per day live in rural areas, and most of them are farmers. The Bank will not be successful in its overall poverty reduction objective unless it helps reduce rural poverty at an accelerated rate.

The Agriculture and Rural Development Department, in close cooperation with the regions and other sector units active in rural areas, has prepared an updated rural development strategy to revitalize IBRD/IDA activities in rural areas by: a) adjusting the strategic framework; and b) formulating a program of concrete and implementable actions. This revision of the strategy responds to changes in the development context:

- in the global environment, especially to changes brought about by the forces of globalization and remaining trade distortions;

- in client countries, especially the challenges of unfinished policy reforms, decentralization, institutional development, still inadequate governance, the increased role of the private sector and civil society, as well as the rising number of conflicts; and

- within the Bank and especially through lessons learned in the past five years in the implementation of *From Vision to Action*.

The world confronts major challenges in rural development as it enters the 21st century. Most of the world's poverty is in rural areas, and will remain so, yet there is a pro-urban bias in most countries' development strategies, and in their allocation of public investment funds. Rural people, and ethnic minorities, in particular, have little political clout to influence public policy to attract more public investment in rural areas. The Bank recognizes that, to be successful in reducing rural poverty, the Bank must focus on the entire rural space, meaning the entire

rural society and both farm and non-farm aspects of the economy. The Bank is convinced that five critical components of a rural development strategy will contribute most to accelerated growth in rural economies and, consequently, to measurable poverty reduction: a) fostering an enabling environment for broad-based sustainable rural growth b) enhancing agricultural productivity and competitiveness; c) fostering non-farm economic growth; d) improving social well-being, managing risk, and reducing vulnerability; and e) enhancing sustainable management of natural resources.

This document outlines a holistic and spatial approach that tackles some tough and long-ignored issues and also addresses old issues in new ways. Most importantly, it recognizes that while top-down, non-inclusive approaches in the past, such as integrated rural development, identified most of the necessary pieces of the puzzle, they failed to put them together in a way that resulted in successful attainment of the Bank's objectives. While the main focus of the strategy is on rural poverty reduction, at the same time it includes key elements of a strategy for the food and agriculture sector. This sector remains a crucial and central component of rural growth and it is vital to success in reducing rural poverty.

The revised action-oriented strategy provides guidelines and focal points for enhancing the effectiveness of the World Bank's rural development efforts. Strategy implementation is based on four main thrusts:

- Raising the profile of rural development in national policy.

- Scaling-up innovations and successful investments in rural development.

- Improving the impact of Bank operations in rural areas.

- Pursuing the Bank's global and corporate priorities.

The implementation of the strategy will transform rural development activities in the Bank from a compartmentalized activity of various sector

2

departments and divisions, into a coherent, multi-sectoral discipline, supported by conducive internal budgetary and planning frameworks necessary for a more efficient implementation. The new approach is flexible, action-oriented, and client-driven. The strategy provides a platform for locally-owned and participatory, national priority-setting. Within that context it allows for a substantive rural development contribution to Comprehensive Development Frameworks (CDFs), Country Assistance Strategies (CASs), and country-owned Poverty Reduction Strategy Papers (PRSPs). It also creates a framework for multi-sectoral cooperation in client countries, within the Bank, and among international donors.

The basic foundations of the updated strategy are the six regional action plans.[1] Each of these was prepared by a regional team of cross-sectoral operational staff. The regional action plans indicate some shared overall priorities that are reflected in the corporate strategy even though the sequencing of the priorities may differ for specific regions. A series of nine regional consultations involving representatives of the respective governments, private sector, NGOs and academia were organized to ensure that the Bank, its clients, and fellow donor agencies are in agreement on the focus of the strategy and that they have had the opportunity to contribute to its formulation.

A detailed portfolio analysis and a number of studies on both global and regional issues were commissioned to support this process. These studies provide a rich empirical foundation for the regional action plans and the corporate strategy. Other sectoral strategies dealing with environment, forestry, water, and private sector development were considered in creating a coherent rural development strategy. A rural strategy seminar series was organized to discuss the findings and conclusions of the most important background studies. These seminars also provided an opportunity for the rural staff to interact with some the world's leading experts on rural development and poverty reduction. The Bank's Rural Weeks in 2001 and 2002 provided a forum for in-depth discussion of the emerging strategy and its implementation within the Bank's Rural Family.

Each chapter in this volume deals with a major building block of the revised rural development strategy. Chapter One presents an overview of the current development context, which provides a foundation for the revision of the Bank strategy. Chapter Two outlines the conceptual foundation, objectives, and strategic priorities of the revised rural development strategy. Chapter Three discusses the enabling policy and institutional environment for broad-based rural growth. Chapter Four provides a discussion of the Bank's renewed approach to agricultural productivity and competitiveness. Chapter Five concentrates on fostering non-farm rural economic growth. Chapter Six enumerates the improvement of the social well-being of rural peoples, managing risk, and reducing vulnerability. Chapter Seven focuses on fostering sustainable natural resource management. Chapter Eight deals with the implementation thrusts and provides a framework to monitor implementation progress.

Annexes to the strategy provide more in-depth analysis of the issues discussed in the corporate strategy. Annex One gives a review of lessons learned from the implementation of the Bank's previous strategy *From Vision to Action*. Annex Two provides an overview of the consultation process that led to the new strategy. Annex Three includes summaries of the regional strategies. Annex Four focuses on water in rural development. Annex Five presents background material on physical and social infrastructure. Annex 6 concerns natural resources. Annex 7 gives examples of successful World Bank operations in agriculture and rural development. Throughout the main text in this volume there are references to further information available in these annexes.

3

ENDNOTES

1 From Action to Impact: the Africa Region's Rural Strategy 2002; Reaching the Rural Poor in East Asia and the Pacific Region 2002; Reaching the Rural Poor in Europe and Central Asia 2002; Reaching the Rural Poor in the Latin America and the Caribbean Region 2002; Reaching the Rural Poor in the Middle East and North Africa 2002; South Asia Strategy and Action Plan for Rural Development 2002.

4

DEVELOPMENT CONTEXT: WHY A STRATEGY UPDATE IS NECESSARY

S imply put, a revision of the rural development strategy is necessary because the environment in which the Bank operates has changed. Globalization opens new doors and poses new threats. The needs of client countries have evolved, as has the way the Bank approaches its mission of "fighting poverty with passion." This section briefly describes the nature and importance of some of these changes at the global, client country and Bank level, and focuses on the developments since the Bank's rural development strategy *From Vision to Action* was adopted in 1997.

THE EVOLVING GLOBAL CONTEXT

Persistent Poverty and Food Insecurity

One of the most frustrating moral contradictions of our time is the **persistence of poverty**. More than a billion people are desperately poor. The number of people living on less than $1 per day has declined only slightly in the 1990s, and best estimates indicate that 1.2 billion persons still live below that poverty line (World Bank, 2001b). Other social and poverty indicators over the same period demonstrate that some regions are a long way from the day when the goals for international development will be met.

Who Are the Rural Poor?

To craft an effective rural development strategy focused on the rural poor requires a clear understanding of who the rural poor are, where they live, and the challenges posed by the prevailing poverty levels in their respective habitats. This is because the rural poor are not a homogeneous group, and behind the aggregate numbers are the various diverse entities that make up the rural poor. They could be broadly classified into five categories: a) the landless (those without any crop land); b) those with a low asset base, or smallholders (farmers with up to two hectares of cropland); c) pastoralists (those who are not settled in any specific area and who derive most of their income from pastoral livestock); d) rural women (especially women-headed households); and e) ethnic minorities and indigenous populations.

Source: Okidegbe, 2001

Poverty is predominantly a rural phenomenon. Approximately 75% of the poor reside in rural areas, and the rural poor will outnumber their urban counterparts for at least another generation (Alderman, 2001). By most quality-of-life indicators, people living in rural areas, on average, have a lower quality of life than urban residents (Box 1.1). Rural public services, as measured by per capita public expenditure are approximately one-half that of urban areas.

There is a disturbing paradox in recent developments: **the existence of pervasive malnutrition in a world of abundant food supplies.** Growth in global food production over the past four decades has more than kept pace with growth in population.

While global production has grown faster than demand, hunger and malnutrition persist. This enigma has been addressed by many eminent economists who conclude that hunger is less strongly related to the level of food availability than to household income, or as Amartya Sen puts it, the "entitlement" to sufficient resources to purchase enough food to live (Sen, 1981b).

The persisting high share of poverty and food insecurity in rural areas has important implications for public policy and in the design of any strategy for its reduction (Binswanger and Landell-Mills, 1995). Because of the geographic dispersion of the rural poor, it is more expensive on a per capita basis for central governments to provide them with public infrastructure, social services, and safety nets equivalent to those provided to urban residents. A willingness to spend more public resources targeted to the rural poor, and decentralizing decision making to localities and communities are first steps, but these are limited by a lack of political voice and influence in many rural areas.

Globalization

The concept of globalization captures the growing interdependence and linkages of the world's economies, markets, and people. It concerns more open international trade in goods and financial services, growth of multinational companies, more uniform labor and environmental standards, and growing global sourcing in supply chains. In the context of rural development and poverty reduction, globalization presents both emerging challenges and new opportunities. The process of globalization, including increasing inter-linkages across countries, lower transaction costs, and expanded trade, financial, and information flows, provides some of the key ingredients for rural development and poverty reduction. But globalization and economic liberalization carry with them risks. There are winners and losers in globalization, and the challenge for policymakers is to provide adjustment assistance or at least partially compensate losers.

Urbanization and Demographic Shifts

Despite higher rural birthrates, between 2000 and 2030 virtually all net population growth in the world will be concentrated in urban areas, as a result of continued rural migration to urban centers. This migration is driven by the desire for higher incomes. The pace of urbanization will be most rapid in developing countries, where the urban population is forecast to increase from 1.94 billion to 3.88 billion in the next thirty years. Rapid urbanization has been accompanied by increasingly strong links between rural and urban economies, and the dichotomy between rural and urban is beginning to blur. Rural households are more and more likely to participate in non-farm employment opportunities available in small towns and cities. Seasonal employment in urban areas, and remittances from household members working in urban areas, frequently enable rural residents to supplement their agricultural incomes. Resulting changes in intra-household division of labor also affect the status of women. In an area of male out-migration women may manage the entire farm often without legal ownership of the assets. In other areas, off-farm employment is an income-generation opportunity for women. The interdependence of rural and urban economies and strong linkages at household levels implies that effective policies to reduce rural poverty also need to be concerned with growth and economic development in urban centers, and particularly with the linkages between smaller cities and market towns in more isolated areas.

Growing Scarcity of the Rural Natural Resource Base with Global Climate Change

Whether the world continues to be able to feed itself depends in large part on the condition of the world's natural resource base in the future, and this depends, in part, on whether poverty will be greatly reduced. Poverty and environmental degradation are closely linked, often in a self-perpetuating spiral where poverty accelerates environmental degradation and degradation exacerbates poverty. Poor people live at the margin of subsistence and are more vulnerable to adverse events than others. Concern by policy makers over environmental degradation is driven by growing scarcity and continued degradation, in both developed and developing countries.

There is consensus among climatologists that the **global climate is changing**. There is, however, considerable controversy over the nature and extent of climate change, and potential impacts, both pos-

itive and negative. Climate change will affect food production, ecosystem function, and farmer vulnerability in many areas of the developing world, especially in Africa and parts of Asia. These changes are likely to have a disproportionate impact on the poorest countries, and the poorest people within those countries, thereby exacerbating inequities in health status and access to adequate food, clean water and other resources.

Clearly the concerns over environmental degradation and global climate change and their links with rural poverty and agricultural development are well placed. Continuing to neglect vulnerable areas where many of the world's poor live will only make degradation and misery worse—continuing present trends is simply not a long-term option.

The Revolution in Biological and Information Sciences

Biotechnology based on molecular biology is generating revolutionary advances in genetic knowledge and the capacity to change the genetic makeup of crops and livestock, which have the potential to benefit poor producers and consumers. Despite this potential, the complex issues of biosafety and food safety, bioethics, and accessing proprietary science for the benefit of the poor must be addressed. Also, early adopters may incur significant risk. Although biotechnology strategies will vary with each country's technological capacity and level of agricultural commercialization, all countries need some amount of investment in public-sector research and regulatory frameworks. The biotechnology revolution in agriculture is only beginning and presents policy makers with a unique set of challenges. There are ethical, safety, health, and property rights issues. Yet the promise of this technology to assist in coping with increasing food demand is enormous—so large that the challenges mentioned above must be addressed.

New information and communication technologies (ICTs) with lower costs combined with the increasing literacy and sophistication of farmers have the potential to revolutionize rural information systems, providing more and better information directly to farmers, extension agents, agribusinesses, and other intermediaries. Application of ICTs in rural areas may increase the flow of information of all types, and facilitate market transactions, changes in employment, emergence of new industries, and social development, but such advances are dependent upon telecommunications reaching remote rural areas and diverse populations, including rural women.

CHANGES IN CLIENT COUNTRIES

Progress in Policy Reform: Unfinished Agenda. The past decade has seen much progress on policy and institutional issues throughout the developing world, yet the policy reform agenda in many countries is still far from complete. Developing countries' own policies may: a) create terms of trade unfavorable to agriculture; b) have higher levels of protection against agricultural imports than developed countries; c) have a prevailing urban bias in public expenditures; and d) create an unattractive environment for private economic activity.

Governance: Decentralized and Improved, but still Inadequate. In the past decade, there has been increasing recognition among development stakeholders that good governance is crucial for achieving sustainable development and poverty reduction. This recognition has brought about improvement in many aspects of governance, but the impact of these improvements has been relatively limited in rural areas.

Increased Role of the Private Sector. One of the most visible signs of change in client countries is the increased role of the private sector in rural development, and the growing recognition that new jobs in the private sector will do the most towards reducing rural poverty. The incentives for private investment depend greatly on the enabling environment. Markets are the vehicle for rural economic development and allow for specialization and diversification into new products. However, markets can be inefficient because of externalities, difficulty in achieving economies of scale, asymmetric information, non-excludability, and excessive transaction costs.

Increased Role of Civil Society. In recent years civil society (including local and transnational NGOs) has become a major force in international development. The civil-society organizations participating in international development serve a variety of functions ranging from service provision to advocacy on issues as diverse as water, forestry, food security, human rights and humanitarian assistance. It is recognized that NGOs/CBOs can be effective in reaching poor communities and remote areas at low cost, as they are more inclined to identify local needs and promote participation, and that engaging these groups in projects and policy dialogue can improve project design, implementation and sustainability.

Continuing Regional and Local Conflicts. The past decade has been characterized by the resurgence of conflicts in several regions. Most of the physical and economic damage resulting from these conflicts takes place in the poorest areas of the countries and regions involved. Many of the recent conflicts have been fought over the use of certain natural resources or have an ethnic origin. These conflicts bring additional hardship to the rural population, particularly women, who are the most vulnerable to their negative impacts.

CHANGES WITHIN THE BANK

The changing global environment has also shaped the Bank and its approach to development. This change has become especially pronounced in the period since the Bank's last rural development strategy, *From Vision to Action* was completed five years ago.

New Approach to Development Assistance
A new approach to development assistance, the "Comprehensive Development Framework" (CDF) was initiated by the Bank and the development community. The CDF builds on lessons concerning development aid effectiveness, such as the need for social inclusion, better governance, and understanding of the complementary roles of civil institutions, the private sector, and donors. It offers an opportunity to approach rural development challenges holistically, by catalyzing local initiatives, taking a long-term perspective on development, and focusing on coordinated "country-driven" strategies among development partners.

8

The Bank's **Strategic Framework Paper (SFP)** identifies two main pillars of the Bank's assistance to
clients in fighting poverty: (a) building a climate for
investment, jobs, and sustainable growth; and (b)
empowering poor men and women to participate
in development. Together these pillars embody the
key elements of sustainable development. The SFP
also calls for selectivity: (i) *within countries* based on
the CDF principles; and (ii) *across countries*, guided
by income, poverty, and performance æ focusing on
countries where the overall policy environment
favors aid effectiveness; and (iii) *at the global level,*
based on clear linkages to the Bank's core institutional objective, its leveraging and catalytic effect,
and a balancing of resources and risks.

Sharpened Poverty Focus

One of the most visible changes in the Bank over
the past several years has been the increasing
poverty focus combined with a growing emphasis
on meeting the Millennium Development Goals
(MDGs) articulated in 2000 (Box 1.2). In late 1999
finance ministers of World Bank and IMF member
countries called for Highly Indebted Poor
Countries (HIPCs) to draft **Poverty Reduction
Strategy Papers (PRSPs)** as a condition of HIPC
debt relief. In Bank practice, these PRSPs have
become central to the preparation of Country
Assistance Strategies (CASs) for all IDA countries.

MIXED RESULTS IN IMPLEMENTING FROM *VISION TO ACTION*

The Bank's performance in rural development during the past several years can be best analyzed in
light of the main principles and objectives set out
by *From Vision to Action*. It was expected that *From
Vision to Action* would revitalize the lending program
for rural areas into a vibrant, broad-based, and
broadly focused high-quality rural development
program. The **major thrusts** of *From Vision to Action*
were clear: the Bank's rural development strategy
would shift from a narrow agricultural focus to a
broader rural development approach, incorporating long ignored issues such as land reform and
nutrition, and finding new ways to address old
issues, such as rural financial services and community driven development. Above all, *From Vision to*

Action sought to integrate rural development more
closely into CASs. To implement those thrusts, the
main **priority actions** included increasing economic
and sector work, enhancing knowledge management and agricultural research programs, and
strengthening alliances with other international
organizations, for example, FAO and IFAD. In terms
of **major outcomes**, the Bank was to be seen by
2000 as the world leader in the fight against rural
poverty, to have significantly contributed to freer
and fairer world trade in agriculture, and to have

**Millennium Development Goals
(1990-2015)**   1.2

1. ERADICATE EXTREME POVERTY AND HUNGER
   ■ Halve the proportion of people with less than $1 a day
   ■ Halve the proportion of people who suffer from hunger

2. ACHIEVE UNIVERSAL PRIMARY EDUCATION
   ■ Ensure that boys and girls alike complete primary
     schooling

3. PROMOTE GENDER EQUALITY AND EMPOWER WOMEN
   ■ Eliminate gender disparity at all levels of education

4. REDUCE CHILD MORTALITY
   ■ Reduce by two-thirds the under-five mortality ratio

5. IMPROVE MATERNAL HEALTH
   ■ Reduce by three-quarters the maternal mortality ratio

6. COMBAT HIV/AIDS, MALARIA AND OTHER DISEASES
   ■ Reverse the spread of HIV/AIDS

7. ENSURE ENVIRONMENTAL SUSTAINABILITY
   ■ Integrate sustainable development into country policies
     and reverse loss of environmental resources
   ■ Halve the proportion of people without access to
     potable water
   ■ Significantly improve the lives of at least 100 million
     slum dwellers

8. DEVELOP A GLOBAL PARTNERSHIP FOR DEVELOPMENT
   ■ Raise official development assistance
   ■ Expand market access
   ■ Encourage debt sustainability

source: www.developmentgoals.org

revitalized rural development in a number of under-performing countries. In conjunction with *From Vision to Action*, at the request of the Bank's President, a special action program was launched in fifteen focus countries, and a budget allocation from the **Strategic Compact** was made available to support rural development in these countries.

Main Outcomes

From Vision to Action has had a significant influence on global thinking on rural development, induced a stronger participatory approach in Bank rural lending and non-lending activities, and, within the agricultural sector, promoted a broadening of the scope of lending. Moreover, the current portfolio, in terms of the mix of instruments, and key quality aspects, has improved, although there has been a slight decline in FY01. Valuable experiences in critical investments affecting the livelihoods of the poor have also been gained. The improvements in project quality achieved under *From Vision to Action* provide a strong platform from which to launch *Reaching the Rural Poor* and move to "scaling-up" quality rural operations.

While significant progress in rural development has been made, major challenges still lie ahead. The revitalization of the lending program for rural areas into a vibrant, broad-based, and high-quality rural development program has not materialized. Although the role of the private sector was recognized, little was done to support the non-farm private sector. **Rural needs are still not adequately taken into account in national and Bank decision-making processes.** Many internal and external constraints to multi-sectoral approaches to rural poverty reduction still exist. Finally, the agricultural development portfolio has not yet met the 80% satisfactory development outcome rating at completion, as targeted by *From Vision to Action*. The quality of the poverty focus, and the sustainability and quality of the institutional development still leave much to be desired. *Reaching the Rural Poor* will address these concerns. One particular concern is the strikingly low resource allocation to support rural women. In the 2001 rural portfolio, 23% of the projects addressed gender issues, but only 2.8% of the funds were allocated towards gender-responsive components (World Bank, 2002b, FY01 Rural Portfolio Review).

Trends in Lending for Rural Development

While *From Vision to Action* did not set specific lending targets, the underlying assumption was that **lending for rural development would grow.** However, the contrary has occurred. While there are no long-term trends available for total lending in rural areas, a special analysis carried out for this review showed that in FY99-01 (aggregated), the

Bank invested $15 billion (about $5 billion annually), or 25% of its total lending, in rural space[1] (Box 1.3) Out of the $5 billion annual World Bank investments in rural space, more than half were IDA investments ($2.7 billion in FY99, and $3 billion in FY01). Projects coded for urban development are 11% of total lending. The remaining national operations cannot be spatially attributed, but experience indicates that these operations are predominantly focused on city dwellers. Taking these two factors together, lending to rural space as a proportion of overall Bank lending is not congruent with the greater incidence of poverty in rural areas. OED also reported a rural under-representation in investment (World Bank 2001c). According to preliminary analysis, this situation has not changed for FY02. Using comparable methodology, total investment in rural space in FY02 amounted to about $5 billion (or 25% of total lending) (Box 1.4).

Lending for agricultural activities declined dramatically as a proportion of total Bank lending, from about 31% in 1979–81 to less than 10% in FY00 and FY01 (Figure 1.1). The reasons for this decline are many; and some are, in fact, positive. A clearer understanding of public and private roles, market functioning and the need for institution building resulted in a shift away from big (but unsuccessful) investments in public infrastructure and government bureaucracies, to more effective inputs into comprehensive rural institution building, which requires less funding. For example, comparing the nature and scope of lending approvals from FY79–81, with those of FY99-01, the largest declines are in the sectors of (a) perennial crops and agro-industry, because of the shift away from support for parastatal enterprises, (b) agricultural credit, because of a shift away from targeted credit, (c) irrigation and drainage, because of the shift away from large new irrigation schemes to institution building and operation and maintenance; and (d) agriculture adjustment operations, because of a much more gradual approach in the Bank's policy dialogue in the sector.

It is highly unlikely that the Bank will revert to those types of investments, and it therefore also unlikely that the Bank will attain those levels again. However, there has been further decline in agricultural lending over the past five years, since *From*

Vision to Action was launched. Between FY96-98 and FY99–01, lending for agriculture declined by more than 30%. The decline was particularly strong in EAP, SAR, and ECA, which experienced an average drop of 40%-50%, over that period. LCR declined by about 13%, while AFR and MNA showed increases of 15% and 74%, respectively, over this period. Preliminary results for FY02 confirm this decline (Box 1.4). This cannot be explained by the shift away from the costly and outmoded agricultural and rural operations of the past. Part of the decline in rural lending is due to the perceived burden of safeguard policies for projects predominantly in rural space.

Current Bank Operations in Rural Space – FY02 Update   1.4

■ Total investment in rural space in FY02 was US $5 billion, or 25% of total lending. Of this, $3.2 billion was IDA investments (40% of total IDA), and US $1.8 billion IBRD lending (15% of total IBRD)

■ Instruments: Adjustment operations, 17%; Investment, 83%

■ Total investment in the agriculture sector (including agro-industry and markets was US $1.5 billion (or 7.9% of total Bank lending). Lending to the Crops sub-sector amounted to 32% of Agriculture Sector lending, while Irrigation and Drainage received 22%, and Agriculture Markets and Trade received 14%. These figures were derived using the new project coding system introduced in July 2002.

Rural Space Lending and the Millennium Development Goals[2]

In undertaking the rural portfolio review, efforts were made to align ongoing (FY99-01) activities to the MDGs (Table 1.1). The bulk of lending in rural space (46%) is allocated towards Goal 1, poverty reduction and the elimination of hunger. Support to social sector goals total 18% of overall rural space lending, with Goal 2 of primary education receiving 8%, and Goals 4–6, the health sector related goals, at 10%.[3] The current information management systems, however, are not yet adequately refined to align or attribute fully the Bank's contributions to the MDGs. For example: lending towards Goal 1 includes all economic activities, access to, and quality of, infrastructure and assets and may not be exclusive to the poverty reduction objective. Similarly, systematic tracking of lending to rural women (MDG 3) has not been possible with the present portfolio analysis tools. Bank-wide systems are now being put in place to achieve better alignment and it is anticipated that the work undertaken in FY99-01 will form part of the baseline for monitoring the rural sectors' contribution to the MDGs.

Improved Leadership Role of the Bank in Rural Development

The Bank has made progress toward achieving a leading **international role in rural development** as was envisaged by *From Vision to Action*, as it has significantly influenced thinking on the holistic nature of rural development, decentralized decision making, and greater stakeholder participation. Several international agencies developed similar strategies afterwards.

In regard to developing **fair and freer** trade and increased access to OECD markets for client countries, the record has been disappointing. The Bank has not taken a forceful position on this until recently, when more active support to client countries in their preparation for WTO negotiations has been offered. Additionally, the Bank's senior man-

agement has spoken on the need for freer trade in several international fora. The Bank's impact remains limited, however, as the Bank has no direct influence over OECD countries in addressing such issues as subsidies and market access.

Why *From Vision to Action* Did Not Completely Succeed

Earlier approaches to rural development often involved significant government intervention frequently leading to inefficiencies, reduced institutional sustainability and pricing and marketing policies that were adverse to farmers. *From Vision to Action* recognized the deficiencies in these approaches and attempted to find new avenues for rural development assistance. Approaches such as community driven development, pluralistic rural service provision and support to producer organizations emerged and have been piloted. The major challenge for the future is to scale up the best practices among these pilot projects.

Why did the envisaged rural development program not materialize? Why were the results under *From Vision to Action* mixed? The Bank has analyzed this question thoroughly. Some reasons are associated with decision making at the client level. Earlier political interests in rural development (for example

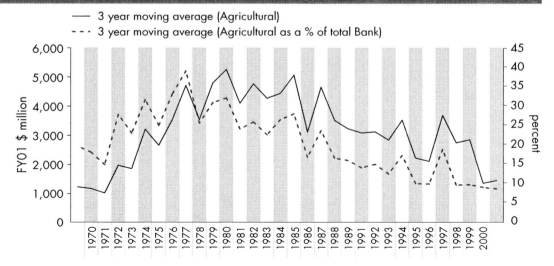

Figure 1.1: IBRD/IDA Agriculture Sector Approvals, FY70-01: FY01 $ million; Percent of Total Bank Approvals

— 3 year moving average (Agricultural)
- - - 3 year moving average (Agricultural as a % of total Bank)

REACHING THE RURAL POOR A RENEWED STRATEGY FOR RURAL DEVELOPMENT

securing food for urban areas) have now been met in most regions, and more focus should be placed on the neglected **political voice of the rural poor** with appreciation for the ethnic, age, and gender diversity of this group. The PRSP process offers new opportunities to get the needs of the rural poor better recognized. A preliminary review of the first set of PRSPs and Interim PRSPs prepared during 2000 and 2001 showed that in all these documents, rural development was stated as a priority (Cord, 2001a). However, the actions were often narrowly defined and tended not to address the broader needs of rural development. The involvement of agencies often considered to be champions of rural development in the PRSP processes such as the Ministries of Agriculture or Rural Development, rural NGOs, and community based groups was felt to be weak.

Systematic implementation of *From Vision to Action* did not last long. With the exception of Africa, after the initial adoption of the strategy, it was never deepened and taken forward by the regions. While this strategy was reasonably well known within rural departments of the Bank, , it was not integrated into the strategies of most Bank client countries. The **lack of baseline data and clear outcome indicators** for *From Vision to Action* limited the value and impact of the monitoring and review processes.

Other reasons for the mixed results of *From Vision to Action* are more internal to the Bank and are mainly concerned **with relative costs, resource levels, and resource allocation mechanisms.** Over the past few years, the Bank has been called to attend to an expanded mandate, thus increasing competition for resources. Against this background, rural projects are perceived as more costly, more complex, riskier, and smaller and slower disbursing. In addition, staff responded to an apparent decline in demand from client countries for rural operations.

Annex 1 presents the major achievements and lessons learned of *From Vision to Action* as derived from OED's rural strategy review (World Bank, 2001c), the Rural Portfolio Review, and internal deliberations within the rural sector units within the Bank.

Table 1.1: **Alignment of Rural Space Lending of the Rural Portfolio with the MDGs (FY99-01) ($m)**

Millennium Development Goals	Total Bank Lending ($m)	Total Bank Lending %	IDA ($m)	IDA %
Goal 1. Eradicate extreme poverty and hunger	6,998	46	3,215	40
Goal 2. Achieve universal primary education	1,134	8	751	9
Goal 3. Promote gender equality and empower women[1]	n/a	n/a[3]	n/a	n/a
Goal 4. Reduce child mortality[2]	178.5	1	132	2
Goal 5. Improve maternal health[2]	178.5	1	132	2
Goal 6. Combat HIV/AIDS, malaria and other diseases	1,251	8	729	9
Goal 7. Ensure environmental sustainability	1,289	8	689	9
Goal 8. Develop a Global Partnership for Development	2,421	16	1,340	17
Rural Space investment ($m) FY99-01 directly aligned to MDGs	13,450	88	6,989	88
Contributing to multiple goals	1,768	12	981	12
Total Rural Space Investment ($m) FY99-01	15,218	100	7,970	100

Notes:
1 The portfolio review ranked this activity but did not differentiate funding allocated.
2 The portfolio review marked Key Components supporting the two Goals (5 and 6) in a combined manner. Due to the methodology used, it is not possible to allocate the actual shares of lending to these Goals. The lending amount for the Key Component has therefore been divided arbitrarily and allocated equally to the two Goals
3 This can be calculated at 3% using a different data set.

ENDNOTES

1 In this report, the term "rural space" includes small and medium sized towns, according to the national definitions and applies to all sectoral investment i.e., social sectors as well as agriculture, natural resources management, infrastructure etc, in rural space.

2 Source: The Rural Portfolio Review FY2001 *Investment Profile of the World Bank's Rural Portfolio—Synthesis Document*. The document provides further details on the analysis and the lending breakdown.

3 When using only the Bank's sector codes and methodology used for defining rural space against Goal 2—achieving universal primary education—a share of some 49% of total Bank lending was estimated as allocated to rural space and for the combined health sector Goals (Goals 4–6) some 54% of Bank lending was estimated to be allocated to rural space.

FRAMEWORK FOR A RENEWED RURAL DEVELOPMENT STRATEGY

2

This chapter presents the overall approach of the World Bank's strategy in reaching the rural poor and reducing poverty in rural areas. At the outset, it must be recognized that reducing poverty requires a strategy flexible enough to be adapted and adopted by individual regions, countries, and even sub-regions within countries. This chapter also describes the Bank's priorities in rural policy and institutional development. While building on previous strategies, the new strategy has five distinct features:

- **Focusing on the poor.** The Bank is moving to holistic pro-poor rural development and the enhancement of returns to labor, land and capital.

- **Fostering broad-based growth.** While reaffirming its commitment to agriculture as the main engine of rural economic growth, the Bank recognizes the importance of non-farm economic activities and the private sector.

- **Addressing the entire rural space.** The Bank is moving to cross-sectoral approaches for the longer term—and away from short-term sector-by-sector approaches—yet addressing directly the shortcomings of earlier top-down, non-inclusive approaches.

- **Forging alliances of all stakeholders.** The Bank is increasing broad-based stakeholder participation in design and implementation, away from working mainly with central governments in project and program design.

- **Addressing impact of global developments on client countries.** The Bank is placing increased emphasis on global development issues, including international trade policy, the subsidization of agriculture and global climate change.

These features are threaded throughout the strategy discussion that follows.

A HOLISTIC APPROACH TO RURAL DEVELOPMENT WITH A FOCUS ON POVERTY REDUCTION

The Bank's revised rural strategy focuses on improving the well-being of rural people and reducing rural poverty in the widest possible sense. Figure 2.1 provides a conceptual overview of this strategy revision. Rural poverty focus entails much more than increasing the average income of rural populations—it envisages improving the quality of rural life. Accordingly, the Bank's vision for the developing world is one in which:

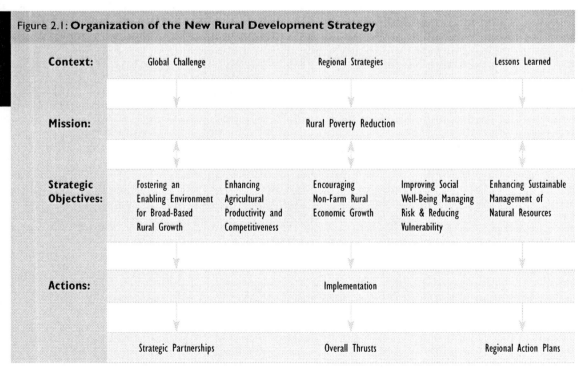

Figure 2.1: **Organization of the New Rural Development Strategy**

Context:	Global Challenge		Regional Strategies		Lessons Learned
Mission:	Rural Poverty Reduction				
Strategic Objectives:	Fostering an Enabling Environment for Broad-Based Rural Growth	Enhancing Agricultural Productivity and Competitiveness	Encouraging Non-Farm Rural Economic Growth	Improving Social Well-Being Managing Risk & Reducing Vulnerability	Enhancing Sustainable Management of Natural Resources
Actions:	Implementation				
	Strategic Partnerships		Overall Thrusts		Regional Action Plans

- Rural residents enjoy a standard of living and a quality of life that is not significantly below that available to urban residents.

- Rural communities offer equitable economic opportunities for all of their residents regardless of income, status, gender, or ethnicity.

- Rural communities become vibrant, sustainable and attractive places to live and work.

- Rural areas contribute to national development and are dynamically linked to urban areas.

- Rural areas adapt to on-going economic, social, cultural, environmental and technological change.

The overall vision of the new strategy, which has been endorsed by the Bank's clients via a number of consultations, requires a clear shift in government and international donor priorities to increase resources available for holistic rural development efforts. Some of the key elements of the holistic approach are as follows:

- Sustainable rural development requires multi-disciplinary and pluralist approaches to poverty, social and gender equity, local economic development, natural resource management, and governance.

- An agricultural focus is necessary, but not sufficient for sustainable rural development. More integrated approaches are also needed—integrating infrastructure and agricultural technologies, institutions and capacity building, non-agricultural job creation, and human capital.

- Solutions in rural development must be based on participation, empowerment, and rural governance; address directly the shortcomings of earlier top-down, non-inclusive approaches; and must also foster growth of the private sector, and the use of market mechanisms.

- Developing rural institutions and capacities requires long-term efforts.

- Piloting and experimenting are desirable, but replicability must be a design objective.

THE RURAL-URBAN INTERFACE IN RURAL DEVELOPMENT

The poor have much in common with each other wherever they live. Nevertheless, rural areas around the world share a number of characteristics that are distinctly different from urban areas. For this reason it is necessary to examine the specific approaches required to address the needs of the rural and urban poor separately. The Bank's rural strategy recognizes that urban and rural areas are inextricably linked in the process of development, and that the strategy must take into account the diverse range of interactions between urban and rural economies when crafting future development efforts. All countries experience a transition from a predominantly rural to a more heavily urban character of their economies as development progresses. Urban and rural areas are a continuum, but they are also internally heterogeneous.

Development strategies need to be differentiated for urban and rural areas. However, there should be an overall coherence between urban and rural development. Economic development is a dynamic process potentially affecting all areas of a society, and urban growth can be a catalyst for rural economic activities. Population flows are ongoing, not static, so the actual boundaries of rural and urban areas are constantly shifting. In fact, despite high rural birthrates, most population growth in the next decades will be in urban areas, largely as a result of continued rural to urban migration. Rural areas can often be more prosperous and productive when they are close to, or integrally linked to, urban centers which provide opportunities for agglomeration, major markets, financial resources, and employment options. At the urban periphery and in small and medium towns, the "rural" and "urban" distinctions can be blurred. Non-farm employment (small manufacturing and services) is important in rural economies, and urban agriculture (household plots) is a significant source of food and incomes in many cities.

Migration is an integral part of rural and national development and societal change. It allows individuals to respond to economic opportunity and helps to manage risks and accumulate assets. Mobility is

17

frequently adopted as a critical livelihood strategy for many households. Patterns of migration are themselves diverse ranging from rural-urban, rural-rural and urban-rural and may be daily, seasonal, annual, or permanent. Part or all of the household may migrate. Much migration remains circular and many migrant household strategies remain based in their villages of origin. The multi-locational nature of livelihood strategies necessitates policies that both understand and recognize population mobility, and which aim to minimize any negative consequences and build on opportunities (de Haan, 1999).

Rural enterprises are generally small and suffer from diseconomies of scale (Table 2.1). Rural areas at low levels of development face specific market failures. In most poor rural areas, transport, energy, and telecommunications and business services are deficient and expensive, if available at all. These deficiencies often have different impacts on male and female farmers. In Sub-Saharan Africa, crops such as cocoa and coffee, marketed by men, are often collected from the farm gate whereas food crops marketed by women have to be transported to the market. Studies in Ghana and Tanzania revealed that women spend nearly three times as much time in transport activities compared with men, and trans-

port about four times the volume. Health and education are almost inevitably quantitatively and qualitatively less developed than they are in urban areas. There are typically low volumes of trade, high margins on goods purchased from distant centers, few competitors, and high transaction and information costs. Many rural markets are highly seasonal and require storage capacities and financial services that are seasonal as well. This restricts trade and employment in the off season. Because of these constraints, the private sector finds rural areas less desirable than urban ones. Therefore, rural infrastructure services must be seen as public goods requiring public support.

SELECTIVITY AT THE REGIONAL AND COUNTRY LEVELS

To support rural development effectively, the principle of selectivity has to guide implementation. The Bank's strategic framework paper (SFP) and strategic direction paper (SDP) provide guidelines for selectivity at corporate, regional, and country levels. The selectivity criteria outlined below indicate that **the Bank does not intend to work on all components of the strategy in all regions, and**

Table 2.1: **Characteristics of Rural and Urban Enterprise Environment and Markets in Developing Countries**

Characteristic	Rural Areas	Urban Areas
Scale of enterprises	Predominantly small	Small, medium and large
Intermediary providers of inputs, credit and services	Few private providers	Many private providers
Public services and infrastructure Markets for products and labor	Scarce, unreliable, and expensive Highly seasonal	Relatively favorable Year-round
Access to markets	Poor access to markets, especially for the poor	Good access
Competition	Thin markets, many nearly natural monopolies	Most sectors have competitive markets
Transaction costs in markets	High due to poor infrastructure, and many small dispersed buyers and sellers	Relatively low

especially, in all countries. Rather, the program has a focused hierarchy of priorities that lead to a tailored and selective program for each of the individual regions and countries. CASs will reflect the specific decisions by national governments and the Bank regarding the degree of support for rural development to be provided by the Bank.

Corporate Priorities

At the corporate level the priorities are set to fulfill the Bank poverty-reduction mandates. The global strategy provides overall priorities for countries at all stages of development. The corporate priorities are also geared to programs supporting global public goods that convey shared benefits world-wide (such as support to CGIAR and agricultural trade advocacy).

Regional Priorities

At the regional level, the strategies exhibit a greater level of selectivity and diversity. Each regional strategy and action plan reflect the specific conditions, stages, and lessons learned in the given region, and the Bank's comparative advantage in that region. The regional action plans also provide region-specific implementation guidelines and concrete programs for delivering Bank support in rural areas.

The foundations of the revised strategy are the six regional action plans, each the product of intensive consultations with the full range of stakeholders including local organizations, national governments, private firms, NGOs, academics, and fellow donor agencies. The six regional action plans reflect rural development agendas fully consistent with the overall Bank rural development strategy. Each has a poverty reduction focus and a multi-sectoral approach with increased emphasis on the private sector, yet they all maintain a region-specific character. The differing foci of the regional action plans reflect the varying conditions and the tailored application of the corporate rural development strategy to reduce rural poverty and contribute to achieving the MDGs.

The **Africa** action plan places major emphasis on the institutional foundation for reducing rural poverty. It advocates support for government efforts to decentralize, and enhance the participation of rural communities. The **East Asia and Pacific** regional plan calls for financing programs that directly attack poverty through targeted productivity enhancing investments in very poor areas. The **Europe and Central Asia** region focuses on sustainable rural productivity growth and the completion of the transition process

19

Table 2.2: Country (or regions within countries) Priorities by Level of Development

	Least Developed	Less Poor	Middle Income
Broad-based Market Growth for agriculture and non-farm economic activity	■ Promote agriculture ■ Integrate subsistence farmers into market economy ■ Develop rural infrastructure and basic institutions	■ Improve agricultural productivity and diversification ■ Non-farm private sector development ■ Improve access to markets	■ Promote competitiveness of the commercial rural sector ■ Promote high-value crops ■ Expand private sector provision of semi-public services
Improving social well-being, managing risk, and reducing vulnerability	■ Basic social services ■ Introduce safety nets ■ Develop social capital	■ Expand social services ■ Promote improved risk management	■ Specialist medical services and higher education ■ Comprehensive national safety nets
Sustainable management of natural resources	■ Property rights ■ Reduce soil degradation and deforestation	■ Getting resource prices right ■ Watershed management	■ Environmental regulation ■ Reduce negative externalities of agriculture

in the rural areas. In the **Latin America and Caribbean** region, the action plan puts special emphasis on rural and urban dynamics, and adopts a Local Economic Development approach to addressing rural development built around increased participation of local actors including local and sub-national governments, private sector and organizations of civil society. The **Middle East and North Africa** action plan places a high priority on rationalizing water management and policies. The focus of the **South Asia** regional action plan is the enhancement of human and social capital development in rural areas, as well as decentralization (see Annex 3 for more information on the regional action plans).

Country Level Priorities

The differences in emphasis among the regional strategies are critical to their ultimate success in implementation. The participation of stakeholders from each individual country ensures that the translation of the regional action plans into country implementation plans will reflect the unique characteristics of each country. For East Asia and Pacific, Middle East and North Africa, and South Asia, the regional priorities have already been translated to country-specific priorities and action programs. For Africa, Europe Central Asia, and Latin America Caribbean, detailed action plans have been developed for major country groups.

At the country level, the priorities and the mix of Bank assistance instruments are determined by many factors, including progress in policy reforms, the size and state of the rural economy, and the access to external finance and markets. Country priorities reflect greater selectivity than the regional objectives. At the country level, the development of country-owned rural development strategies will provide the framework for translating the corporate strategic framework into reality for the given country.

The country and sub-regional priorities obviously reflect regional and country conditions, but, at the same time, they share common features across the regions corresponding to their levels of development, their policy and institutional environments, and their natural resource endowments (Table 2.2).

THE COMPARATIVE ADVANTAGE OF THE WORLD BANK IN RURAL DEVELOPMENT

The World Bank is the largest single provider of loans for rural development, including 60% of all agricultural lending by the international financial institutions. Because of this substantial involvement and experience with rural development, the World Bank has a comparative advantage in rural development. Bank support to agriculture equals roughly one-third of total official development assistance (ODA) to agriculture specifically, and about 20% of all assistance to agriculture-related activities. It is estimated that the Bank also provided at least the same amount ($2.5 - $3 billion) of resources to other themes in rural areas (including, infrastructure, health and education). The Bank's strong partnerships with most of the major bilateral and multi-lateral development agencies, and key UN Agencies such as the FAO and IFAD in supporting rural development, gives it a depth of knowledge and experience in assisting the world's rural poor. Specifically, the Bank has comparative advantages in the following areas:

- **Power to Convene.** The Bank is the only global institution capable of bringing together all stakeholders and donors, including the private sector, to discuss important issues and set objectives for assistance strategies. This convening power allows the Bank to play a catalytic role in bringing forth new directions and agendas in rural development programs globally, regionally, and for individual countries, and lever the efforts of donors and other international institutions.

- **Ability to Provide Both Finance and Policy Advice.** The diversity of instruments available to the Bank enables it to provide policy-oriented technical assistance and also to support the implementation of Bank-endorsed policies through a variety of investment programs.

- **Ability to Approach Rural Development Holistically.** As a multi-sectoral institution, the Bank is able to provide a cross-cutting and holistic perspective to the truly multi-dimensional nature of rural development (including agriculture, non-farm economic production and rural physical and social infrastructure), and integrate these into a broader, comprehensive development framework and PRSPs.

- **Depth of Knowledge and Experience.** The Bank's physical presence in almost every client country provides an unmatched depth of knowledge. The economic and sector work produced by the Bank in individual countries, in the regions, and globally provides an invaluable knowledge base for donors and governments alike.

- **Ability to Provide Clients with Advice Based on World-Wide Best Practices in Rural Development.** The world-wide scope of Bank operations, as opposed to regional, or national development efforts, allows for the diffusion of knowledge and experiences on a global basis. This also allows for the development of partnerships and communities of interest and practice that cut across countries and regions.

- **Impartial Long-Term Development Agenda.** The Bank is a collectively owned international institution that is not driven by narrow profit maximizing objectives. This reality allows the Bank to provide its clients with impartial, multi-year support to rural development, even when political or economic conditions, or conflicts in a given country do not provide immediate business opportunities attractive to private financial institutions.

STRATEGIC OBJECTIVES

The strategic objectives are now addressed by returning to the Bank's objectives in rural poverty reduction (Figure 2.1), which are geared to accelerate broad-based rural growth by:

- fostering an enabling environment for broad-based and sustainable rural growth;

- enhancing agricultural productivity and competitiveness;

- encouraging non-farm economic growth;

- improving social well-being, managing and mitigating risk, and reducing vulnerability; and

- enhancing sustainability of natural resource management.

The elements of the strategic objectives conceptually all fall under the two key headings identified as the critical foundations for successful poverty reduction (Stern, 2001), namely, creating an investment climate conducive to rural growth, and empowering the poor to share in the benefits of growth. The entire strategy approach, as well as its specific strategic objectives, are fully consistent with the 2001 World Development Report on poverty and the 2003 World Development Report on sustainable development. Addressing rural space in its entirety naturally draws on the principles underlying the Comprehensive Development Framework. The rural strategy must emphasize and utilize the linkages and coherence among all sectors operating to meet the needs of the rural poor and rural communities, such as Health, Education, Transport, Infrastructure and Communications, Agriculture, Public Sector Reform, Private Sector Development, and Social Protection. As such, it recognizes and draws upon the many sectoral strategies of the Bank including the links between urban and rural strategies.

The five objectives represent individual components of rural development that must be implemented in an integrated fashion, tailored to each particular situation. The successful implementation of these objectives in each country requires a coherent institutional and public policy environment for rural development. The five objectives are discussed in turn in the five following sections. A holistic set of strategies and actions must be developed for each setting.

21

FOSTERING AN ENABLING ENVIRONMENT FOR BROAD-BASED AND SUSTAINABLE RURAL GROWTH

3

The strategy *From Vision to Action* correctly recognized that the rural development challenge could be met only if international and domestic policies, institutional frameworks, and public expenditure patterns were conducive to sustainable rural development. In spite of progress in our client countries, the process of policy and institutional reform is far from complete. This strategy stresses the need to complete the traditional policy reform agenda and to address new policy issues in client countries. In addition, rural financial services and good governance are also essential components of an enabling environment for successful rural development.

The Bank will continue to place emphasis on the enabling policy and institutional environment for rural development, fully embedded within the wider country economic policy and institutional framework. In addition, however, no amount of progress will be sufficient for agriculture to fulfill its role as an engine of economic growth until a global environment conducive to commerce is established, with the elimination of high international trade barriers to agricultural products. The Bank will thus also enhance its role in, and contribution to, international policy for dealing with agricultural trade and subsidy issues.

3.1 Current Farm Support Levels in OECD countries as measured by the Producer Support Equivalents (PSEs)

Producer support levels (PSEs) vary widely across countries within the OECD. PSEs for farmers ranged from 1% in New Zealand and 4% in Australia to 60% or more for some countries (for example Japan, Korea and Norway). For the US, the average PSE is about 20%; for the EU 35%. PSEs also vary greatly among commodities: rice 81%; sugar 45%; wheat 36%; beef and veal 36%; poultry 16%. The highest levels of support are directed at temperate products, and it is sometimes argued that these are not the products of greatest interest to developing countries. However, not only are these products significant in some developing countries, but the heavy subsidies discourage growers of tropical products from diversifying into these temperate crops.

Source: OECD, 2002.

OECD AND DEVELOPING COUNTRY TRADE POLICY REFORM CRITICAL TO DEVELOPING COUNTRIES

Developing countries have a huge stake in the full integration of agriculture under multilateral trade rules. In many of the least developed countries agriculture often constitutes the single most important sector in the economy. Many developing countries have a comparative advantage in agriculture because of their relatively large endowments of land and/or unskilled labor. Furthermore, a large number of the poor derive their livelihood directly, or indirectly from agriculture. Agricultural trade, therefore, is crucial for

poverty reduction and economic growth in the developing world. However, while the volume of global merchandise trade grew by a factor of 17, the growth in agricultural trade has been relatively modest, approximately matching the six-fold increase in world production. Further, although developing countries as a whole have increased their share of world trade in manufactures, this has not been the case in agriculture (World Bank, 2001b).

OECD Trade and Domestic Subsidy Policy - a Major Barrier to Agricultural Growth in Developing Countries

A major reason both for the limited growth of agricultural trade and for the inability of developing countries to capture a larger share of agricultural trade is that protection, especially in the large OECD markets, has remained high (OECD, 2001a). Barriers to imports in OECD countries, together with export-limiting policies in a number of developing countries, have limited the volume of trade. At the same time, high levels of farm support in OECD countries have led to surpluses that have been exported (sometimes with the use of export subsidies) onto world markets, depressing world prices, and further undermining the ability of agriculture to contribute to global prosperity (Box 3.1).

Total agricultural support amounted to $311 billion in OECD countries in 2001 (OECD, 2002). This amounts to 1.3% of their own GDP, and is roughly equivalent to the GDP of all of sub-Saharan Africa. On average, prices received by OECD farmers were 31% above world prices (compared to 58% in 1986–88) and almost one-third of total farm receipts originated from government programs. Of this support, 69% is administered via price support and output payments, mechanisms that are the most distortionary for production and trade (compared to 82% in 1986–88).

Reflecting current levels of support, agricultural tariffs in OECD countries remain extremely high, in spite of the reductions introduced with the Uruguay Round Agreement on Agriculture (URAA). Recent estimates indicate average agricultural tariffs are about six times as high as industrial tariffs. Tariffs of over 50% exist for 60 tariff lines in Canada, 71 in the EU, 14 in Japan and 8 in the United States (McCullock et al, 2001). These cover nearly US$5 billion of developing countries exports (despite the high rates) and are almost exclusively focused on agriculture. Given these extreme levels of OECD countries' trade barriers— for example, 129% for sugar in the United States and 162% for grains in the EU (Elbehri et al., 1999)— improved market access offers the potential for huge increases in income in developing countries that can supply these products.

Protection also escalates with the level of processing, particularly in markets for processed tropical products, reducing the scope for profitable development of value-added activities in developing countries. Tariff escalation essentially taxes developing countries for trying to process their products.

High levels of export subsidies in some OECD countries remain a major factor in world food markets and have wide effects on world prices and market conditions. Between 1995 and 1998, global export subsidies amounted to over $27 billion cumulatively, of which over 90% is from the EU (Elbehri and Leetma, 2002). For potential agricultural exporting countries OECD export subsidies reduce prices and make it difficult for them to compete. For importers, they can bring short-term benefits in terms of lower import prices. But for both groups of countries they can be detrimental to agricultural development in the longer run.

In addition, agricultural imports into OECD countries and other major markets face an array of health controls, referred to as sanitary and phytosanitary (SPS) barriers. While ostensibly designed to protect human, animal and/or plant life, such measures can potentially restrict trade and pose major market access problems for developing country suppliers. Further, even when legitimate standards are imposed, developing countries may have serious difficulties proving that their exports actually meet these standards, due to the high cost of some testing and certification procedures. Technical capacity constraints—both in the public and private sectors—may also seriously hinder developing country compliance, as testing procedures are very expensive. Current rules do not recognize the real difficulties that developing countries have in imposing the standards with the emerging array of international standards and technical requirements.

Policy Bias Against Agriculture in Many Developing Countries

Policies of developing countries also discriminate against their own agricultural sectors. Krueger, Schiff and Valdes (1988) found that in the past developing countries have typically taxed their agricultural sectors, to some extent directly (for example by taxes on exports or controlled food prices), but even more so, indirectly, through trade barriers and macroeconomic policies that overvalued the exchange rate, turned the internal terms of trade (manufactures prices vis-à-vis agricultural prices) against agriculture, and kept the prices of agricultural inputs high. These indirect policies affected production incentives by making agriculture relatively less attractive than other sectors of the economy. This tends to draw resources away from the agricultural sector towards the manufacturing sector, diverting resources away from the sector that has comparative advantage.

Many of the direct measures have also been equivalent to a tax on agriculture, depressing the prices received by agricultural producers below levels that would otherwise prevail. Commodity and input markets have been characterized by heavy government interventions through centralized procurement measures (government parastatals and marketing boards), input subsidies, quotas on exports of agricultural commodities, direct taxation of such exports, and various regulatory rules and decrees. Other direct interventions have attempted to hold down the costs of food for urban consumers. Some direct interventions have benefited agricultural producers, however. Governments have often subsidized the costs of farm credit and important agricultural inputs, such as fertilizer.

During the 1990s many of these interventions have been eliminated or reduced in scope. Developing countries have reduced the explicit and implicit taxes on the sector and have often reformed marketing arrangements. In addition, exchange rate overvaluation and high industrial sector tariffs are less prevalent. In many countries, tariffs on industrial products have been lowered more than in agricultural products, reducing relative distortions against agriculture.

25

Although the magnitude of the bias has been reduced, it still remains significant. Average tariff on agricultural products remain high—at 113% in South Asia, 75% in sub-Saharan Africa, 71% in North Africa, 54% in Central America, 49% in Eastern Europe and 48% in the Middle East (Gibson et al., 2001)—and continue to create barriers to greater South-South trade in agricultural products, which has the potential to improve productive efficiency based on true comparative advantage. Most reforming countries have eliminated export taxes, but there are still some cases of export restrictions. Also, the operation of inefficient state-owned marketing enterprises for key agricultural exports continues in some countries. Despite significant improvements in their macroeconomic and trade policies in the last two decades, many developing countries still retain a policy bias against agriculture.

Large Potential Gains from Agricultural Trade Liberalization

A recent World Bank study on the potential economic welfare benefits of global agricultural trade reform estimates that the increase in aggregate welfare of the developing world could be some US $142 billion annually. This does not include any economic welfare gains from liberalization of trade in services, or investments, or reductions in imperfect competition. Most of these gains would come from trade policy reforms within the developing countries themselves (about US $114 billion), while the impact of liberalization in OECD countries upon developing countries is about US $31 billion—amounting to more than 50% of the official development assistance given to developing countries in 2001. When more dynamic effects of liberalization are considered including productivity gains, the benefits are potentially much larger (Table 3.1).

Overall, the potential gains from liberalization of agricultural markets are estimated to be substantially higher than the potential benefits from liberalizing manufacturing, even though agriculture accounts for a much smaller share of total world merchandise trade. For the most part this is due to the relatively higher level of agricultural protection (Figure 3.1).

Table 3.1: Gains from Multilateral Trade Liberalization in Agriculture and Food, billions of 1997 US dollars

Liberalizing Region	Benefiting Region	Static gains: fixed productivity	Dynamic gains: endogenous productivity
High Income	High Income	73	144
	Low Income	31	99
	Total	104	243
Low Income and Middle Income	High Income	23	53
	Low Income	114	294
	Total	136	346
All Countries	High Income	106	196
	Low Income	142	390
	Total	248	587

Source: World Bank, 2001, p.171
Note: Static gains refer to the results holding productivity constant. Dynamic gains allow productivity to respond to sector-specific export-to-output ratios.

Figure 3.1: Gains from Full Multilateral Trade Liberalization, as a percentage of income

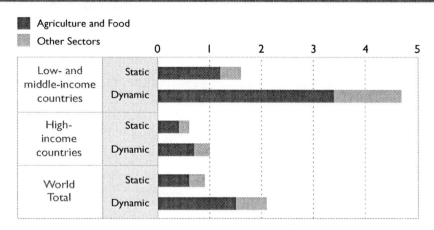

Note: Static gains refer to results holding productivity constant. Dynamic gains allow productivity to respond to sector-specific export-to-output ratios.
Source: World Bank, 2001.

Developing countries themselves would net 83% of the benefits from liberalizing their own agricultural trade policies. And the gains from developing countries' liberalization contribute almost half of the gains from those countries' overall merchandise trade reform. These large shares reflect not only the significant distortions in those countries but also the fact that the food and agricultural sector is such a large part of the economy of developing countries.

From the scale of these numbers, it is clear that there are big potential welfare gains from a successful negotiation of the Doha round, for developing and developed countries alike. The importance of the multilateral approach to liberalization cannot be overemphasized. The model simulations, in fact, assume that in achieving these gains unemployment is fixed, so that, once market barriers are lowered in a given country, all the farmers who were producing the now imported foodstuffs will shift to producing export crops or to work in nonfarm occupations. With other markets closed, the former cannot happen, and the latter is difficult to achieve. In other words, if only one country liberalizes, foreign producers would enter that new market causing a need to shift production. If trade barriers in other markets and have not been lowered, however, there is little chance of entering

new activities, and liberalization results in unemployment and lower incomes. It is especially important, therefore, that OECD countries, which represent the largest market for developing countries, remove first their trade barriers.

In addition, developing countries have extra reasons to support the full integration of agriculture under multilateral rules. First, and most basic, are the potential gains from the strengthening of a "rules-based" global trading system. Developing countries as a group would benefit most when all trading countries play by a common and more liberal set of rules. Second, multilateral agreements and trade negotiations should help developing countries to undertake and "lock-in" their own trade and domestic policy reforms needed to advance their development objectives. Reciprocal trade agreements can facilitate the political economy of policy reform in developing countries by enlisting the support of other sectors of the economy that would gain from trade reforms, thus helping to sustain the pressure of domestic lobbies for protection. Third, the new round of trade negotiations should expand trade in agricultural products, thus reducing the volatility of world prices that is so high partially because of the current thinness of markets. Since producers and consumers in poor countries are especially vulnerable to large price fluctuations, they have a special interest in the reduction of international commodity price volatility.

World Bank Actions in the Trade Arena

The World Bank will continue to assist its clients to improve their own trade policies, and to use the system of multilateral trade rules to expand their trade and thereby enhance their development prospects. The Bank's role is particularly important in integrating the complex multilateral and sectoral trade policy issues (especially on agriculture) with economic growth and poverty reduction objectives. The Bank's

comparative advantage is that it can combine trade policy analyses with significant sectoral expertise into a comprehensive view of how agricultural trade liberalization, globalization, and market integration can promote growth and rural sector development. This capacity can be used to support better agricultural and trade policies through:

- Advocacy of trade liberalization in both OECD and developing countries. The Bank supports developing countries in their efforts to increase their market access for agricultural products in OECD countries. This will, first of all, require that the Bank be clear and outspoken in regard to market liberalization in the OECD countries. It should also advocate that the removal of current protection levels not be replaced by non-tariff barriers.

- Mainstreaming agricultural trade liberalization and trade capacity development in the Bank's country assistance and operations (for example in national rural development strategies, CASs, and PRSPs).

- Facilitate capacity building through technical assistance and training on trade-related issues. The Bank will support developing countries in equipping themselves with policy and institutional tools to manage their integration into the global economy. Bank programs in trade capacity building are geared towards: institutional capacity building; development of country specific statistical databases for policy monitoring; and, providing training to participate effectively in trade negotiations and develop national trade capacity necessary to capture the benefits from trade integration.

- Increase assistance in the area of Standards and SPS regulations. In addition, improvements in developing countries' food safety and sanitary conditions is a prerequisite to be able to take advantage of any trade liberalization. The Bank is engaged in different capacity building programs, including: analytical research on the costs of regulation and compliance, and quantitative assessment of standards and regulation as barriers to trade; diagnostic assessment of the current situation in country supply systems and regulato-

---

3.2 **Turkey - From the Economic Reform to the Agricultural Reform Implementation Project**

In 1999, a new and reform-minded Government came to power in Turkey. The Government formulated a wide-ranging program of macro-economic stabilization and adjustment. The Government's agriculture reform program encompasses three main initiatives designed to reduce the heavy burden on the budget and Turkish consumers, while promoting agricultural growth. The first is to introduce a unified national program of direct income support to improve the access of smaller farmers to budget support and to encourage new income generation initiatives by farmers. Second, the Government is phasing out the system of subsidies for fertilizer, credit, and price supports, which disproportionately benefit large farmers and regressively tax consumers. The third initiative is to privatize state enterprises in agriculture to reduce Government involvement in the marketing and processing of agricultural products.

The Bank has been supporting adjustment in agriculture and other sectors through a separate Economic Reform Loan (ERL), approved by the Bank's Board in May 2000. Agreement on operationalizing the recommendations made by the Bank on agricultural policies (in agricultural support policy notes) was reached during ERL preparation. However, full implementation requires financial support over a time horizon extending well past ERL. This is being provided through the Agricultural Reform Implementation Project (ARIP) approved by the Bank in 2001. This operation, not only supports the policy reform described above, but also includes components to assist in setting up the direct income support system, to transform the government-dominated cooperative system into a true member-operated coop network, and to help farmers switch crops as price supports are removed and the crop-specific state economic enterprises are privatized.

ry/certification arrangements, including the preparation of country-specific action plans; and, production of toolkits to help countries and donor agencies identify problems and formulate action plans in the area of food safety issues.

- Analytical work at both global and country levels identifying key areas for future policy reform. The Bank is conducting rigorous research on the impacts of WTO agreements, agriculture trade liberalization and the implications of new trade agenda issues on developing countries. Further quantitative research will be carried out to assess impediments to agricultural trade integration and development at the country level, and to measure the impacts of trade reform on food security and rural poverty reduction.

CREATING A DOMESTIC POLICY FRAMEWORK TO STIMULATE RURAL DEVELOPMENT: THE UNFINISHED AGENDA

For long-run benefits from trade liberalization to accrue, it is also essential that developing countries adopt domestic policies that facilitate adequate supply responses. This includes an overall macroeconomic policy environment conducive to agricultural growth and investment, a sound set of agricultural sector policies, and the development of complementary markets for credit and agricultural inputs and services. In addition, the ability to translate improved market access for agricultural products into significant poverty reduction depends significantly on having a structure of land ownership that encourages increased productivity.

In spite of major improvements over the past decade, many developing countries still need to introduce significant policy reforms in agriculture. The nature of the reforms will be influenced by the degree of agricultural trade and subsidy reform in OECD countries. The World Bank will continue to assist its clients in their efforts to improve their own policy environment for rural development and thereby enhance their development prospects. The Bank's role is particularly important in combining macroeconomic policy analyses with significant sectoral expertise into

Bulgaria - Agricultural Sector Adjustment Loans I & II 3.3

A new government was elected in 1997 with a strong commitment to market reform. Government eliminated export bans and controls on profit margins of agriculture and food, eliminated most import quotas and duties on cereals, liberalized markets and abolished subsidies for cereal products. The government also has a program with the IMF. The objectives of the sector adjustment loans were to promote efficiency in the agricultural sector, contributing to rural employment generation, better living standards and more consumer choice through:

- Promotion of a land market, including restitution of 80% of land area eligible and several administrative measures to facilitate land transactions.
- Development of a private grain market by privatizing the grain marketing agency, and limiting the State Grain reserves stock levels to agreed amounts.
- Privatizing agricultural enterprises including agreed numbers of grain mills, seed, and food industries.
- Privatizing irrigation systems through decentralization transfer of management of operation and maintenance to water users associations on at least 100,000 ha.
- Improving agricultural financing according to agreed criteria.
- Liberalizing trade in most agricultural products.
- Improved forest legislation and increased community based participation in forest management.

Each loan was a one-tranche operation, supporting a medium-term program. The Government took all of the designated steps before each of the loans went to the Board. A key feature of the Bulgaria adjustment program is that it had the full support of the elected government and Parliament. Another feature was the willingness of the Bank to adjust the state reserves condition in response to perceived risks of food shortages by the Government in light of tensions in Kosovo over the period of the loan.

29

a comprehensive view of how agriculture can promote growth and rural sector development, building on its knowledge of international experience and best practice. The Bank can support its policy-oriented technical assistance with provision of finance for a variety of investment programs (Box 3.2).

Improving the Macroeconomic Context for Agricultural and Rural Growth
The major areas of domestic policy reform are macroeconomic policy, sectoral price and trade poli-

cies, land market policies, policies in other input markets, and legal and regulatory policies (Box 3.3 summarizes the Bulgarian agricultural adjustment loan which supported a comprehensive reform program). Specifically, the World Bank will assist its clients in the implementation of the following policy agenda:

- Correct remaining biases in macroeconomic environment. Economic growth in rural areas requires an undistorted exchange rate policy that does not discriminate against agricultural exports and/or imports of agricultural inputs. Macroeconomic and trade policies should seek to eliminate remaining implicit taxation from currency overvaluation and high tariff and non-tariff barriers to improve agricultural production and investment incentives.

- Adopt the principle of non-discriminatory taxation. Agriculture taxes should not be higher than those for other sectors, and should be integrated with general value added, profit, income and wealth taxes. Output and input taxes should be minimized. High levels of agricultural taxation

need to be reduced and taxation instruments need to be made explicit.

- Stabilize macroeconomic policy and enhance the institutional framework and the credibility of rules. While macroeconomic polices have improved significantly in many countries, macroeconomic stability remains fragile and uncertain. Evidence suggests that the credibility of reforms in many developing countries is poor due to unpredictable changes in rules and policies (Brunetti et al, 1998). This instability and fragility has an adverse effect on investor confidence and growth. Improving credibility or the reliability of the institutional framework within a country is a critical requirement to encourage private sector activity and investment in all sectors, including agriculture.

Supporting an Enabling Policy Environment for Agricultural Trade and Market Access

Trade policy measures need to foster agricultural trade and create an institutional environment that facilitates exports, while protecting the poor from sudden price fluctuations:

- Reduce trade barriers and anti-export bias to foster growth in agricultural trade. Despite reforms, average tariffs on agricultural products remain very high in developing countries, and there are still some cases of export restrictions. To realize the potential benefit of greater agricultural trade, developing countries must liberalize their own agricultural trade policies. This must be done carefully, and not unilaterally, however; with more rapid liberalization possible if OECD countries reduce trade barriers and subsidies. If OECD countries do not liberalize, the pace and structure of liberalization needs to take into account the pace of change in the global trade regime.

- Improve access to foreign markets. Developing countries need to be prepared to play a greater role in international trade negotiations to promote international agreements that achieve their market-access goals. Developing countries will also need to build their capacity in meeting the international sanitary and phy-

3.4 Strengthening Private-Sector Development and Market Approaches in Rural Areas

- Create a level-playing field for the rural private sector by removing anti-rural biases in the investment climate.
- Tune the methods for surveying investment climate to suit the needs of rural areas, include the rural private sector in country-level surveys as well as in detailed surveys in rural areas and use the results for policy dialogue and interventions to improve rural investment climates.
- Conduct pilot operations in rural areas with market solutions as alternatives to public services, and with Output-Based Approaches for delivery of agricultural services, infrastructural services and social services; promote mainstreaming where intervention is proven effective.
- Promote access to markets for the poor.
- Facilitate expansion of privately operated financial services to all rural areas.
- Promote private associations and public-private cooperation that can help in solving market failures and in reducing high transaction costs of public services.

tosanitary standards, which will become more important to gaining market access.

■ Reduce protection on non-agricultural goods. Developing countries need to re-examine their trade policies beyond agriculture. Large import tariffs on transportation equipment, machinery and agricultural materials impose higher costs on exporters who use these imports as intermediate inputs in production. This cost disadvantage erodes competitiveness and inhibits growth. Non-tariff barriers in fertilizer markets continue to be widespread and inhibit private sector entry and competition in these markets. High average import duties create a general anti-export bias for the economy discouraging gains in efficiency and diversification in general, including in agriculture.

■ Cope with world commodity price decline and fluctuations. Commodity price volatility implies a need to complement liberal trade policies with policies to provide an adequate safety-net for the poor. Useful strategies to cope with the cyclical trends include adopting prudent monetary and fiscal policies, avoiding higher export taxes, avoiding cartels, using hedging instruments and prudent financial management in times of commodity price booms. Some countries have avoided reform largely out of fear of domestic repercussions from food price variability. This reality brings to the fore the importance of accompanying measures such as safety nets and compensation. Useful strategies to cope with secular trends include export diversification and more rapid adoption of new technologies.

Introducing Sound Food and Agricultural Policies, and Supporting Effective Markets for Agricultural Inputs and Services

In addition to removing the anti-agriculture bias of policy, there are also large long-term gains to be made from improving competition in agricultural input and commodity markets:

■ Food subsidies and social safety nets need to be more effectively targeted towards the poor. In many developing countries, food prices are maintained at a low level largely to benefit urban consumers. Because everyone benefits from the low food prices, the subsidies are very expensive straining government budgets while not targeting the poor. The Bank will work with developing country policy makers to design safety-net and compensation policies that are more effectively targeted.

■ Removing remnants of marketing boards. Controlled marketing systems continue to distort market price signals in many countries. Substantial gains are attainable through careful introduction of foreign and domestic competition into the domestic markets for marketing, distribution and import/export services. Governments, however, need to ensure that the institutions are replaced by satisfactory arrangements, that trader entry is not constrained and that newly liberalized markets function adequately.

■ Remove other obstacles to effective operation of input markets. Much progress has been made in the past two decades in reducing government intervention in these markets. The main area where additional progress is needed is in creating a market-friendly environment that will permit the private sector to provide agricultural inputs without excessive government regulation. Fertilizer is one input that was often heavily subsidized in the past. Governments need to establish labeling regulations for grades and standards (for example for fertilizers and animal feeds), but the private sector should be permitted to deliver inputs to farmers in a competitive market environment. The Bank will continue to work with governments to create a policy environment that will be conducive to private sector participation in agricultural input markets and does not restrict farmers' choices of seed and other inputs to government-approved varieties.

■ Sequencing is important to successful reforms. In the short run there can be large adjustment costs associated with improving the competitiveness of domestic firms by liberalizing markets. But in the long term improved competition encourages faster growth of the sector than

31

3.5 Good Practice in Land Tenure and Administration

The BThe Bank has accumulated broad expertise and a good track record in the policy dialogue and investments dealing with land administration. The main focus of these operations is formalizing and registering land rights to provide security of tenure, improve access to credit, and thereby reduce the vulnerability of rural poor, particularly for women. Comprehensive, public sector managed, free registration, as now promoted in Central and Eastern Europe on a large scale, ensures that security of tenure is available to everyone, not only to those who can afford to pay for the service, as is the case in demand-driven systems. There is also extensive Bank experience with land reform and land administration in Latin America and East Asia. The ongoing portfolio of 50 projects has a 96% satisfactory supervision rating as far as expected development impact is concerned, compared with 89% for the overall agriculture portfolio.

3.6 Promote Equal Access to Secure Ownership for Women

There is also a gender dimension to land ownership, because land tends to be held predominantly by men in most countries. For example, in much of Sub-Saharan Africa conflict between customary and statutory law in land rights is common. Women's use rights to land are generally guaranteed through customary channels, but customary prejudices against women owning land mean that they are generally denied titles to land. Even where local norms give women rights to use land, these rights are acquired through men—thus these rights are precarious and contingent on a woman's marital status (Engendering Development, World Bank, 2001a). In Cameroon just 3.2% of land titles, representing just 0.1% of the registered land mass, were issued to women. (Fsiy 1992). This often has the consequence of depriving women access to credit and security in old age, and where women farm land independently of men, also discourages them from investing in productivity improvements. The Bank will seek to promote equal access to secure ownership for women in its rural operations.

would have otherwise occurred and releases public resources for investment in other needed actions. Nonetheless, where reforms are likely to have immediate negative effects, choosing an appropriate sequencing and speed of reforms may mitigate the impact on the poor and allow time to design compensatory policies to safeguard the livelihoods of the poor during the transition period. Careful sequencing of subsidy removal and liberalization is therefore a key issue for a successful reform process.

Complementary Legal and Regulatory Frameworks that Facilitate Private Enterprises

Promotion of Efficient Markets and Private Enterprise. In addition to correcting the remaining urban biases in the enabling environment and promoting a level playing field, governments are responsible for creating an environment that is conducive to the development and functioning of markets, business enterprises and farms. Governments need to adopt policies, and legal and regulatory frameworks that facilitate private enterprises and marketing cooperatives and improve the investment climate for farmers and other private sector entrepreneurs. The Bank's Private Sector Strategy provides evidence of the importance of private-sector solutions for boosting growth and poverty reduction. In line with that strategy, actions of particular importance to rural areas are given in Box 3.4.

Introducing Effective Legal and Regulatory Policies for the Efficient Functioning of Markets. Many developing countries have complicated systems of business regulations that increase costs of private sector operation and open up avenues for corruption. These regulations need to be streamlined, and training is needed for judges and lawyers on the modalities of the streamlined systems. The problem of efficient and fair adjudication of contract disputes is one of the major issues in many developing countries. To achieve development success, an efficient and fair contracting system is essential. Contract enforcement is required for the efficient functioning of markets. The Bank will work with developing countries to help create a legal framework and enforcement mechanisms for contracts to enable efficient market transactions.

Continuing Land Reforms and Improving Land Administration

Improve the Operation of Land Markets and Land Administration. Land is a key input in the rural economy and functioning land markets are important for the development of agriculture. For land to be allocated and used efficiently, it is essential that land markets operate. But for land markets to function, owners need to have secure tenure; tenants need to have secure tenancy rights; rental fees and contractual arrangements should be freely negotiated; titling and recording of land transactions should be in place; and a court system to enforce rights should function. Much progress has been made on these issues during the 1990s, and World Bank lending for land administration has grown several fold (Box 3.5).

Promote Land Reform for Countries with Inequitable Land Distribution. Some countries have a highly unequal pattern of rural land ownership. For example, in Brazil, for the year 2000 the wealthiest 5% of the farmers owned 69% of the nation's agricultural land, while the poorest 40% owned only 1.2% of the land. A more equal distribution of land can produce greater social harmony, higher productivity, and poverty reduction. Land ownership has a significant gender dimension as well (Box 3.6). But the record of land reforms has been poor. Several countries (notably Brazil, Colombia, South Africa) have been experimenting with community-managed agrarian reform programs that are often referred to as "market-assisted." Under such programs, groups of landless people negotiate directly with willing would-be sellers of land, and then, with credit and follow-up infrastructure investment provided by the state, proceed to establish a smallholder farming structure backed by strong community organizations. The experiment with this approach for land reform, which in some countries is sponsored or financed by the Bank, is still ongoing. The Bank is also active in supporting land reform and the transformation of the farming sector of transition economies, focused on the provision of secure land tenure rights and creating a system of land administration.

DEVELOPING EFFECTIVE RURAL FINANCIAL SERVICES

In order to achieve broad-based economic growth and reduce vulnerability, people and enterprises in rural areas need access to a range of services for saving, borrowing, remittance transfers, transaction pay-ments and insurance. There is also need for a wide range of service providers, formal as well as informal (Box 3.7). Many rural areas are poorly served. Supply-driven agricultural credit has generally proven unsuccessful and is no longer supported by the Bank, although still pursued in many countries. Although new approaches to rural finance are emerging, it is generally felt that these approaches only partially meet the immediate challenges of broad-based rural growth and poverty reduction. The Bank will strengthen its support for the development of a diversity of products and institutions that fill the finan-

---

Diversity in Rural Financial Services 3.7

The range of rural finance services includes many forms of savings, such as membership of a savings and credit association or a funeral society, savings accounts in a bank, and holding financial papers. People can borrow from relatives, friends, money lenders, micro-credit institutions, savings and credit cooperatives, banks, processors, traders and shopkeepers. Equity participation may be available as an alternative source for investment. Remittance transfers and transaction payments can be made through banks, postal offices, or special services. Insurance can be obtained through policies for health and other hazards, but also through forms of risk sharing in production, buying and selling.

New Approach to Rural Finance 3.8

There is a growing consensus on rural finance:
- Credit cannot compensate for urban bias.
- Credit subsidies almost never reach the poor.
- Providing financial services to poor people can be good business.
- Rural financial systems and institutions must be judged by outreach and self-sustainability.

There is also consensus on the characteristics that make rural finance institutions successful. Successful institutions are:
- Rural-based but not specialized on agriculture.
- Autonomous.
- Able to charge market interest rates.
- Able to mobilize savings and reduce reliance on donor or state funds.
- Able to collect on loans and have few losses.
- Able to provide staff incentives.

cial needs of low-income rural clients in income generation and reduction of vulnerability. The Bank will also try to reduce knowledge gaps about the relation between financial services and poverty and about the effectiveness of various instruments.

Financial services develop in interaction with demand. In a subsistence economy informal institutions generally suffice and modern financial institutions often are not viable. In a developing market economy, however, modern financial services are essential to enable farmers and enterprises to flourish (Box 3.8). In all societies households need access

3.9 Latvia -Agricultural Development Project (ADP) and Rural Development Project (RDP)

These two projects have supported the newly emerging private rural economy in Latvia. When ADP was launched, there were no commercial banks in Latvia with interest in serving small scale private farmers. The Agricultural Finance Company (AFC) was set up with a flying squad of mobile credit officers who took financial services to the farmers rather than waiting for them to come to a fixed and often far away site for such services. The concept of "a bank coming to the clients" helped overcome the transportation problem frequently faced by farmers. During four years of implementation, with only 42 staff, AFC approved a total of $43 million for 2,860 sub-loans including reflows, and the repayment rates remain high at around 93 percent. The loans made at market interest rates offered both in Lat and US $. AFC was subsequently merged with a commercial bank in Latvia and continues to serve the rural population today.

RDP, approved in 1998, supports a wider range of rural entrepreneurs and was aimed at helping the Government to build its rural policy making capacity for EU membership. A particular innovation was the "Special Credit-line" with government subsidy of a matching grant for small-scale farmers and rural entrepreneurs borrowing for the first time. First time borrowers received a small portion of the loan in grant form, once they had repaid their loan amount in full. To date, some 1,300 of these small loans, each for a maximum of $4,000 equivalent, have been made. The bulk went to a wide range of rural entrepreneurs, including rural tourism, hairdressers, tailors, doctors, and other rural service providers with only 20% going to farmers. RDP also successfully introduced participatory approaches to rural development by creating Local Action Groups (LAGs). Two leaders of LAGs in Latvia received a United Nations Award of Excellence for community-led development. Repayment performance continues to be good, at around 98%.

to safe saving facilities and insurance mechanisms to smooth consumption, diversify risk, and cope with vulnerability. In a developing market economy demand for formal forms of savings, credit and other financial services increases. This means that liquidities have to be generated in rural areas and allocated to evolving priority uses for production, innovation and managing risks. The Bank's objective is to support the institutional and economic factors that play a role in this process.

The development of modern financial institutions in rural areas meets serious obstacles: (a) high transaction costs due to spatially dispersed population and weak physical infrastructure; (b) high probability of large income fluctuations and the prevalence of covariate price risks as well as yield risks; (c) small sizes and volumes of savings, loans, payments and insurance contracts; and (d) difficulty of contract enforcement and lack of physical collateral for lending. Often informal providers of services and non-financial enterprises can cope better with these obstacles. But they face limitations in providing efficient support to the commercial sector because of their small scale and limited geographical reach. Given the inherent constraints to developing sustainable financial markets in rural areas, government policy may need to specifically address these obstacles.

In many developing countries financial institutions are poorly functioning. Many countries still look at their financial sector as a political instrument that can be used to influence the political landscape and favor allies in business. Often the policy and regulatory environment hinders the development of commercially viable financial institutions. Common features are targeted credit and interest rate caps. Formal financial institutions are often not or hardly available in rural areas. Policies to use state-owned institutions to provide subsidized credit have produced at best a very modest development impact. Subsidized credit is often appropriated by wealthy farmers, and repayment is poor. Consequently, directed credit drains public resources and is counter-productive for the development of viable financial institutions.

Alternative approaches to rural finance are emerging. In recent years, innovative micro-finance methods have been successful in helping households to smooth their consumption and support their economic activities. They have been able to overcome lack of collateral, and often achieve high repayment. However, their spread into less densely populated areas is limited, and their role in agricultural and term credit almost negligible. New approaches to crop and livestock insurance are being based on readily monitorable indicators such as rainfall and commodity prices, though coverage so far is limited. Information technology and credit scoring are enabling commercial institutions to better reach small enterprises and lower-income clients, though more in urban than rural areas.

The Bank Group will continue to support credit in rural areas to farm and non-farm enterprises where market failures inhibit the flow of liquidity, while observing sound market development approaches and discipline in financial intermediation (Box 3.9). The Bank recognizes that there are many suppliers and demanders for rural finance, and a range of mechanisms. Strategic priorities for rural finance are:

- Pursue a proper enabling environment for the provision of financial services. Policy reform for the financial sector is a high priority for many countries. This may include removal of supply and demand constraints, privatizations and contract management for state owned financial institutions, and appropriate licensing and supervision of a wider range of financial institutions. Good commercial laws and effective enforcement are necessary for all providers of financial services. Communication and infrastructure services facilitate the supply of efficient financial services.

- Support the development of efficient, viable financial institutions and products. The development of financial markets requires viable financial institutions. This often involves improved management, organization, and human capital of the financial institutions. Development of financial instruments is important as well. Generating local savings is a success factor, both in providing services to the poor and in providing a sustainable source of funds for investment. Institutions with activities diversified over various sectors can better cope with agricultural risks than agricultural development banks. The Bank Group will support capac-

ity building of private institutions by helping them to overcome market failure and providing public goods. Matching grant-based programs are often needed. The Bank will develop good practices in using matching grants. A basic requirement for the way grants are given is that they enhance and not destroy market development.

- Promote investment in social and economic infrastructure. A new focus on capacity building facilitates greater access by lower-income and poorer clients through training in business culture and financial management skills, building up business development services, assistance in group formation and in the creation of viable savings and credit associations. Alternative interventions may be needed for extremely poor clients and communities that lack an adequate economic base for credit and financial institutions to succeed. The Bank will work flexibly with poverty-focused programs to develop packages of grant, credit, and savings-based programs that are suited to the circumstances and economic potential of client communities, while pursuing the discipline needed for viable financial institutions.

The Bank will develop indicators of access to financial services in rural areas and financial performance of intermediary institutions, and monitor progress. Basic knowledge about the relation between reduction of rural poverty reduction and the role of financial services is still thin. Consequently, knowledge about effectiveness of interventions is limited. For this purpose, the Bank will produce a strategic paper to fill these knowledge gaps.

SUPPORTING EFFECTIVE INSTITUTIONS AND GOOD GOVERNANCE FOR RURAL DEVELOPMENT

Good governance and institutions are needed to support rural development. Empirical analysis has confirmed that poor governance significantly lowers development achievements (Kaufmann et al, 2000). Similarly, there is increasing recognition that the highly centralized institutional structure that characterizes many government administration systems can lead to losses in effectiveness of development investments and policies. An adequate transfer of resources must accompany administrative decentralization, so that local governments have the fiscal resources needed to carry out decentralized functions effectively. Political decentralization is also necessary, as it leads to better accountability and governance reforms at the local level.

Improved, But Still Inadequate Governance

In the past decade, there has been increasing recognition among development stakeholders that good governance is crucial for achieving sustainable development and poverty reduction. This recognition brought about improvement in many aspects of governance in general. However, the speed and impact of these improvements in governance has not been felt as much in rural areas due to the lower average level of education, the lower average qualification of civil servants, the smaller enforcement ability of governments, and more widespread traditions of paternalism. In general, several factors contribute to determine the quality of governance in Bank's client countries:

- Better processes by which governments are selected, monitored and replaced: More accountability and public representation, greater civil liberties, more political rights, better procedures for disclosure, and greater independence of the media, which serves an important role in monitoring those in authority and holding them accountable, lead to more effective public development activities.

- Improved capacity of government to effectively implement sound policies: Such capacity depends on the quality of services provided by the public sector, the quality of the bureaucracy, and the competence of civil servants, and their independence from political pressures. Higher quality was achieved in many countries by adopting personnel policies based on merit, rules of conduct that entail checks and balances, and budgetary processes that limit waste.

- Media and civic organizations have increasingly exposed and battled cronyism and favoritism, and have championed non-tolerance of corruption. All these improved the ability of a society to develop

an environment in which fair and predictable rules form the basis of economic and social interactions.

Administrative Decentralization and Development of Effective Institutions

The delivery of public sector functions that are necessary to achieve rural development in our client countries is hampered by the fact that many different sectoral ministries or agencies operate within rural space (for example, agriculture, health, education, public works, water resources and environment) each with a high degree of centralization. Furthermore, the formulation and implementation of effective rural development strategies is also hampered by the fact that public administration in the rural sector typically has lower capacity, poor personnel training, and inadequate budgetary resources, and that rural institutions generally have a low level of transparency, responsibility, and responsiveness to clients.

Experience shows that decentralization offers great scope for more efficient delivery of public sector functions. Decentralization allows local decision-makers to make better decisions based on their superior knowledge of local conditions and needs, and allows greater local participation in the decision-making process. Local government has a greater stake at being responsive to local priorities and needs (especially if elected in some popular or democratic manner). For that reason, it is more likely to engage in participatory procedures that can identify local priorities, and that provide feedback on actual implementation progress and difficulties.

In recent years, the Bank has increased its emphasis on institution building and related capacity development, with special attention to the Africa region.

Fiscal Decentralization is an Essential Component of an Improved Administration System

Financial responsibility is a core component of decentralization. If local governments and private organizations are to carry out decentralized functions effectively, they must have an adequate level of revenues—either raised locally or transferred from the central government—as well as the authority to make decisions about expenditures. An adequate decentralization of resources is particularly important for rural development, as it is generally associated with a net increase in the amount of resources benefiting rural areas. Fiscal decentralization can take many forms, including: a) self-financing or cost recovery through user charges; b) co-financing or co-production arrangements through which the users participate in providing services and infrastructure through monetary or labor contributions; c) expansion of local revenues through property or sales taxes, or indirect charges; d) intergovernmental transfers that shift general revenues from taxes collected by the central government to local governments for general or specific uses; and e) authorization of municipal borrowing and the mobilization of either national or local government resources through loan guarantees.

Political Decentralization

Political decentralization is also important as it leads to better accountability and governance reforms at the local level. Political decentralization aims to give citizens or their elected representatives more power in public decision-making. It is often associated with pluralistic politics and representative government, but it can also support democratization by giving citizens, or their representatives, more influence in the formulation and implementation of policies. Political decentralization has a great importance for rural areas in light of the fact that the rural people generally have a weaker political voice. Decisions made with greater participation will be better informed and more relevant to diverse interests in society than those made only by national political authorities. The selection of representatives from local electoral jurisdictions allows citizens to know better their political representatives and allows elected officials to know better the needs and desires of their constituents. International experience has shown that when local institutions are empowered, within a democratic system, they become more responsive to local development needs and more effective at supporting a favorable business climate.

The Role of the World Bank in Supporting Development of Effective Institutions and Good Governance

In spite of the progress achieved, the institutional reform agenda in many countries is still far from complete, and the environment for private economic activity is still unattractive. The development of good rural institutions is of particular importance, since, in general, rural areas have populations that are less assertive politically, and often do not have a tradition of participatory government.

Good public institutions are characterized by transparency, accountability, responsiveness to clients, checks and balances, participatory approaches, and concern for the interests of the disadvantaged. They also practice independent audit procedures for both financial and substantive affairs and adopt monitoring and evaluation systems as part of the management system. The Bank will encourage governments to concentrate on the provision of public goods and on the establishment of supporting legal, administrative, and regulatory systems that correct for market failures, facilitate efficient operation of the private sector, and protect the interests of the disadvantaged.

Facilitating further decentralization in rural areas is an important component of the policy agenda outlined in the strategy, which incorporates future World Bank assistance programs to support decentralization efforts in the rural areas of client countries. In order to promote the development of effective institutions for rural development the Bank will support the following actions:

- Upgrading local administrative capacity. Local governments often lack the skilled staff, equipment, and working methods needed to implement complex programs efficiently. A history of limited funds has deprived local governments from gaining knowledge and skills in designing and managing interventions. This implies that the Bank should support investment in capacity building in a well-coordinated sequence along with decentralization.

- Transferring responsibility also requires a transfer of resources and power. Fiscal decentralization must accompany the decentralization of institutions and administrative functions. Bank support for decentralization should include a thorough assessment of the likely local financial requirements associated with decentralization, and installing a realistic capacity (and authority) to raise revenue and retain it locally.

- Enhancing accountability. Where democracy and transparency have not been traditionally practiced at the local level, it cannot be taken for granted that local government is more accountable to the local constituency. In such cases, the transfer of responsibilities, budget, and power, coupled with the absence of checks and balances, can produce very undesirable outcomes, where the benefits of public activities are captured by narrow interest groups dominated by the wealthy and influential, to the detriment of the poor. Some of the activities in capacity building discussed above could ameliorate these risks.

- Support Participatory Approaches. Participation is the process through which stakeholders influence and share control over priority setting, policy-making, resource allocations and access to public goods and services. Participatory processes or civic engagement in the administrative process allows authorities to share information with other stakeholders and thereby increase the transparency of their decision-making. This in turn will improve government accountability to the people and, as a result, increase the overall governance and economic efficiency of development activities. The World Bank is increasingly relying on participatory approaches as an instrument towards better governance.

- Retaining economies of scale in certain government functions. Training of public employees and updating their knowledge are easier to accomplish when they all belong to a central organization. The establishment of training centers is not efficient if compartmentalized. Similarly, some procurement and requisition functions are easier and more efficient when handled centrally, as well as the development of monitoring and control systems. The Bank should facilitate the improvement and retention of functions of this nature under central government responsibilities.

- Involve private sector as much as possible in provision of public services. Many government functions can be carried out more effectively by contracting specialized private sector firms and NGOs under competitive bidding. Certain functions that need to be performed by public agencies can be better accomplished if the agencies are organized as financially autonomous entities, capable of securing much of their funding through the recovery of costs from users. This is typically the case with "toll goods" and "natural monopolies" such as water utilities, power suppliers, and land registration and titling bureaus. Some services may prove too expensive for the poor, and require graduated tariffs, direct income subsidies, or targeted vouchers for the needy. The financial viability of these public service entities requires that commercial and social objectives must be kept separate and distinct.

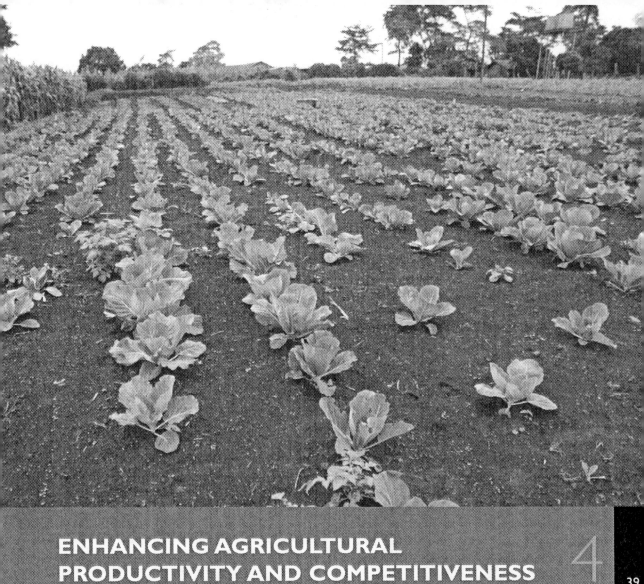

There are 900 million poor people living in rural areas in the world today. Rural poverty is as diverse as are the rural poor in their livelihood strategies. While acknowledging this diversity, certain common threads can be identified. In many poorer developing countries agriculture is the principal source of overall economic growth and *agricultural growth is the cornerstone of poverty reduction.*[1] Agricultural development, however, needs to be undertaken in a sustainable manner.

AGRICULTURE'S ROLE IN RURAL POVERTY REDUCTION

Agriculture is faced with fundamental change. Human population growth, improved incomes and shifting dietary patterns are increasing the demand for food and other agricultural products. At the same time, however, the natural-resource base underpinning agricultural production is under threat, with growing threats to genetic diversity and the degradation of land and water resources. Revolutionary advances in biological and information sciences offer great potential to address these resource constraints. However, making their benefits available to small-scale farmers is a major challenge, especially women with limited access and control of productive resources. International trade is increasing rapidly bringing with it a set of global governance treaties and regulatory frameworks whose implementation requires local capacity. How to lever these shifts so that small and impoverished farmers reap the benefits is a major challenge.

Agriculture employs nearly one-half of the labor force in developing countries. Indeed, a high share of rural communities and especially the rural poor are directly or indirectly dependent on agriculture through farming, food processing, fishing, forestry, and trade. A paradigm shift is underway from agriculture being an often protected and sometimes closed sector highly influenced by state interventions toward an open, diversified and highly competitive sector, tightly interlinked with other economic sectors and more strongly influenced by macroeconomic policies. This shift is occurring only slowly, however.

To reach the millennium goals of cutting hunger and poverty, agricultural growth must be put back on top of the development agenda—but 'business as usual' will not suffice. The dynamic changes now influencing agricultural production, diversification and competitiveness require a thorough re-analysis to develop better ways to support tomorrow's agriculture.

Given the poverty-reduction focus of the World Bank, agricultural growth and competitiveness are seen in the context of broad-based rural growth with the following overall objectives:

- improve the income-earning capacity of family farmers through improved technology and better access to input and product markets;

- boost rural employment creation through competitiveness and access to global markets; and

- enhance the availability and quality of food produced in rural areas, through increased supply, sustainable production methods, and efficient markets.

Agriculture's Multiple Contributions to Achieving Development Goals

Given the number of poor in rural areas and the changes in the agricultural sector—all compounded by the deteriorating natural resource base—the

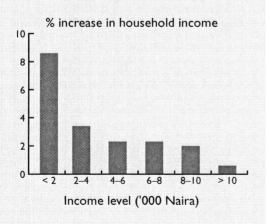

4.1 Distribution of Benefits of Enhanced Cassava Productivity in Nigeria

Cassava is the most important food staple in Nigeria. The Nigerian Roots and Tubers Research Institute in collaboration with IITA introduced improved cassava varieties in the 1980s that resulted in yield increases of about 30% on 50% of the cassava area. Falusi and Afolami, 1999 estimated that consumers captured 72% of the benefits of this research through lower prices. In addition poorer consumers captured a disproportionate share of these benefits. And since poor farmers consume most of their produce, they gained relative to larger farmers.

% increase in household income

Income level ('000 Naira)

40

role of agriculture in achieving Bank goals has never been larger. Agriculture impinges on the following goals: a) economic growth; b) poverty reduction; c) food security: and d) the conservation of natural resources. Subsistence agriculture is the ultimate safety net for many of the poorest rural people.

Reducing poverty through economic growth. In low-income countries, the agricultural sector is the primary engine of overall economic growth, due to its size and its important growth linkages to the rest of the economy. Agriculture is by far the largest employer in these countries, providing 68% of the labor force and 25% of GDP. In middle-income countries the share of GDP falls to 10% but agriculture still accounts for one quarter of total employment. Many of the world's poor depend directly on agriculture for their livelihoods. Increased agricultural productivity also provides cheaper food, which makes up a high share of expenditures of poor households (Box 4.1). In addition, an evolving agricultural sector creates jobs in agricultural processing and marketing, input supply and consumer products and services, and indirectly generates jobs for those leaving the farm. Finally, for the poorest rural dwellers, subsistence agriculture often provides a survival strategy in the absence of jobs, and in the absence of commercially viable agricultural activity.

Improving food security. Future food and feed needs are large and expanding, driven by population and income growth and rapid growth in demand for grain for livestock feed. Projections by Rosegrant (2001) indicate that unless there is a renewed commitment to agriculture through increased public and private investment and favorable policies, the long-term trend to lower food prices will not be maintained to 2020, and millennium targets for poverty reduction and malnutrition will not be met. Agricultural growth also makes important contributions to other dimensions of food security (Box 4.2)—access to food (by increasing incomes of the poor who depend on agricultural production for their livelihoods), and utilization of food (through more nutritious, higher quality and safer foods).

Conserving natural resources and the environment. Agriculture depends fundamentally on natural resources and has an important role in their conser-

vation. The deteriorating land and water base in many regions presents a concern for many producers, and wider public awareness of environmental issues is bringing urgency to conservation issues æ many global in nature. Protecting natural resources and the environment will require greater efforts to ensure sustainability of intensive agricultural production systems, and to manage natural resources in less-favorable and more fragile production environments.

PAST FAILURES AND SUCCESSES IN AGRICULTURE: UNDERLYING FACTORS

There have been significant achievements in terms of global agricultural productivity in recent decades. Commodity prices on world markets have shown a decline as a result of productivity gains and the increased availability of food from industrial countries that subsidize agriculture (Figure 4.1). Rapid technological progress in the production of the major staples across much of the developing world has brought impressive results: low food prices, improved farm income, and the generation of employment in the farm and rural non-farm sector.

Empirical Illustrations of Relationships Between Agricultural Growth and Poverty Reduction 4.2

- A 10% increase in crop yields leads to a reduction between 6% and 10% of people living on less than $1 a day, according to a recent study (Irz, et al., 2001). For African countries, a 10% increase in yields leads to a 9% decrease in the percentage of those living on less than $1 a day
- Wheat prices would have risen 34%, and rice prices 41%, more between 1970 and 1995 in the absence of international agricultural research efforts (World Bank, 2001d)
- The average real income of small farmers in southern India rose by 90% and that of landless laborers by 125% between 1973 and 1994, as a result of the Green Revolution (World Bank, 2001d)
- One percent increase in agricultural GDP per capita led to a 1.61% gain in the per capita incomes of the lowest income fifth of the population in 35 countries analyzed (Timmer, 1997)

41

Over the past three decades, irrigated area doubled and fertilizer use increased 18-fold, resulting in a 20% increase in per-capita food production. Increased agricultural productivity and lower unit costs of food production have led to a sharp decline in real prices of cereals in world markets, providing significant benefits to poor consumers. The major ingredients for this Green Revolution-led growth were public investments in irrigation and roads, public research on high-yielding varieties, and reliable (sometimes private but often public) supply of inputs such as fertilizer. Returns on these investments have often been high, especially in agricultural research (often over 40%), but variable. However, the yield growth experienced since the 1970s has slowed sharply in the 1990s due to diminishing returns to further input use, the rising cost of expanding irrigation, a slowdown in investment in infrastructure and research (in part induced by declining commodity prices), and resource and environmental constraints.

The agricultural development track record in developing countries is rather uneven. In many developing countries, especially in sub-Saharan Africa, agricultural performance has not kept pace with other regions, and is a major cause of continuing, or even deepening rural poverty. The sector has been subject to policy and institutional failures, in particular:

■ agriculture suffers from quantitatively inadequate support, excessive taxation, and discrimination in macro, trade, and industrial policies;

■ agricultural marketing institutions, particularly parastatals, providing services to farmers, have been inefficient, uncompetitive, and poorly linked to international markets;

■ reform of parastatals has been incomplete and support to alternative private sector structures has been inadequate;

■ local and regional markets are underdeveloped and hampered by poor infrastructure, lack of security, and bureaucratic obstacles;

■ rural financial systems have failed to stimulate and capture agricultural savings and channel these into agricultural investment;

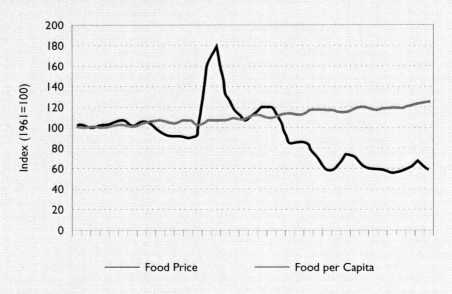

Figure 4.1: **Index of Global Food Availability per Capita and Food Prices, 1959–1997**

Source: IFPRI & WRI, 2001

- political institutions are weak, both within government and in civil society (e.g., farmers' organizations);

- insecure property rights have inhibited investment in land improvements; and finally,

- OECD agricultural and trade policies have limited market access, depressed world market prices, caused greater price volatility and inhibited processing to add value within poorer countries.

In terms of agricultural development, the majority of successful examples are found in East Asia. Here agricultural development created a dynamism in rural areas, which, in later stages, was combined with rapid industrialization. The major lessons of this success are as follows:

- policies must not discriminate against agriculture, nor give it special privileges and agriculture should be taxed lightly, using the same progressivity and instruments as for other sectors;

- the economy should be open, employment sensitive, and oriented towards smallholders;

- the importance of external, including specialty and niche markets, should be fully recognized and exploited;

- FDI should be an integral part of the agricultural development process;

- land reform is essential where land is very unequally distributed;

- rapid technological progress is needed, for which both the private and public sectors have important roles in research, extension, and financing;

- rural areas need substantial investment in education, health, and infrastructure; and

- the needs of women, who constitute an important component of farmers and farm laborers, must be built into programs.

DIRECTIONS FOR FUTURE BANK OPERATIONS IN ENHANCING AGRICULTURAL PRODUCTIVITY AND COMPETITIVENESS

This strategy treats agriculture as the leading sector within the rural economy, with significant forward and backward linkages to the non-farm sector. Accordingly, agricultural productivity enhancement is considered as a crucial component in reducing rural poverty. The strategy recognizes that the production of staple foods is the primary source of income for many poor rural households, but to get out of the poverty trap, diversification into livestock, cash crops, and non-farm activities is essential. In particular for those higher value products, experience has shown that, for sustained development, it is essential to support backward and forward linkages. Agricultural development induces economic growth in other rural sectors by creating demand for inputs, and providing materials for processing and marketing industries. Experience has also shown that agricultural investments are more effective if they are set within appropriate policy and institutional environments with adequate infrastructure and market development. This strategy, therefore, puts agricultural growth and competitiveness in the context of broad-based rural growth. In designing future Bank activities in agriculture, the new strategy incorporates the successful aspects of the lessons learned and focuses on the following areas:

- provide an enabling policy and institutional environment and advocacy and assistance for greater market access in the global trading system (OECD, WTO);

- support sustainable intensification of production through the use of new technologies and scientific advances;

- encourage, in part through demand-driven extension services, more efficient use of farm inputs and a reduction of post harvest losses;

- increase the productivity of water use in agriculture;

43

- support the diversification of agriculture and boost the share of high-value products;

- strengthen farmer-to-market linkages;

- enhance food safety and address competitiveness through quality assurance and supply chain management;

- apply differentiated strategies to fit various farm types; and

- support the development of rural physical and financial infrastructure[2] services.

This agenda expands and refocuses the Bank's existing support program for agriculture with a number of important new features. These include shifting the emphasis:

- from narrow agricultural focus to broader policy context—including global impacts;

- from agriculture to rural space;

- from focus on crop and livestock yields to market demands and incomes;

- from staples to high value crops;

- from primary production to entire food chain;

- from a single farm type approach to heterogeneity;

- from public to public-private partnerships, including community driven development;

- from avoidance of issues to head on approach (biotechnology, forestry, water).

This chapter provides directions along these lines for both the Bank and client countries. Support to the preparation and implementation of *national rural development strategies* is one of the primary implementation thrusts of the strategy, providing detailed programs for agricultural development in a national context. In many cases, agriculture will remain the key economic driver in the rural economy and in reducing rural poverty. Agriculture will be reflected in the priorities of national rural development plans and correspondingly, in the Bank's country assistance program (which entails dialog, technical assistance, and financing). Additionally, to deepen the conceptual framework for agriculture and the policy directions of the future, the Bank will prepare an *agricultural approach paper* which will present greater operational detail to guide the Bank's future agriculturally-related interventions, with particular reference to scaling-up good practice and innovations. Together, these efforts will go a long way towards addressing the "micro" agenda required to support country-level agriculturally related planning processes and interventions.

4.3 Agricultural Technology Generation and Dissemination

The Bank is promoting new models of partnerships between the private and public sectors, through competitive and contractual resource allocation schemes, building producer organizations, and providing farmers with a menu of technology options. In Brazil, Colombia and Ecuador, national competitive funds have forged new research partnerships involving the national research institutes, universities, farmer organizations, NGOs, the private sector and foreign and international organizations. Projects in Venezuela, Uganda and Burkina Faso are building the capacity of rural producer and community organizations and local governments to contract extension services and monitor their implementation, resulting in services that are responding to farmer demands, including information on marketing and business management. Several projects are incorporating new technologies, such as research in the new field of genomics to more precisely target crop breeding in India, and multi-media approaches with new information and web-based approaches to disseminating information, as in Russia. These models replace the pure public-sector delivery model of the past, which had significant efficiency, relevance, and sustainability problems in many countries.

44

Providing the Enabling Environment for Transforming Agriculture

Despite much progress in privatization and liberalization, many of the Bank's client countries still do not provide a business-friendly environment for private investment. Clearly, macroeconomic stability and good governance are necessary conditions for a positive investment climate, including a climate that is favorable to private farm investors. The Bank's overall approach to creating a pro-poor rural policy and institutional environment is discussed in Chapter 3.

Sustainable Intensification Through the Application of Science

High Priority to Public and Private Investment in Science and Technology. Most high-potential agricultural areas have now reached the limits of land and water resources that can be exploited. The closing of that land frontier—not to mention the acute water scarcity in many areas, diminishing returns and negative environmental effects from high levels of external inputs—means that future growth in these areas will largely depend on knowledge. This means that future agricultural growth in high-potential areas will be increasingly knowledge-based. The growth in total factor productivity that accounted for about one-third of growth in the past will now need to be the major source of growth in the coming decades (Box 4.3).

Therefore, investment in science and technology will play a larger role in the future, as agricultural sectors in all regions face increasing land and water scarcity, and greater demand for quality assurance in national and global markets. For very poor countries, increasing food staple productivity remains the main opportunity for growth and poverty reduction. Science, technology, and knowledge-based investments are also important to support market-driven diversification into high-value crops and livestock products, and for the development of sustainable production and marketing systems. Therefore investments need to support traditional research areas such as crop and livestock breeding (Box 4.4), integrated crop management, and crop-livestock systems, post-harvest technology and food safety, as well as provide new funding for biotechnology research in many countries and regions.

The Bank will continue to support institutional reforms to promote demand-driven and financially sustainable national research and extension systems that include public research institutes, universities, the private sector, NGOs, and producer organizations. Strategic alliances with foreign and international public and private research institutions, including collaborative R&D activities with CGIAR centers and other global programs, will be emphasized to promote access to knowledge. Innovative financing arrangements will be explored to develop mechanisms for regional research programs. The Bank will also foster global policy dialogue to ensure equitable access to new technologies, and continue to provide the leadership and financing to put the CGIAR system on a sustainable footing as a major provider of international public goods in agriculture.

It will be impossible to achieve the level of research investment needed from the public sector alone.

Meeting the Challenge of the Livestock Revolution 4.4

Projections by IFPRI (Delgado et al, 1999) shown an almost doubling of demand for animal products over the next two decades. Along with the dramatic expansion of demand in developing countries has come major pressure for change. Traditional production systems frequently cannot compete with intensive, industrial production systems, especially for poultry, but also increasingly for swine, fish, and cattle. New intensive production systems confront serious issues regarding:

- environmental sustainability, especially relating to waste management;
- animal health, both to maintain productivity and to avoid international spread of disease;
- food safety for livestock products;
- genetic diversity and loss of germplasm of local breeds;
- animal welfare, a growing concern, at least in industrialized countries; and
- employment standards and conditions for employees in processing plants.

45

Increased private investment in agricultural research is essential. To stimulate that investment, the Bank must contribute to the creation of an economic environment wherein the private sector has a reasonable chance of obtaining a return on its investment. This requires protection of intellectual property rights, input market systems that permit introduction of new varieties and technologies, and other policy reforms conducive to an efficient market system.

The Challenge of Biotechnology. The Bank is committed to helping developing countries assess, explore, and safely use new technologies. There is an emerging consensus in the scientific community that biotechnology is likely to be a valuable tool in addressing production and nutritional constraints and to commodities important to poor producers and consumers. The Bank recognizes that strategies and priorities for biotechnology will be specific to individual countries and/or regions, and that benefits and risks will be specific to the country/region in which it is applied. Therefore, where justified in the context of CAS priorities and tradeoffs, the central pillar of Bank approach to biotechnology will be to build capacity so that policymakers, scientists, consumers, and farmers in client countries can make informed decisions about options for, and risks of, research and technology release. The Bank will participate in dialogue with partners on global, regional, and country-specific policy issues and, in selected cases, will provide leadership and leverage. Key issues include access to, and adaptive capacity for, using proprietary tools and technologies, management of biological assets, assessment of risk, and benefits in food and environmental safety, especially in regard to biodiversity and genetic integrity of local species. Other issues include models of technology transfer, regional harmonization of regulatory frameworks, and development of international public goods. The Bank will look to current international protocols for guidance on the formulation and implementation of regulations and will continue to contribute to discussions on international agreements on bio-safety, intellectual property rights, and genetic resources. In this regard, the Bank will convene a consortium of interested institutions to assess the status of agricultural science, including biotechnology.[3] The Bank recognizes the critical role of public funding of research and development, including risk assessment and food safety, if biotechnology is to meet the needs of poor producers and consumers safely and sustainably.

Promotion of Environmentally Sustainable Pest Management Systems. Excessive use of chemical pesticides can be a risk to human health and the environment. The Bank will continue to promote integrated pest management (IPM) systems to reduce the reliance on synthetic chemical pesticides. Accordingly the Bank will seek to enhance the adoption of agro-ecological and biological plant protection approaches guided by the framework of its safeguard policies. The promotion of IPM in Bank operations includes support to technology generation in IPM (for example, through the CGIAR system and through lending for R&D), support to national policy reforms (for example, elimination of pesticide subsidies), and inclusion of IPM in exten-

---

4.5 Mali IPM Special Initiative—A Comprehensive Approach to Capacity Building and Policy Reform

Mali depends on cotton production as a cash crop for farmers and for export revenues. About 90% of the pesticides imported into the country are used on cotton. In the 1990s, due to pesticide resistance and inappropriate use practices, pesticide costs increased steadily while yields remained stable or declined. Evidence of occupational health problems and pesticide residues in food was mounting. Based on a comprehensive status report produced by a local research institution and a stakeholder policy workshop, a Special IPM Initiative was developed. The initiative cuts across project components and takes a problem-focused view. Policy reform elements include the expansion of existing participatory farmer training for IPM, the strengthening of regulatory controls, capacity building for monitoring of environmental and human health impacts, and the adjustment of the fiscal and economic incentive framework (elimination of hidden subsidies of cotton and food crop pesticides, provision of sustainable funding for regulatory and training activities through elimination of import duty exemptions for pesticides).

sion and farmer education programs. The Bank is updating its strategy and guidelines on pest management and monitoring IPM implementation in the lending portfolio. The demand for IPM technology can be served in research support projects, as was done in Ecuador and the Uttar Pradesh Agricultural Research Project, where comparatively large shares of project funding were allocated to IPM through competitive research grants. Another approach in some countries has been to support the development of regulatory and economic frameworks to promote IPM (Box 4.5).

An Evolving Concept for Agricultural Extension

Agricultural and rural development extension programs will be critical to achieving the rural development objectives. Delivering scientific and technical advances in most developing countries requires effective extension programs. New approaches in extension services will be important in bringing together the rest of the ingredients for successful productivity gains in agriculture æ new technologies, modern inputs, credit, and efficiently functioning product markets. Some approaches need to recognize the specific requirements of small and poor farmers, while other approaches which are designed to serve large and commercial farmers should encourage the participation of the private sector in delivering extension services and be based on joint financing and monitoring among stakeholders in order to improve efficiency and increase cost recovery. But extension must be more than just a delivery vehicle for agricultural technologies. Extension can play an important role in delivering social services such as information on rural development, business development and marketing, and other areas. Key principles in creating extension systems to accomplish these objectives are outlined in Box 4.6.

Increasing the Productivity of Water Use in Agriculture

Fresh water is indispensable for agricultural production, yet this input is under increasing pressure due to population increase and competition with other consuming sectors (Annex 4). It will be a great challenge to meet growing food demands, which is expected to double during the next 50

years under such water constrained environment. Another challenge is that most of the available quality land is already brought under irrigation and any further expansion would be in marginal land or at the cost of valuable forest resources. Therefore, future investment will need to focus on improving the productivity of existing cultivated land, meaning, 'more crop per drop' and 'more crop per land area.' This would require promoting new

---

Key Principles in the Design of Effective and Efficient Extension Programs 4.6

1. Productivity gains in agriculture are essential for reducing rural poverty, and technical agricultural extension (for example on adoption of new technologies, use of water retention technologies and fertilizers) is necessary to achieve these gains. Generally, demonstrations in farmer fields of new varieties and technologies are needed to assure widespread and rapid farmer adoption.

2. Technical extension can be combined with information dissemination in other areas such as HIV/AIDS, and especially for women farmers, information on health and nutrition. Priorities for extension delivery should be determined and managed locally.

3. Extension services will have to be publicly financed in the poorest countries. But in many cases they can be privately provided even though they are publicly funded. Existing and new institutions such as NGOs, universities, private firms, and even public agencies can compete for delivery of publicly funded extension services.

4. Modern information and communication technologies need to be employed to ensure that most people are reached with a wide range of information.

5. To assure effective management of privately provided extension services, local institutions will need to be strengthened to minimize waste and corruption. In many areas, this will require some assistance in developing local institutional capability and in assuring that the poor are adequately targeted.

6. As rural areas develop and agricultural productivity increases, some of the extension, especially the technical agricultural part, can move towards private farmer funding.

7. Periodic review and quantitative evaluation of all programs should be designed into the local operation and management systems.

Source: Alex, Zijp, and Byerlee (2002)

47

policies, institutional arrangements, technologies and management practices, which lead to improved water use efficiency and increased overall agricultural productivity of the already land under irrigation. To improve irrigation efficiency the Bank will focus on: ensuring the integrity of existing infrastructure that can be economically viable (primarily a challenge in low-income countries and in Central Asia); addressing adverse environmental impacts; providing demand-driven irrigation to improve livelihoods of poor producers; and raising improving cost-effectiveness (Box 4.7).

Future irrigation projects must be designed in concert with agricultural policies and include user - ownership and incentives for efficient and equitable water use, as well as cost recovery, and transfer of system responsibilities to autonomous private user groups or water users associations. The Bank will support innovations to improve water use efficiency, including, where appropriate, pricing of water, and

4.7 Egypt Irrigation and Drainage Program

The drainage program in Egypt represents a long term commitment towards growth and sustainability. The shift to a high intensive agricultural production system following the construction of High Aswan Dam in the 1960s depended largely on a reliable irrigation supply and highly efficient water management system. Adequate drainage has been timely planned and provided to mitigate the effect of the irrigation induced waterlogging and salinity. The government of Egypt in a partnership with the Bank invested about US $3 billion (in FY2001 Dollars) since the 1970s to provide main and farm drainage systems to 5 million acres. The program is expected to continue till a full coverage of the irrigated area (about 6.5 million acres) is achieved by the year 2017. The government and farmers have shown great commitment to the program through adopting appropriate technologies, improving the irrigation system, transferring management to WUAs and adopting a well functioning system of cost recovery. With remarkable increase of the crop intensity (230%), the yield per unit area of crops in Egypt stands now among the highest in the world especially for wheat, rice, and cotton. The share of improved drainage accounts for 15-25% of the yield increase. Re-use of drainage water in irrigation guided by appropriate criteria and guidelines contributed to the raise of the overall water use efficiency to one of the highest in the world.

shifting from staple food production to higher value products. The focus on the entire watershed, including attention to downstream environmental impacts, accountability and transparency mechanisms, knowledge and information systems, and modernization and rehabilitation will help realize the potential of existing irrigation systems and reduce the need for new construction. New systems will generally be smaller scale, and existing larger-scale systems will be renovated in conjunction with management improvements. Attempts will be made to focus management at the greatest level of decentralization possible. A poverty focus underpinning new investments will use irrigation investments to increase the assets of subsistence and small-scale family farmers. The IFC will explore financial structures that can attract private financing for the development of irrigation systems.

Promoting Diversified and Sustainable Production Systems for Expanding Markets
The food and agricultural systems of today face more rapid changes than at any time in history. They also face greater opportunities than ever before. These changes and opportunities are being made possible by consumer demands and by the liberalization of markets and trade.

With market liberalization taking hold in most countries, the private sector—traders, processors, and retailers—is expanding in many fields, including technology, information, and marketing services. Markets are now the driver for agricultural growth, making cash crops attractive, and allowing specialization and diversification into new products. Private investment is creating more value added and employment in rural space, more competition and thus better services for consumers, farmers and non-agricultural businesses. Technological progress is central to competitiveness and can boost production for markets and promote specialization and diversification. National food markets are rapidly changing with urbanization and more affluent populations who are demanding a richer, more diverse diet, with higher value products. Increases in demand for meat, fruits, vegetables, specialty and processed foods will provide new market opportunities to farmers, especially those who have sufficient access to resources, information and skills. The dramatic shift in food consumption to urban areas will also place special demands on food supply chains, market infrastructure and transportation.

Rapidly expanding export markets are providing a new source of rural growth, especially for middle-income countries and the more commercially oriented farmers. Many high-value products such as fresh fruit, vegetables, fish and flowers have created an opportunity for developing-world farmers to compete for a share in export markets. Diversification to high-value export commodities offers farmers new opportunities to increase incomes without increasing farm area. It also offers them wage employment in processing and packing sites. Another new phenomenon is the fact that large food retailers and processors are increasingly sourcing their supplies globally. As a result, international trade in high-value agricultural products is growing by some 7% annually compared to 2% annually for staple commodities. This expanding global market provides exciting possibilities for export, but it also forces farmers to compete with the world's most efficient producers. In addition, the expansion of supermarkets and chain retail outlets in many developing countries is already having an impact on national production and market systems. In Latin America and Southeast Asia, for example, the supply of local commodities to local markets is having to compete with globally sourced commodities (Box 4.8). To achieve such gains from diversification requires adequate infrastructure and investment in research and extension.

Growing public awareness of environmental values is leading to new opportunities to produce environmentally friendly products at premium prices. These opportunities include such things as organic produce, environmental services (such as carbon sequestration or biodiversity conservation), and new products related to multi-functionality of agriculture, including rural landscape management.

Coping with these new market opportunities will require technologies tailored to specific groups of farmers in more narrowly-defined production environments. The Bank's agricultural programs will emphasize technologies that promote more precise use and efficiency of inputs, conservation tillage, and integrated nutrient management. Integrating livestock into small farm systems will provide a means of recycling nutrients, and create income generation opportunities, especially for women farmers and poor landless people. For both extensive and intensive livestock systems, special attention will be given to environmental and food safety issues. Driven by market liberalization, urbanization, and income growth, there are rapidly expanding options for diversification of agriculture and boosting the share of high-value products, serving niche markets (for example, organic produce, cut flowers), and meeting the fast increasing demand for livestock products. As indicated by international experience, the increased focus on export crops does not imperil staple food production or food security (Box 4.9). The Bank will focus on strengthening private initiatives to export, implement post–harvest initiatives to improve product quality and reduce post-harvest losses, diversify and develop new products, and link poor producers to markets through supply-chain management systems and strengthening producer and community development groups. Public-private partnerships in science and

Export Oriented Agricultural Growth Based on Cash Crops: The Malaysian Example 4.8

Malaysia has achieved success by nurturing its export-oriented cash crops, namely rubber and oil palm and pursued a three pronged strategy encouraging rubber production on plantations, the development of an oil palm industry on small farms, and increasing rice production in fertile alluvial river basins. The post colonial government nurtured the rubber industry by developing rural infrastructure and industry, supporting research that transferred knowledge to farms and promoting credit and extension programs. The government also initiated world-class research in oil palm. The export earnings from rubber and containment of rice imports provided the resources that kicked off rapid industrialization. Poverty declined and the Malaysian economy rapidly transformed itself into an industrial nation. In the case of Malaysia, political factors positively contributed to agricultural development since the majority of farmers and the government were Malay while business people were Chinese. The only way to avoid income disparities between the two dominant ethnic groups was to create a prosperous agricultural sector.

technology will be supported to enhance and retain the momentum for competitiveness and sustainability of diversified production systems. Finally, the Bank will assist clients in developing arrangements for product certification (for example, for organic products).

Strengthening Farmer-to-Market Linkages

Strengthening farmer-to-market linkages is a crucial objective in promoting agriculture. In implementing this objective, the Bank will focus its interventions in ways that maximize participation of the private sector and impact on poverty reduction:

- improving conditions for private investment and the functioning of markets by helping overcome market failure;

- improving the performance of agencies providing key public goods and services that underpin the productivity of agriculture, with a focus on cost-effectiveness, client-responsiveness, and sustainability;

- promoting market solutions for service delivery, including co-financing and cost recovery mechanisms, where they are efficient and effective for poverty alleviation;

- empowering the poor, especially women, through collective action to profitably participate in markets, manage their risks, and access public services;

- promoting selective direct support to groups of farms, farmers, small enterprises, and rural laborers, with a high potential for sustainable poverty reduction; and,

- promoting supply chain management as a means to secure market linkage, quality control, and reduction of logistic costs.

Strong *producer organizations and community-driven groups* can help to link farmers to markets and technology providers, combined with an enabling environment conducive to private investments. The strategy gives special attention to building local capacity through producer and community organizations. In this regard:

- Bank lending will strengthen the capacity of producer organizations to link to markets and access technology, as well as provide a voice in policy formulation and governance.

- Producer organizations will participate in new Bank lending in roles ranging from consultation and advice to direct planning and implementation of technology and marketing services.

- Trade associations for exporters, processors, seed companies and others will be promoted and included as stakeholders in agricultural sector development and contributors to consultations on policy reforms, project design, and sector development.

New *information and communication technologies (ICTs)* with lower costs, combined with the increasing literacy and sophistication of farmers, have the potential to revolutionize rural information systems, providing more and better informa-

---

50

4.9 Is it better to Focus on Food Crops or Export Crops?

Countries should focus on producing the crops that they can grow most profitably. The International Food Policy Research Institute has undertaken extensive research on this question. The main research findings are:

- Countries that treat agriculture and rural areas favorably tend to do well in producing both food and export crops.
- Where smallholders shift some land to export crops, they continue to produce high levels of staple foods.
- Smallholders use their increased purchasing power to improve their farming operations overall, not just their export crop operations.
- As employment (including hired labor) and incomes rise, child nutrition often improves.

Thus, what matters most for impoverished household food security is income growth. It rarely matters whether the source of income growth is higher production of food crops or export crops.

Source: International Food Policy Research Institute

---

tion directly to farmers or to extension agents, agribusinesses, and other intermediaries that serve them. Application of ICTs in rural areas may increase the flow of information of all types, and facilitate market transactions, changes in employment, emergence of new industries, and social development.

Enhancing Competitiveness and Food Safety through Quality Assurance

Investments in strengthening the capacity of institutions and structures responsible for food safety will play an important role in improving public health and facilitating access to export markets. Food safety, especially that relating to microbial contamination and residues, is a major problem for domestic consumers and is emerging as a major issue in international markets. Poor countries need to improve their food sanitation standards as an integral part of poverty reduction efforts, and if they want to increase access to international markets. Food safety typically belongs in the public domain, as there are externalities and moral hazards involved. Where capacity exists, it is often good practice to rely on private certification and investments, under government supervision. On the other hand, the introduction of quality grades, in particular if it is linked to brand name development is a pure private good and should be left to the private sector. The Bank would support its clients in:

- identifying the level of assistance in food safety regulation to provide measures appropriate for domestic and export markets;

- strengthening legal frameworks, regulatory and incentive policy reforms related to pesticides, HACCP training, and food-chain management;

- investments in basic hygiene, disease control and eradication campaigns, laboratory capacity for residue testing, quarantine facilities, and systems of product traceability; and

- preventing the use of food safety issues from becoming protectionist non-tariff barriers to exports from low-income countries.

Differentiated Strategies to Fit Various Farm Types: The Transition to Commercial Farming

In many developing countries, agriculture is already in transition from subsistence orientation and government dominance to a dynamic sector that is well integrated into markets and has access to modern technology. However, this transition is incomplete and varies enormously by region and locality within countries. Most agricultural sectors have a combination of farm types, with different needs for public services and investments. A useful framework for analyzing different entry points for assistance delineates different farm types by their asset base and level of access to markets (Berdegué and Escobar, 2001):

- **Commercial farmers** who produce entirely for the market, and who dominate some cash crop and livestock markets and increasingly some niche export markets, such as cut flowers. These farmers prosper where there is a market-friendly enabling environment for private investment and initiative, especially infrastructure, policies that provide a level playing field and protection of property rights, and economies of scale in the production process.

- **Small producers on family farms** who are linked to markets, but have limited assets. Globally, they produce a large share of the developing world's food products including rice in Asia, vegetables for the domestic market all over the world, and milk in India and East Africa. These farmers—often poor and operating in both favored and less-favored areas—generally rely on diversified production systems and may have important off-farm livelihood activities. With improved market opportunities, many of these farmers can build their asset base and make the transition to commercially oriented farming.

- **Subsistence-oriented farmers** frequently operate in less-favored production environments and lack most types of assets. They have varied livelihood strategies, often operate outside of the market and are prone to high levels of poverty and food insecurity. Within this group, part-time farming is growing in importance accounting for a significant share of family income. Many of these farmers are also located in marginal areas with limited infrastructure and few options for agricultural improvement. While many in this group of farmers in middle-income countries are exiting agriculture, many will remain simply because there are few other options.

4.10 Options for Farming Operations in Developing Countries

Essentially farmers have five possible means of improving their economic well-being: a) get larger; b) become more efficient; c) do different things on farm; d) engage in non-farm activities; or, e) exit from agriculture. Getting bigger means acquiring control of more land and other assets. Usually this requires efficient land markets and an enabling environment for growth. Becoming more efficient means getting more productive in existing farming operations. Doing that usually requires effective agricultural research and extension, efficient input and output markets, good marketing and market information systems, transportation infrastructure, etc. Doing different things (different mix of crop and livestock enterprises) requires some of these same support systems plus farmer education in the new technologies. Adding non-agricultural activities requires an economic policy environment conducive to new business ventures and a marketing and transport system that permits trade with low transactions costs. Finally, the choice to leave agriculture and take up other means of gaining livelihood requires that economic opportunities be available outside the farm.

4.11 Rural Roads Help Connect the Poor to Markets: Peru Rural Roads Project

The Peru Rural Roads Program Team, through an innovative design that emphasized a strong poverty focus, grassroots participation, and collaboration among key players—the Ministry of Transport and Communications, the Inter-American Development Bank, the World Bank, and more than 20 NGOs— succeeded in improving physical access to about 3 million poor inhabitants of the rural Sierra. The program reduced the isolation and facilitated the integration of the beneficiary communities. It also enhanced economic opportunities and spurred local entrepreneurship. Over 11,000 km of rural roads were rehabilitated, and 32,300 seasonal unskilled, and 4,700 permanent jobs were created in 410 local road maintenance enterprises. An institutional collaborative framework was established to make most of the comparative advantage of each stakeholder. This innovative partnership program was one of the recipients of the 2001 World Bank President's Award for Excellence.

The transition of farmers between the different farming types (Box 4.10) under liberalization offers unprecedented opportunities for small farmers to lift themselves out of poverty. It may, however, also lead to more differentiation if the economic environment does not enable family farms to become more market oriented, there is a policy bias toward large commercial farms, and if land markets constrain adjustment. Farm consolidation and expansion, allowing more efficient farms to compete, is one way that this will occur in regions where good infrastructure and a conducive policy environment favor growth of non-farm employment so that less efficient farmers can leave agriculture. Contract farming and outgrower schemes are other mechanisms for small farmers to link to input and product markets, credit, and technical expertise.

The Bank fully recognizes that the farmer is the lynchpin in rural development, and is committed to employ differentiated strategies toward the various farm types to achieve the objectives of this strategy. These strategies are summarized in Table 4.1.

Development of Rural Physical Infrastructure and Infrastructure Services

Both farms and households need a minimum level of infrastructure services to function efficiently. Lack of safe drinking water is a major contributor to diarrhea, a frequent cause of death among children in rural areas. Trade requires transportation infrastructure and services. Markets require information systems. Adequate infrastructure is a *sine qua non* for agricultural and rural development (see Annex 5).

Despite widespread recognition of the potential positive impact of rural infrastructure investments, the availability of transport, energy, water supply, sanitation, and telecommunications services in rural areas remains limited. A review of investments in 15 developing countries reveals wide disparities in infrastructure availability between rural and urban areas (Komives, Whittington and Wu, 2000). Average access to electricity, inside water supply, and telephones were two to five times higher in urban areas than in rural areas. The rural-urban disparity exists across all regions, except in the case of electricity in Eastern Europe and Central Asia. In order to improve the availability, quality, and affordability of

Table 4.1 Strategies for Enhancing Poverty Impacts through Growth of Different Farm Types		
	Strategy	**Enhanced Poverty Impacts**
Commercial Farm Sector	■ Assistance to develop and employ food and biosafety regulations and systems for quality assurance, traceability and certification of agricultural produce (labeling, organic certification, fair trade label, etc.). ■ Strengthening of legal frameworks for property rights to promote private R&D and secure tenancy. ■ Strengthening producer organizations to represent member interests and promote initiatives in the industry. ■ Supporting development of diverse and competitive agricultural/agro-industrial innovation systems based on user-financing and private service delivery.	■ Develop labor-intensive high-value systems to generate employment for the poor. ■ Increase productivity to reduce food prices for non-tradables.
Small, Market-Oriented Farm Sector	■ Developing an efficient agricultural technology system to meet the needs of small farmers. ■ Supporting innovative communication systems to supply relevant information on production, markets and alternative crops. ■ Promoting small-farmers' organizations to coordinate input and marketing needs.	■ Broad-based growth to generate income for small-scale farmers. ■ Increase productivity to reduce food prices for non-tradables.
Subsistence-Oriented Farm Sector	■ Strengthening of local institutions and organizations that can best support farmers with scarce resources. ■ Facilitating participatory development of local infrastructure and technology in collaboration with NGOs. ■ Supporting local organizations that hire support services to develop market-oriented enterprises.	■ Introduce participatory research and extension approaches to build human and social capital necessary to address wider problems. ■ Identify niche commodities such as organic produce that are labor intensive. ■ Target investments to poorer regions.

53

infrastructure services to rural households and enterprises, rural infrastructure constitutes a substantial and growing component of Bank activities. This trend needs to be continued.

4.12 Ghana Community Water & Sanitation

In the early 1990's the Government of Ghana created the National Community Water and Sanitation Strategy and Action Plan (CWSP), the product of a national policy reform to which all donors signed. The first Ghana Community Water Supply & Sanitation project was intended to support the reform program and complement the existing activities of the central government water authority, which would focus on building larger systems.

The program evolved out of a set of national workshops on improving water supply and sanitation in Ghana. These workshops, which involved stakeholders from all sectors of society, produced a strategy and action plan for reorganizing the development of rural water supply and sanitation (the CWSP). It used the community-driven, demand responsive approach where rural communities identified their needs and the level of services they could manage and for which they were willing to pay. The new institutional arrangements included all levels of government, NGOs, communities, and the private sector to provide and co-manage services.

In terms of impacts, the rural water supply program more than achieved its physical targets. Beyond that, it increased the capacity of NGOs, so that they could provide technical assistance for water supply. It also built capacity of small entrepreneurs to supply equipment for the infrastructure. The increased competition, created in response to increased demand from communities, led to a 50 percent reduction in the price of boreholes. The project also made specific achievements in gender representation with women comprising 50% of water and sanitation committees (WATSANs). In addition, the WATSANs began diversifying into other areas — such as environmental services.

The follow-on project is helping the government scale up the approach to a national program. Progress began slowly with the first 18 months spent working with the government agencies and communities to learn and accept their new functions in the reformed system. Now two years into implementation, the project has taken off and is working simultaneously in 1000 rural communities. The program is also piloting community contracts (currently the local government contracts) based on lessons learned at a World Bank international conference on CDD held in April 2002. District level agencies manage the program and now handle most of the procurement for infrastructure — now decentralized from the national level, and many districts are supporting the operating costs for water supply themselves.

Transport and trade are initially the most important drivers for the rural economy (Box 4.11). Investment in infrastructure is important in reducing the high costs of marketing for small producers. With improved transport services, markets develop and farmers and other rural households have the opportunity to produce surplus for sale, to specialize in producing those goods in which they are most productive, and to diversify for distant markets. High returns to investment in rural roads, in particular in less-favored areas (Fan, Hazell, and Thorat, 1999), reflect the potential of growth through increased trade. Increased mobility through transport and information also increases participation of rural labor in income-generating activities that can add significantly to rural growth and poverty reduction. Therefore, the Bank intends to provide an enhanced support to clients in their efforts to improve rural physical infrastructure and ensure that the basic physical infrastructure (roads, ports, telecommunication, electricity, drinking water, sanitation, etc.) needed for rural economic growth is in place (Box 4.12). Specifically, in implementing rural infrastructure projects, the Bank will:

- support the formulation and implementation of sound sector policies to enhance the sustainability of investment programs;

- promote decentralized arrangements for providing local infrastructure;

- advocate participatory, gender inclusive, and demand-driven approaches;

- facilitate private sector involvement in the production and financing of infrastructure;

- ensure accountability to users in rural infrastructure projects; and

- encourage adequate cost recovery and upfront contributions from users.

54

ENDNOTES

1 Two studies that were completed as supporting documents for this chapter provide greater detail on the issues discussed in this section. These are: *Investing in Science for Food Security in the 21st Century, ARD 2001, and Farming Systems and Poverty,* FAO/World Bank, 2001.

2 Rural finance issues are discussed in section 3.3.

3 The consultations will include all relevant stakeholders, will discuss the full range of S&T issues and will not just focus on transgenic crops.

55

FOSTERING NON-FARM ECONOMIC GROWTH

5

Sustainable rural development requires multi-disciplinary approaches to poverty reduction. The agricultural focus is necessary, but not sufficient for sustainable rural development (Box 5.1). The Bank's updated rural development strategy recognizes the importance of non-farm economic activities, and the essential role of the private sector in rural development, including rural infrastructure and financial services.

Rural Development Strategies: Marginal Versus Favorable Areas

In many cases, policymakers and donors call for more research on marginal areas as a way of reducing poverty and arresting resource degradation. This is appropriate, as the situation is usually complex. In some of the most difficult areas, the rate of gain from improved technology may be very slow. Providing infrastructure, education and non-farm opportunities may bring earlier, greater and more sustainable benefit (to both poverty alleviation and the conservation of natural resources) than is possible with agricultural intensification. This is especially true for areas with high production risks and/or a fragile resource base. In addition, there are often substantial spillover benefits from productivity gains in favored areas through the operation of labor markets (migration from marginal areas, etc) and food markets (e.g., lowered cost of food).

Source: Renkow 1993; David and Otsuka 1994.

5.2

Rural Non-Farm Investment Benefits the Poor: Madagascar Aqualma Project

Aqualma was established in 1992 to produce and process shrimp for export in a remote area of Madagascar. The project was supported by IFC. Aqualma has established itself as one of the leading private companies in the country, with exports of US $26 million in 2000 and a profound impact on the local economy and living conditions. Aqualma in 2001 has about 1,200 employees, 80% of whom were never previously involved in wage-paying employment. Employees and local villagers have been able to access education and health services through the primary school and clinic established by the company. The project has generated many linkages with small local enterprises during the construction and operational phases. Future plans include expanding production on a new site, for which a community development plan and a conservation management plan to protect biodiverse habitats are being developed.

Source:: Karmokolias, 1997.

STRATEGIES TO SUPPORT NON-FARM ENTREPRENEURIAL ACTIVITIES

In addition to agriculture, growth of non-farm rural income producing activities offers important opportunities to reduce rural poverty. A common feature is the wide diversity of non-farm income sources at the household level including income derived through mobility of labor markets and remittances.

Many non-farm activities are derived from agriculture and natural resource use via upstream or downstream linkages and they can have important multiplier effects (Box 5.2). Other activities are essentially similar to those in urban settings including manufacturing, services and commerce. With the opening of markets, many non-farm enterprises will feel increasing competitive pressure and some will be forced to adjust or abandon the activity.

To design proper supporting strategies for the development of the rural non-farm economy, linkages to agriculture and to the process of urbanization must be fully taken into account. As is summarized by Ashley and Maxwell (2001), these relations develop according to a four-stage model:

- In pre-modern and subsistence societies, characterized by high rural remoteness and low urbanization, the rural non-farm economy is small, and has only local service provision;

- In the next stage, as the agricultural economy grows, the rural non-farm economy is able to capitalize and expand;

- Later, as the urban economy grows and new roads connect rural to urban areas, the rural non-farm economy faces new competition and may decline; and

- Finally, in the fourth stage, as the economic and social costs of urban congestion grow, new forms of rural non-farm economic activity may develop, perhaps benefiting from new outsourcing or clustering arrangements, and the unique circumstances offered by a rural environment (tourism, etc).

Of course, such a model does not apply everywhere and the poverty impacts of increased rural non-agricultural entrepreneurial activities are not evenly distributed. Many observers have pointed out that the relatively high-return activities in the rural non-farm economy are usually accessible only to those with capital or skills, while the low return activities are often the only ones open to the rural poor. It is essential, therefore, that the interventions designed to support rural non-farm activities include actions needed to enable the poor to over-come entry barriers and allow them to participate in the more productive aspects of non-farm economic activities. The informal segments of the non-farm rural economy are especially important for the poor and should also be taken into account when design-ing assistance programs. Strategies to support rural non-farm economy activity can be grouped into four main types (Start, 2001): a) removing general con-straints to growth; b) facilitating urban-rural links; c) facilitating enterprise growth; and d) sector or sub-sector specific interventions (Box 5.3). The creation of an enabling policy and institutional envi-ronment for non-farm entrepreneurial activities is discussed in Chapter 3.

SPECIFIC BANK ACTIONS TO SUPPORT RURAL NON-FARM ENTREPRENEURSHIP

The development of effective methods of support to the rural non-farm economy is an essential objec-tive of the rural strategy. Interventions will focus on strengthening existing opportunities, seeking new opportunities and removing barriers to entry by rural people to diversified employment and enter-prise activity. Specifically:

- Strengthening skills and organization capital. The Bank will help build the labor market and enter-prise development needs of rural communities and address the means whereby such capacity building can be offered and accessed. Such skill needs range from functional literacy and numer-acy, to specific skills in labor markets, and to management and administrative skills for enter-prise development, including market assess-ments and detection of business opportunities. Specific attention will be given to the demands and needs of women and to the rural poor. Common interest associations, trade and pro-fessional associations and cooperatives will be promoted. Rural Producer Organizations (RPOs) will be encouraged and supported to be able to perform economic and social advocacy, information sharing, capacity building, and coor-dinating functions and to develop market and negotiating power. The Bank should support the emergence of these organizations and develop working partnerships with them.

- Promote local economic development and inter-sectoral linkages. Recognizing that the sec-toral responsibility for the rural economy falls between many line ministries and private play-ers, the formation of cross-ministerial working groups and structures to support the rural economy will be encouraged. These working groups need to be fostered at both national and local levels and should involve the participation of both public and private sectors. Such groups at sub-national and local levels should aim to address local-level competitiveness and the wider enabling environment of both the farm and non-farm sectors, identify and seek means to remove barriers (legislative, regulatory frame-works, taxation, infrastructure, financial institu-tions, etc) and address opportunity creation for the community and the private sector.

5.3 Strategies for Supporting the Rural Non-Farm Economy

REMOVING GENERAL CONSTRAINTS TO GROWTH; FACILITATING URBAN-RURAL LINK
- Invest in transport, communication, education, and health
- Facilitate labor movement and remittances
- Increase the flow of market and price information to rural areas
- Set regulations/standards that facilitate out-sourcing and sub-contracting
- Develop rural recreational amenities for the urban population
- Identify options for increasing access to social-business networks
- Foster local economic development planning, combining rural and urban administration

FACILITATING ENTERPRISE GROWTH
- Develop infrastructure in small towns
- Support producer associations for marketing & sourcing
- Remove regulatory or bureaucratic burdens on small/medium enterprise
- Support business advisory services

SECTOR OR SUB-SECTOR SPECIFIC INTERVENTIONS
- Support industrial clusters
- Provide incentives for industry relocation
- Use concessions to encourage local economic linkages

Source: Start, 2001

- Strengthening the supply chain and product linkages. Trends in consumer markets, quality requirements and competition require better planning and coordination of supply chains from input suppliers, primary producers, traders and processors to retailers. Competitiveness depends on effective and flexible logistics and low transaction costs in the chain. The role for the public sector is to create adequate conditions for the development of efficient private-sector supply chains and to promote investment in physical infrastructure, to support effective sub-contracting systems and quality inspections through appropriate legal frameworks and enforcement systems.

- Support micro-, small-, and medium-scale enterprises. Lack of a skilled labor force, and lack of public and private services, including financial and technological services, are obstacles for the development of small enterprises, especially in rural areas (Box 5.4). The Bank will promote small rural enterprise development through support for commercial business development services. The Bank will promote efficient service provision through SMEs, in particular, in rural infrastructure services.

- Recognize and support labor mobility. Migration and labor mobility are essential aspects of economic development, employment creation, and poverty reduction. The Bank will provide support to policies that increase mobility through information on, for example, labor legislation, communications, skills development, and addressing welfare and entitlements, including access to services, and those policies that minimize the potential for social tensions and environmental damage.

- The non-farm sector is an important source of employment for rural women. Research in Ghana and Uganda has shown that non-farm activities are linked to falling poverty rates for both male and female headed households, but the rate of decline is faster for woman-headed households. Increased women's employment in the non-farm sector is also a direct contribution towards one of the MDGs.

In most countries knowledge about the rural non-farm private-sector is insufficient for effective development interventions. Surveys and sector work will be carried out to obtain better information. For this purpose, the Bank will include rural specificity in surveys on the investment climate, and to conduct more detailed surveys in rural areas, including rural towns. Where relevant, findings will be addressed in a rural section in country Private Sector Strategies and CAS documents. In preparing rural strategies, surveys will be conducted to assess the investment climate, and findings will be analyzed to find possible interventions for improving competitiveness. Outputs can also feed into the PRSP and other national processes. More work will be done on rural labor markets and policy interventions for enhancing broad-based growth and employment generation, including addressing the relationship between the formal and informal sectors in a diversified rural economy. Efforts will be made to identify strategies strengthening the poverty impact of non-farm private-sector development.

5.4 Kenyan Entrepreneurs Build Market for Business Services

Since 1998 an innovative World Bank project with a rural component, the Kenya Micro and Small Enterprise Training and Technology Project, is using vouchers to enable jua kali entrepreneurs to purchase skills and management training. As a demand-side instrument, the voucher project departs from the old approach of supporting public training institutions. Now, diverse suppliers are packaging their services for jua kali clients. Skilled craft workers have emerged as the leading providers of training. Local private agencies handle allocation of the vouchers. More than 25,000 vouchers have been issued, 60 percent of them to women entrepreneurs. There has been a 50 percent increase in employment and income among training recipients. The project currently subsidizes up to 90 percent of the cost of each voucher, but cost-sharing percentages rise with second and third vouchers. Jua kali now frequently purchase training without vouchers from providers who have demonstrated the value of their services.

Source: Riley and Steen (2000).

KALAMA, MUUMANDU P.H.C PROJECT.

LUMBWA LOC. ACTIVITIES DONE.	1990	1991	1992	1993	1994	1995	1996
1 NEW LATRINES.	36	148	74	59	74	84	
2 REFERAL FOR IMMUNIZATION.	80	21	32	29	67	134	
3 No. OF CHILDREN BORN AT HOME.	12	62	54	129	134	202	
4 SAFE WATER POT SYSTEM.	11	14	10	—	8	10	
5 FRUIT TREES PLANTED.	26	1645	1040	196	103	94	
6 LEAKY TINS.	188	117	92	55	114	86	
7 DISH RACKS.	96	198	200	83	104	132	
8 KITCHEN GARDEN.	24	49	42	55	118	131	
9 REFERAL FOR FLP.	25	16	20	383	431	516	
10 OTHER TREES PLANTED	5	566	120	50	64	76	
11 INCOME GENERATING ACTIVITIES	—	33	10	7	34	6	
12 No. OF ORS ISSUED.	—	10	5	—	311	—	
13 CASES TREATED ON DIARHOEA	—	13	5	—	18	—	
14 No. OF CONDOMS USED.	—	1938	1969	1344	2434	4321	
15 COMPOSITE PITS DUG	62	133	84	45	69	14	
16 MID WIFERY HOUSES	—	2	8	3	4	3	
17 HOME VISITS	672	1008	1344	1182	1004	1332	
18 PILLS DISTRIBUTED (CIRCLES)		530	680	940	730	616	

IMPROVING SOCIAL WELL-BEING, MANAGING RISK, AND REDUCING VULNERABILITY

6

I mproving social well-being, managing risk, and reducing vulnerability are key to improving the quality of life of rural people. These investments will also make substantial contributions towards increasing productivity, promoting the rural non-farm economy and enhancing economic growth. The Bank's activities to improve social well-being and address and minimize the vulnerability of the rural poor will be focused on: a) improving access to nutrition and health; b) HIV/AIDS; c) increasing access to and improving the quality of rural education; and d) managing and coping with food insecurity and risk for the rural poor (Annex 5). To achieve these objectives, foster broad-based growth, and enhance the sustainable management of natural resources, the Bank will also promote inclusiveness and remove barriers that exclude individuals on the basis of gender or ethnicity from economic and social opportunities.

IMPROVING ACCESS TO NUTRITION AND HEALTH

Disease and illness are frequent consequences of living in poverty, while at the same time illness and disease are leading factors pushing families into poverty. Communities routinely mention that poor health is a characteristic of their poorest members (Narayan et al., 2000). Disease and illness also affect labor productivity and economic growth. Current health and nutritional status of adults affects participation in the labor force and the intensity of work-effort. Among children, nutrition and health status affect cognitive development and learning abilities. Childhood malnutrition can also affect future labor-force participation and work-effort since it is associated with increased risks of morbidity and mortality during adulthood.

The area of reproductive health—and in particular culture-specific family planning—is essential to achieve the goals of the rural strategy. For example, experience in Latin America shows that attention to reproductive health care would have direct pay-offs by facilitating increased and effective participation of women in productive activities. Lessons from Bank projects including Ecuador and Argentina indicate that better development outcomes can be achieved if childcare and domestic responsibilities are considered in projects addressing agricultural and non-farm productivity.

Rural areas are also the scene of widespread malnutrition, which compromises natural immunity and contributes to disease burdens. In 2000, an estimated 32.5% of children under the age of five in developing countries were stunted (ACC/SCN, 2000). While the global prevalence of stunting has declined considerably during the past two decades, there are still unacceptable numbers of children suffering from malnutrition. There is mounting evidence that child malnutrition rates are static or increasing in Sub-Saharan Africa. Micronutrient malnutrition also continues to be a significant problem affecting both children and adults throughout the developing world.

To improve health and nutrition outcomes the Bank will:

- advocate the interests of the rural poor to ensure that government resources for health are not biased toward urban constituents;

- place greater emphasis on improving dietary quality and micronutrient status (fortification and supplementation are important strategies to combat micronutrient deficiencies, however plant breeding may provide an alternative sustainable and affordable long-run solution);

- promote community-driven multi-sectoral approaches to improving health and nutrition as these are more likely to yield high returns; and

- promote the status of women in rural development to improve health and nutrition (as primary care-givers, women are key to improving health and nutrition but their ability to invest in their own and their children's health and nutrition is hampered by their lack of control over household incomes, poor education, and the health risks arising from their reproductive role).

HIV/AIDS: A THREAT TO RURAL DEVELOPMENT AND FOOD SECURITY

HIV/AIDS is threatening the progress made in the past 40 years of agricultural and rural development, undermining gains in life expectancy and threatening productivity. The disease is no longer just a health problem—it has become a major development issue, posing enormous challenges to governments, NGOs, and the international community.

Of the 36.1 million people living with HIV/AIDS, an overwhelming 95% live in developing countries. The situation is particularly dramatic in Sub-Saharan Africa, where approximately 9% of all adults carry the disease. Sub-Saharan Africa accounts for only one-tenth of the world's population, but nine out of ten new cases of HIV infection. In nine countries in Sub-Saharan Africa, more than 10% of the adult population is HIV positive. In Botswana, Namibia, Swaziland and Zimbabwe, 20 to 26% of the population aged 15–49 is living with HIV or AIDS. Other parts of the world are also hard hit, however. In India, around four million people are currently infected with HIV. Further, it is estimated that by 2010 Asia will overtake Sub-Saharan Africa in absolute numbers (Barnett and Rugalema, 2001). The incidence of the disease is high in several Caribbean countries, although the spread of the epidemic in Latin America has been slower than in other regions and the epidemic is concentrated in urban areas.

Although HIV/AIDS has traditionally been regarded as an urban problem, it is gradually being recognized that rural communities are perhaps more vulnerable to it (UNAIDS, 2001). In absolute numbers, more people living with HIV reside in rural areas. For example, more than two-thirds of the population of the 25 most-affected African countries live in rural areas (FAO, 2001). Information and health services are less available in rural areas than in cities. Rural people are therefore less likely to know how to protect themselves from HIV and, if they fall ill, less likely to get care. In addition, the costs of HIV/AIDS are largely borne by rural communities because many urban dwellers, at least in Africa, return to their village of origin when they become ill. At the same time, HIV/AIDS undermines agricultural systems and affects the food security of rural families. As adults fall ill and die, families lose their labor supply, as well as knowledge about indigenous farming methods. Families spend more to meet medical bills and funeral expenses, drawing down savings and selling assets. HIV/AIDS undermines the incentives and the ability to invest in farms, infrastructure and education, threatening future prospects for rural and national development.

HIV/AIDS disproportionately affects economic sectors such as agriculture, transportation and mining that have large numbers of mobile or migratory workers. AIDS reduces productivity as people become ill and die and others spend time caring for the sick, mourning and attending funerals. The result is severe labor shortages for both farm and domestic work. Labor-intensive farming systems with a low level of mechanization and agricultural input are particularly vulnerable to AIDS. The FAO has estimated that, in the 25 most-affected African countries, AIDS has killed seven million agricultural workers since 1985. Up to 25% of the agricultural labor force could be lost in countries of Sub-Saharan Africa by 2020. This is particularly worrisome because more than one-third of the GNP of the most-affected countries comes from agriculture. According to a recent FAO/UNAIDS study, agricultural output of small farmers in some parts of Zimbabwe may have fallen by as much as 50 percent in the past five years, mainly because of AIDS.

In East Africa, labor shortages caused by HIV/AIDS have led to a range of farm changes, including a reduction in land under cultivation, a decline in crop yields and a shift from cash crops to subsistence crops. In general, farmers have shifted away from labor-intensive cash crops, such as bananas and coffee, to subsistence crops that demand less work, such as cassava and sweet potatoes. As a result, incomes have fallen. The impact of AIDS on farming communities differs from village to village and country to country.

The epidemic is tragic and made more so because it is preventable, through education, behavioral change, appropriate public policy, and treatment. The World Bank has developed an instrument to make resources available rapidly to countries wishing to implement their own programs to prevent the spread of HIV/AIDS and to help communities cope with its impacts, including care for orphans. The HIV/AIDS operations are a core element of the Bank's strategy to support rural development, especially in Africa. The Bank will:

- **Give high priority to stopping the spread of HIV/AIDS and helping communities cope with its impacts.** Poor households facing HIV/AIDS are less able to cope with loss of labor and are more likely to dispose of assets to meet medical and funeral expenses than are more prosperous families. Governments and development partners should target assistance to the poorest households, especially in the period immediately following death, when families are struggling to reorganize their production systems. Programs managed by communities that allow rural people to design and implement their own approaches are proving effective when they are linked to local and national governmental structures. As costs of treatment for HIV/AIDS begin to fall and access to medication increases, measures should be taken to assure that rural people as well as urban can benefit.

63

- **Mainstream HIV/AIDS in Bank operations.** Because of the catastrophic implications of HIV/AIDS for African development, prevention and mitigation of HIV/AIDS has been mainstreamed into most of the projects in the Bank's Africa rural portfolio, either in the design stage or through retrofitting of components. In addition, the Africa region has designed a generic rapid-response multi-sectoral intervention called the Multisectoral AIDS Program (MAP) that makes resources available through streamlined approval procedures to multiple countries in support of rapid responses where commitment to addressing HIV/AIDS is demonstrated. A significant portion of funds flows directly to communities to carry out programs of their own design under simplified procurement guidelines.

INCREASING ACCESS TO AND IMPROVING THE QUALITY OF RURAL EDUCATION

Education plays an essential role in reducing poverty. By enabling individuals and households to harness knowledge, increase and diversify incomes, manage risks, and increase social mobility, education offers the prospect of breaking through the cycle of poverty. In rural areas, education also improves agricultural productivity and efficiency. Skills acquired though both formal and informal education enhance farmers' ability to acquire and decode market and technical information, select optimal cropping patterns, and purchase the right mix of inputs. Education also plays a critical role in facilitating off-farm employment and economic development. In addition to the direct impact on incomes, there are significant positive externalities that are associated with investments in education. Most notably, higher levels of women's education are associated with lower malnutrition, lower fertility and population growth rates, and better child survival rates.

There are two educational needs in rural areas. The first need is for general education (primary and secondary schooling), while the second, more specific need is education for agricultural and natural resource management.

The following Bank actions are envisaged to promote rural education:

- place top priority on achieving free universal primary education;

- advocate gender equality in rural education;

- advocate quality improvements in rural schools;

- ensure that public funds for education are distributed equitably;

- encourage greater community participation in rural education;

- increase investments in rural secondary education, particularly in countries close to attaining universal primary education;

- promote literacy and training opportunities for unschooled rural adults;

- ensure that investments in agricultural training programs are in line with current needs; and

- support experiments with private delivery of educational services.

MANAGING AND COPING WITH HOUSEHOLD FOOD SECURITY AND RISK FOR THE RURAL POOR

Managing the risks with which rural communities and individual residents must cope received only brief mention in *From Vision to Action*. Yet, as clearly articulated in the *2000/2001 WDR*, an effective strategy for reducing poverty needs to enhance security by reducing the risk of natural, financial and health shocks and by enabling households to mitigate their consequences.

Many features of economic development indirectly reduce the riskiness of rural incomes as they facilitate growth (Anderson, 2001). For example, investment in irrigation as well as improved roads, telecommunications, and modern banking systems reduce vulnerability. But there remains a need to design and adapt policies, institutions, and investments that directly manage, reduce, or counteract the risks facing rural residents, particularly the poor. This need may be evolving with climatic change and with changing market structures.

In many areas, women have predominant responsibility for household food security. Removing constraints and improving conditions that enable women to carry out their roles more effectively would promote food security both within the household and outside.

Strategies to Manage and Cope with Risk
Management of risk can be seen as policies or other actions taken to deal with or reduce risks faced by poor rural households, whereas coping generally implies actions after the fact to help households deal with shocks they have experienced. The Bank is promoting a number of policies and instruments that help in managing and coping with climatic and financial risks (Box 6.1), yet avoid market distortions. Among the new instruments being developed are a diverse set of financial products that are market-based but historically have not been readily accessible to many of the poor, such as forward contracting, hedging, and pool pricing. The Bank is also exploring means to assist poor individuals learn about and use insurance, and to reduce the costs to primary insurers and re-insurers.

Social Safety Net Policies and Strategies to Maintain Food Security. Targeted transfers serve to convey income to the poor and vulnerable. However, such programs face special challenges in rural areas due to the difficulties in defining targeting criteria, in collecting beneficiary contributions, and in administering programs in communities with low population densities and undeveloped infrastructure. Many of the most successful programs in rural areas, such as Mexico's Progressa and South Africa's Old Age Pension, are administered in middle-income countries (for example, Cord 2001b). The poorest countries with the greatest need for poverty programs also have the greatest need to be selective to avoid compromising macroeconomic stability or investment in human and physical capital.

Some Management and Coping Strategies for Risk Related to Agricultural Production 6.1

- **Providing More and Better Information:** Access to reliable information significantly reduces uncertainty in a risky world. Such information relates to markets and weather, as well as technologies.

- **Insurance:** The principle of insurance as a risk-sharing device is that, by accepting appropriate premiums from a large number of clients, the insurance company is able to pool the risks. New mechanisms for insuring against price risks are being explored in a donor-supported initiative operated out of the Agriculture and Rural Development Department of the World Bank (Commodity Risk Management Program). Such yet-experimental price insurance arrangements will operate in conjunction with credit instruments to reduce downside risk to both lenders and small-scale borrowing producers. To overcome some of the well-recognized problems of traditional crop insurance, the World Bank and several partners are testing novel rainfall-based insurance policies. IFC is investing in a global facility to develop weather-index insurance in emerging countries and financing the establishment of such an insurance scheme in Morocco. The Bank is testing a weather based insurance scheme for poor pastoralists in Mongolia.

- **Contract Marketing:** In many countries, farmers have the opportunity to reduce price risks for commodities not yet produced, or for inputs needed in the future, by various marketing arrangements. The most important alternatives, from a risk-management perspective, include cooperative marketing with price pooling and forward contracts for commodity sales or for input delivery.

- **Income Diversification:** This includes a range of cropping practices, investments in livestock and non-farm income, and migration that are used to reduce fluctuations in income. Traditional risk coping strategies may also serve this function.

World Bank-supported programs and policy advice are based on the experience that many targeted food security programs are more cost-effective than generalized food subsidies. Food security at the household level is essentially a matter of access or purchasing power. In most situations, cash transfers or the provision of vouchers will allow the recipients to purchase the food they require using normal market channels, although in a few cases, mainly famine situations in Africa, it may be necessary for outside agencies to transport food to remote areas. While food assistance

65

may be given to families (as opposed to individuals), such transfers can be a small part of a broader program aimed at improving nutrition for vulnerable children or of health programs for pregnant women. These programs stress food *utilization* as much as household food security.

Another principle to be emphasized by the Bank is the strengthening of informal support programs that build upon traditional rural community structures. While these frequently fail in times of shared hardship, this shortcoming may be reduced with support from a central government. The Bank also supports a third form of intervention for smoothing consumption in times of economic crisis by having government provide employment in public-works programs. Such programs generally allow self-selection by offering wages slightly below market rates. The value to the poor of such programs is not measured only in terms of income support but also in terms of the benefits they receive from the infrastructure created.

Disaster management. Many disasters have a low probability of occurring in any given area, yet incur high costs when they occur and, thus, are unsuited to private insurance. The Bank supports disaster prevention or relief programs, while facing the challenge of designing publicly funded programs that stabilize income or consumption without creating inducements that encourage excessive risk taking. For example, investments in afforestation reduce the risk of flooding. The Bank's overall Social Protection strategy provides guidance that is also relevant to rural development (Holzmann and Jørgensen, 2000). The Bank also assists in disaster early warning and has recently redrafted its Operational Policies and Bank Procedures for emergency reconstruction to clarify guidelines. An issue that is related to that of disaster management is that of reconstruction after conflicts. As with many types of disasters, rural areas may be particularly vulnerable to devastation, since isolated communities often are targets in insurgencies. It is important to understand the involvement of the local communities in their own reconstruction. Women have been recognized as critical but often invisible players in post conflict societies. They also have been recognized as a force for peace, often crossing borders and ideologies.

SOCIAL INCLUSION, GENDER AND ETHNICITY

An important priority of the rural strategy is to help make institutions more responsive to the rural poor thereby improving social well-being and reducing vulnerability. One approach includes empowering rural people through their increased participation in the work of the Bank. This means that any barriers to inclusion must be removed. Particularly vulnerable to exclusion are refugees, ethnic minorities, indigenous populations, women, landless and the disabled.

Principles of Bank actions in ensuring inclusiveness are envisaged as:

1. **Reforming institutions to establish equal rights and opportunities for both genders, marginalized populations and ethnic minorities**

- Advocate legal reforms and regulations that ensure equitable ownership of assets (particularly, land and livestock) and user rights (including water use, forest management) and promote equal opportunities (labor laws, corporate laws, equal opportunity laws).

- Improve rural financing opportunities and mechanisms for rural women and entrepreneurs and marginalized groups.

- Promote social safety nets and protection for vulnerable groups.

2. **Fostering equal access to resources for women, marginalized populations and ethnic minorities**

- Promote an enabling environment for rural women and minorities to benefit from new economic opportunities.

- Improve access to markets through improved availability of information by ICTs, better infrastructure services, especially transport and communication facilities.

- Reduce the opportunity costs of women's time and energy in carrying out their multiple roles, through investments in water, fuel, transport etc.

3. Strengthening the political voice of women and ethnic minorities

- Ensure equality of opportunity for women and ethnic minorities in community and producer organizations, and local, regional and national governing bodies.

- Promote leadership training for rural women and ethnic minorities.

Aligning the rural and gender strategies. The rural development strategy of the World Bank is complemented by the Bank's recent strategic document on gender and development.[1] Gender disparities in power and resources, gender-based division of labor and gender inequalities in rights and entitlements contribute to poverty, undermine economic growth and reduce the well-being of men, women and children. The strategy calls for gender mainstreaming in the Bank's work by working with member countries to identify gender issues important for poverty reduction and growth and by aligning Bank policies, processes and resources. The Bank's rural development and gender strategies support and reinforce one another. It is now widely acknowledged that one of the critical factors in revitalizing rural development is to raise the productivity of women farmers. In most of the developing world, women do most of the agricultural work. Women are also in charge of household food security, yet in some areas are constrained in their access to, and control of, productive resources such as land and money.

Decentralized development efforts such as **community driven development (CDD)** offer the potential for increased community participation and ensuring the inclusiveness of all groups of society in rural decision making, irrespective of gender, social class, or ethnicity. In addition to devolving control and decision-making power to poor women and men themselves, these initiatives help communities build social capital by expanding the depth and range of their social networks (Box 6.2). Past experience reveals that decentralization is not always synonymous with participation and that transparency in decision making and an oversight or review process that does not stifle community initiative is necessary to ensure that all groups participate in decentralized projects.

Community Driven Development Principles 6.2

1. Empower communities: participatory decision making, resources and authority to implement;

2. Empower local governments: fiscal and administrative decentralization;

3. Re-align service delivery of central government: policy and enabling environment; information to communities for decision making;

4. Ensure transparency and accountability at all levels;

5. Make it a learning by doing process and build capacity along the way; and,

6. Commit to long-term reform for the institutional development to take hold and be sustainable.

ENDNOTES

1 Integrating Gender into the World Bank's Work: A Strategy for Action, January 2002

ENHANCING SUSTAINABLE MANAGEMENT OF NATURAL RESOURCES

7

Natural resources provide fundamental support to life and economic processes in rural areas. Many of the natural resource issues have already been treated in chapters 4–6, but this chapter adds some additional important considerations related to the objective of enhancing sustainable management of natural resources (see also Annex 6).

THE BANK APPROACH

Soils are the foundations of agriculture, forests help to protect water sources and provide income for more than 1.6 billion people, and water is essential for human life and agriculture. Biodiversity is the basis for protecting and improving all domestic plant and animal varieties and safeguards food security. Inappropriate use of these resources threatens rural livelihoods and creates formidable new challenges, such as global warming. The degradation of the natural resource base affects the poor more than others, as they tend to rely on more fragile natural resources for their livelihoods. Sustainable natural resource management and agriculture are generally quite compatible. Decisions on the use of natural resources are not made by governments or international organizations, but are made daily by millions of farmers and rural inhabitants. In particular, women's indigenous knowledge of seed selection and preservation, medicinal and other special use of plants as well as genetic resources for food and agriculture makes them essential to the process of conserving agro-biodiversity. Policies that do not consider the roles of women and indigenous groups in NRM can result in inefficiencies and non-compliance in policy implementation.

The Bank's recently developed **environment strategy, the forthcoming water and forestry strategies,** and the **2003 World Development Report** (Sustainable Development in a Dynamic World), give overall guidelines in approaching rural natural resource management (NRM) issues, and set the framework for linking rural development and the environment, as well as forest management. The Bank's specific objectives in relation to rural development to improve the sustainable use of natural resources include:

- Reducing land degradation;
- Improving water management;
- Promoting sustainable production of forest products while protecting the environment;
- Supporting sustainable fisheries resource management; and
- Incorporating global warming into rural development planning.

This strategy promotes an innovative approach to NRM based on ecosystem management. This approach provides an opportunity for the Bank to respond to the lessons learned from past Bank experiences in NRM and issues that have been raised in Bank reviews of the NRM portfolio. Both objectives can be met by adopting an integrated natural resources management approach that optimizes the use of the natural resource base to meet agricultural productivity goals, protects the long-term productivity and resilience of natural resources, and meets communities' goals. (Izac and Sanchez, 1999). These goals would include the welfare of future generations, poverty reduction and environmental conservation. This approach avoids dealing with strategies that address the principal resources individually; rather it will focus on interactions between soil, water, solar energy, and plant and animal germplasm. For example, bad forestry practices will have an adverse effect on water supply and lead to land degradation. Land conversion from agriculture to urban use puts greater stress on marginal zones that in turn leads to conversion of forests to agriculture and further erosion. Also, there is a confirmed relationship between female illiteracy and population growth, the latter being a significant driver of rapid deforestation throughout various ecoregions. All of these, in turn, have adverse impacts on biodiversity. However, at the operational level, natural resource management strategies will be broken down into manageable investment, institution building and policy programs/projects, often at the single-sector level (for example, forestry or water supply, fisheries, energy, or environmental protection projects).

FUTURE BANK ACTIONS

The Bank's current natural resource management portfolio includes three distinct types of projects, as well as several combinations, each of which addresses technical, institutional and policy constraints, as well as different implementation challenges. Some projects combine production and conservation, or conservation and institutional objectives (Box 7.1). Virtually all have some institutional development component. By and large, the projects were designed to: (a) promote sustainable agricultural, forestry, and fisheries development and/or water resource use through the use of environmentally sound resource management techniques; (b) conserve or protect specific ecosystems and associated biodiversity (such as national parks and wildlife reserves); and (c) strengthen national and/or sub-national institutional capacity to achieve improved NRM.

The strategy proposes future investments with the potential to promote interventions and policy responses to the major market and government failures that are at the root of natural resource degradation. These investments will ensure the successful application of the framework described above for integrated natural resources management programs at the landscape and watershed level.

Under the revised strategy the Bank will support capacity building for the integration of indigenous land, water, forest, and biodiversity management methods with scientific knowledge, and the dissemination of the resulting knowledge to producers. At the community level, investments will also be made to promote appropriate incentives for community-driven resource management programs. The Bank will also promote incentive systems that influence how resources are used by strengthening or establishing property and tenure rights, removing government-induced distortions, and piloting new mechanisms to deal with market failures, such as systems of payments for environmental services.

Specific investments in technical interventions for land, water, forest, and biodiversity will be directed as follows:[1]

- Investments in **land and water** will be made to cover a number of crucial interventions such as the restoration of soil structure and chemical content, reducing the flow of water and wind over land surfaces, and reducing the mining of soil nutrients and carbon through recycling, fertilizer use, and crop residue management. Investments will also be considered to improve the management of water quantity and quality within a watershed-management context (upstream-downstream demand components), as well as investments in the devel-

opment of additional water supplies. An irrigation and drainage business plan will be prepared as part of an agriculture and food review paper in FY03.

- With regard to **forests**, significant investments will be targeted toward scaling-up collaborative forest management and promotion of forest products. Catalytic investments for sustainable harvesting and forest management will be considered, but only in situations that have been independently verified or certified.

- With regard to **biodiversity**, the promising areas of future investment are in the conservation of the genetic variation within species and populations for crops and livestock, conservation of the number of species for subsistence and cash income, and habitat preservation, especially in modified habitats (farmland, rangeland and forests). Other potential areas for investment are to promote synergies between biodiversity conservation and agricultural development.

Good Practice in Watershed Development 7.1

Highly satisfactory results (outperforming the average of the Bank, with 90% satisfactory development objective, of which 17% highly satisfactory, compared with, respectively, 89% and 4% for the overall rural portfolio) have been obtained in the areas of community driven rehabilitation of degraded watersheds. The Bank's OED rated 92% of the 42 watershed development projects completed between FY90 and FY99 at least satisfactory in achieving their development objectives. Projects such as the *China Loess Plateau Watershed Rehabilitation* project reduced erosion by 20-30 million tons annually, and improved the income of the poorest households by an average of 20%. The combined impact of project and non-project activities benefits 6 million people and protects over 5.5 million hectares of forested land. Common key factors of success include high government and community ownership. Other examples of successful watershed development programs include the *Eastern Anatolia Project* in Turkey and the *Tunisia Northwest Rural Development Program* is another positive example.

Investment in the area of **climate change** must be associated with agriculture's role in cost-effective approaches for reducing greenhouse gases. Investments should be in three key areas: a) mitigation of greenhouse gas emissions; b) reduction of vulnerability and adaptation to climate change; and c) capacity building to promote and implement these themes. Actions would include: i) better management of agricultural soils, rangelands and forests; ii) improvement in the efficient use of fertilizer; iii) restoration of degraded agricultural lands and rangelands; iv) improving ruminant digestion through better feed; v) improving rice farming to reduce the amount of methane escaping into the atmosphere; and vi) slowing deforestation by reducing slash-and-burn agriculture and establishing appropriate tree plantations (CGIAR, 2000).

The World Bank has a long history of involvement in the **fisheries sector,** focusing in the past on fisheries development assistance intended to increase production and provide critical infrastructure. However, by the 1990s, experts confirmed that roughly two-thirds of the world's major marine fisheries had been fully or over-fished, and their exploitation is becoming less and less economically viable. Given these adverse trends affecting marine fisheries throughout the world and the fact that 95% of the over 30 million people engaged in fisheries live in developing countries, consensus clearly emerged that governments and communities need assistance to sustainably manage fisheries resources. In response, the World Bank is now focused on strengthening coastal developing countries' capacity to sustainably manage their fisheries sectors, through:

■ capacity-building and technical assistance for sustainable fisheries resource management, including support for reduction of fishing capacity, and institution building to improve the effectiveness of our client countries in international negotiations on fishing rights, fees;

■ coastal rural development, particularly the creation of additional economic opportunities for artisanal fishermen; and,

■ assistance to encourage aquaculture production.

This strategy is currently being articulated in a Fisheries Approach paper and is being implemented on a 'pilot' basis in several countries in East Asia, Latin America and West Africa, through technical assistance to help improve these countries' policy framework for fisheries management. The World Bank expects to continue to learn from these efforts in order to increase its own portfolio and capacity for sustainable fisheries management and to respond to the growing demand from developing countries around the world.

As critical as the investments in land, water, biodiversity and climate change is the investment in **human capital**. Reducing the mining of soil nutrients and carbon through recycling, fertilizer use, and crop residue management demands training and education of the rural poor. The promotion of sustainable forest products means the involvement of the men and women who harvest and market non-timber forest products. Investment in natural resources requires an understanding of how rural people use those resources and benefit from them. It means a respect for local knowledge. The Bank recognizes the importance of investment in the partnership of human and biological resources if sustainable rural development is to be achieved.

72

ENDNOTES

1 Some of these investments will be supported by the Global Environment Facility (GEF).

IMPLEMENTING THE STRATEGY: KEY THRUSTS AND CHALLENGES

8

The previous chapters outline a framework and objectives for revitalizing Bank activities to reduce poverty in rural space, which was endorsed by clients (Box 8.1). The four implementation thrusts discussed in this chapter outline an agenda which enables the implementation of the strategic objectives of *Reaching the Rural Poor*. These thrusts are firmly embedded in the six regional strategies, reinforce and add incrementally to the value of global, regional, and national programs, and take into account the key constraints and lessons learned during the implementation of *From Vision to Action*.

THRUST I—INTEGRATING THE NEEDS OF THE RURAL POOR IN NATIONAL POLICY DIALOGUES

One of the main characteristics of the development process, advocated by *Reaching the Rural Poor*, is its strong client-driven nature in national policy making. However, this policy making process often still has a pro-urban bias. Redirecting national attention to the plight of the rural poor will only occur through internal advocacy within the World Bank and more importantly in individual country capitals. The experience of *From Vision to Action* shows clearly that unless there is broad country ownership of the recommendations, there will be little impact on the country programs. Under *Reaching the Rural Poor* the focus will therefore be on fostering strong advocacy processes in the client countries. This can best be done through support to the preparation of client-owned and client-driven national rural strategies and to enable client country institutions to better articulate and advocate the needs of rural inhabitants, and specifically, the rural poor. To have an impact such processes must be aligned with, and integral to, national development strategy processes (for example Poverty Reduction Strategy Papers and national development plans), and be supported by Bank diagnostic, analytical and strategic documents (Poverty Assessments (PAs), Country Economic Memorandums (CEMs), Country Assistance Strategies (CASs), Country Gender Assessments (CGAs), etc). **The principal focus of this thrust is to strengthen the voice of the rural poor, in national processes for strategy formulation.** This would be accomplished through two related activities:

- Rural institutions in client countries will be supported in preparing broadly owned **national rural development strategies** focused on rural poverty reduction. To do so, the Bank will partner with all stakeholders involved in rural space; i.e., organizations of producers, women's organizations, local NGOs, line ministries, academic institutions, and the private sector, to support both advocacy and policy processes by nationals through, for example, the organization of stakeholder workshops and consultation processes, the preparation of policy notes, undertaking diagnostic, analytical and strategic work on rural issues

focused on poverty reduction. The Bank will encourage a holistic approach reflecting the multisectoral dimension of sustained rural poverty reduction. Such national rural development strategies and associated policy and analytical work by nationals should be integrated into the national processes and will be the key driving force in bringing the attention of Ministries of Finance and the Bank's Country Directors and Country Teams back to rural development. When such work is done by nationals, local ownership is likely to be enhanced.

- Bank staff will support the national rural development strategy formulation processes, as well as provide analytical work to acquire a better understanding of the rural areas in client countries. This would be done by supporting the enhancement of the rural aspects of Poverty Assessments, Public Expenditure Reviews, and the preparation of Rural Policy Notes. Such an improved Bank analytical platform will be a condition for improved decision making on resource allocation in rural space, more effective advocacy by both rural representatives in client countries and members of the Bank's rural staff, and in discussions with other development partners.

This thrust is therefore envisioned as one of the key activities at the country level. Backing of national processes for the rural strategy formulation (Box 8.2) is the overall priority in this regard, and its supportive analytical work will concentrate on up to 12 countries or themes per year. In selecting the countries and themes, priority will be given to those with: a) widespread rural poverty; b) opportunity for impact, i.e., focus on countries with an overall policy environment and rural development policy conducive to poverty reduction in rural space or willingness to establish such policy; c) windows of opportunity for influencing the CAS, PER, PRSP, CGAs and other country-driven processes to ensure maximum impact, accepting that there are many opportunities to ensure increased attention and improved quality of decision making in country and donor-agency processes; and d) opportunities to translate the rural poverty strategy into increased lending, learning through pilot operations, and/or close cooperation with the other development partners. This thrust is based on the regional strategies. This initial group of countries in which national rural development strategy work will be focused does not exclude similar, though probably less intensive work in other countries. The Bank will provide support for the development of improved rural development strategies in any client country requesting such assistance through the country assistance strategy process.

To take this thrust forward with the necessary level of commitment and funding requires enhanced donor collaboration to ensure coherence of work at country level following the principles of CDF within the rural space. Donors need to support the increased national dialogue on rural development at national and local levels, and undertake essential and supportive analytical, diagnostic and policy work. The inputs required from the Bank and its partners to assist the national rural policy formulation process

will include consultancy contracts with key stakeholders for the preparation of rural poverty-reduction-focused strategies and key policy notes, and the organization of national workshops and media contracts. For the economic and sector work, it may include critical Bank or consultant staff inputs. The Bank will build upon its existing global and national alliances with other development partners to support this effort.

Within the Bank, the Agriculture and Rural Development Department will work with internal units and external partners to provide training for Bank-wide staff to help them acquire the necessary expertise in rural poverty reduction for both operational and analytical work and the preparation of enhanced tool kits and guidance and training material for pro-poor rural development. A gender dimension will be included in training materials.

Client Views on the Strategy

8.1

Both the corporate and regional strategies reflect inputs based on a broad set of outreach activities and consultations conducted over eighteen months (see Annex 2).

The holistic approach towards rural development and the increased focus on poverty, vulnerability, risk mitigation, and social issues has been endorsed in consultations with the Bank's stakeholders. There was widespread agreement among the stakeholders on the continued emphasis on agriculture in the new strategy. At the same time, the stakeholders endorsed the Bank's holistic framework for rural development within which agricultural development will take place, including activities to promote a vibrant non-farm economy; an increased role of the private sector, and social sector services. Some of the new directions for Bank operations have also been strongly supported by the stakeholders. These included support for decentralization; community-based implementation; and increased flexibility in project and program design and implementation. Other issues emphasized by stakeholders included increased attention to political economy and governance, conflict and disaster management, and institutional development and capacity building.

There were requests that the new strategy should give consideration to the diversity of conditions among countries (and especially inside large countries) and the heterogeneity of the poor.

There were strong calls for assistance in the development of country driven rural development strategies and the underpinning economic sector work to support national processes, including the PRSP, and to raise advocacy at national levels. The importance of the human factor was emphasized, in terms of demographic trends and their impacts, migration from rural areas to urban areas as well as migration within rural areas, and education of rural people. While the increased emphasis on the private sector was endorsed, the continued role of the public sector was also underscored. It was felt that the previous Bank strategy did not properly elaborate the new models for public/private partnership which are required for rural development to succeed. Stakeholders emphasized the need for the rural strategy to highlight Bank support of the private sector, especially where rural SMEs and agro-processing development are concerned. Land reform and land policy reform are important issues across all regions, and the active participation of the Bank in this process is expected, beyond the efforts outlined in the previous strategy. The consultations confirmed that natural resource management issues need attention. In this regard, smaller projects and community based implementation was emphasized. It was clearly apparent from the consultations that stakeholders expect the Bank to implement the strategy in a more client-specific, more flexible, simpler, less bureaucratic, more "bottom-up" fashion, and be more accepting of local experience and expertise.

8.2   Essential Content for National Rural Development Strategies

- *Alignment with wider national planning processes:* provides direct inputs for PRSP; and, subsequently, CAS development.

- *Participation for broad stakeholder engagement and ownership:* reflects wider moves toward democratic decentralization.

- *Diagnosis:* good analytical work , informative household surveys, review of past policies, understand causal linkages and transmission, understand livelihood strategies, assets and vulnerability, understand economic drivers, all these influencing ultimate content.

- *Content: naturally must be tuned to the specific situation of the country but typically:*
  - holistic, covering the entire rural space;
  - tune strategic options to locational specificity of different areas;
  - favor livelihoods-strengthening diversification options for multi-occupational and multi-locational households;
  - advance market institution development in tandem with liberalization steps;
  - explicitly take on inequality, in assets and incomes, with targets, timetables and concrete measures;
  - propose measures to take advantage of technical change, recognizing the need for public support to research;
  - demonstrate that agricultural strategies, the cornerstones of rural poverty reduction efforts;
  - recognize the importance of investment in infrastructure and human capital;
  - respond to the 'obligation' to protect the poor, with cogent social protection measures, including for conflict areas and for HIV/AIDS; and,
  - propose pragmatic steps toward greater de-concentration and devolution.

- *Targeted M&E:* recognize multi-sectoral within rural and disaggregation for monitoring (by local communities etc.) and local and national planning.

- *Priority actions:* prioritization based on realistic assessment of institutional capacity, macroeconomic feasibility, governance situation and the policy environment.

- *Fostering partnerships:* new instruments, sharing, public-private, – civil society organizations etc., fostering intersectoral linkages and coherence.

Unlike *From Vision to Action*, where financing could not be strategically and systemically sustained, this program will be supported by annually earmarked ("off the top") funding, in part already secured by a specific allocation by the Agriculture and Rural Development Sector Board from the FAO/CP resources, and partly by a reallocation of the departmental budget. This will supplement Bank allocations made by the regional departments. Moreover, by not restricting the actions to a limited number of focus countries, as was done under *From Vision to Action,* but by opportunistically supporting key activities at the national level in a variety of countries, a greater impact can be expected.

THRUST 2—SCALING-UP INVESTMENTS AND INNOVATIVE APPROACHES IN RURAL DEVELOPMENT

The Millennium Development Goals will not be met if greater numbers of rural poor do not have dramatically increased access to resources for proven investments. *Reaching the Rural Poor* will therefore give particular attention to identifying and scaling-up good-practice investments to other regions within the country, to other countries, or to other continents. Recognizing that there are definitional issues surrounding the term "scaling-up" and that more work needs to done to further clarify boundaries, the Bank proposes as a working definition of scaling up as "increase positive socio-economic impacts from a small to large scale of coverage." Neither the approach or type of intervention to be scaled-up, nor the regions listed are exclusive and new interventions may be added over time. This thrust recognizes that where appropriate experience in key development interventions has demonstrated to have sustained and positive impacts on rural poverty reduction, all reasonable effort should be made to address wider application within and between countries and regions.

Scaling-up Rural Investments at the Country Level

Scaling-up good practices must be seen an integral part of national rural development strategies. Good practices are acquired after years of development experience. These should have been piloted successfully before being scaled-up. Innovation and pilot projects will therefore be supported as well. Effective intervention must be **locally validated and adapted** including its socio-economic and gender impacts. Scaling-up does not mean that the Bank will apply the same approach everywhere. Innovative methods of learning and information sharing between countries and among development partners need to be supported. Mechanisms for capturing, validating, disseminating and adapting good practices need to be developed concurrently.

A **checklist for readiness** for assessing the features of a practice and the policy and institutional context has been developed (Box 8.3). It will form an important tool for assessing the readiness of a practice for wider scaling-up and will provide other development partners, governments and communities with a better understanding of the state of the practice and associated risks and opportunities. The Bank, with its partners and member governments, will assess the fit of good practices within the national rural development strategies and processes, the PRSP and the CAS.

Broadly, the **selection criteria** for investments to be scaled-up are based on achieving the highest return in sustainable poverty reduction per unit of investment. The investments selected should: a) make a clear contribution to one or more of the objectives of *Reaching the Rural Poor*; b) cover a large population of rural poor, which, in some situations, implies an emphasis on, for example, remote areas, areas with poor resources and women farmers; c) have a low investment cost per beneficiary so that countries and beneficiaries can afford the required investment; d) have a good track record in terms of development outcome; and e) be suitable for partnerships with other donors, so that funding can be leveraged. Different weights need to be given to the individual criteria in each region or country.

The Initial Program for Scaling-Up. The regional strategies set out the initial program for scaling-up. In strategy implementation, there will be a continuous process of selecting new projects for scaling-up, driven by the regional departments, based on country programs. Table 8.1 shows the first phase in the region/country good practice scaling-up program.

What is known about *impact?*

- Level of social, environmental or economic impact
- Cost of delivery of benefits
- Nature of beneficiaries
- Timescale

What is known about *success factors?*

- Organizational process and institutional factors
- Cultural, environmental and social factors
- Characteristics of beneficiaries
- Policy and sectoral environment
- Technical aspects and inputs supply

What is the *"state of practice"?*

- Innovation — minimal objective evidence
- Promising practice — anecdotal evidence
- Models — positive evidence in a few cases
- Good practice — clear evidence from some settings
- Best practice — evidence from multiple settings
- Policy principle — proven in multiple settings

What are the *organizational strategy options?*

- Direct organizational growth — internal replication; program expansion
- Indirect organizational growth — catalyzing and supporting others; joint venture
- Direct institutional mainstreaming — capacity building; partnerships; replication by others
- Indirect influence — diffuse concepts and models; policy advocacy

The selection for consideration in the first round is based on regional demand and topics where the Bank has accumulated solid experience (see also Chapter 2). This choice is reinforced by the high percentage of project in the current portfolio that are rated satisfactory or highly satisfactory in Bank Project Supervision Reports for meeting their development objectives. Annex 7 provides a collection of successful Bank operations in rural areas.

The above list is not exclusive. Other types of projects demonstrating success in a particular country will also be scaled-up. Scaling-up good practices will require: (a) widespread advocacy from senior management to audiences beyond the typical rural constituency, and with special focus on Finance Ministries, Central Banks, and the international media; (b) special incentives for proj-

ect preparation and supervision, through "off the top" allocation of the budget of the Cooperative Program with FAO, to be supplemented by Bank funds, Trust Funds and partnerships; (c) the development of a structured learning process and priority funding for knowledge management in these areas; and (d) working closely with other partners and clients in the identification and sharing of good practice and innovation.

Promoting New and Innovative Approaches in Rural Development

Together with the scaling-up of good practices, *Reaching the Rural Poor* proposes to accelerate

Table 8.1: **Potential areas for scaling up and innovation**

Objective	Theme
Policy and Institutions	■ agricultural policy reform ■ development of rural strategies ■ institutional reform and capacity building ■ participatory planning
Agricultural Productivity and Competitiveness	■ land reform and administration ■ research and extension ■ information technology – marketing and knowledge ■ irrigation and drainage ■ support for producer organizations/user groups ■ food safety and agribusiness ■ rural finance – including micro finance
Non Farm Rural Economy	■ rural non-farm economy including business development ■ private sector role in service provision ■ infrastructure, including small towns
Strengthening Social Services and Reducing Risk and Vulnerability	■ health and education: specific rural issues ■ community driven development/district programs ■ social inclusion, including women and girls ■ commodity, climate, and disaster risk management ■ emergency reconstruction
Sustainable Natural Resource Management	■ soil fertility ■ watershed development ■ community natural resource management ■ community forestry ■ fisheries

work on rapid learning in new ways of working and in innovative areas reflecting the dynamic and changing economic, social, environmental and institutional context of rural development and the increasing potential for impact of externalities on the rural poor. These themes are again based on the demands from the regional strategies and include the priority need to develop effective means to enhance multi-sectoral coordination and the role of the private sector in rural development. The continuum between innovation, good practice and policy principle is recognized and work on innovation will be set within and tested against the framework as set out in Box 8.3.

THRUST 3—IMPROVING THE QUALITY AND THE IMPACT OF BANK OPERATIONS

The poverty focus, poverty impact, and sustainability of the Bank's operations in rural space all need to be improved. This will require strengthening the understanding of the key characteristics of a pro-poor operation, improving sustainability, social inclusiveness, and maintaining quality standards as set by the Bank's Quality Assurance Group and OED, and achieving a better development outcome of completed projects. This thrust will have three components.

Improve the Poverty Focus
To improve the focus of the Bank's operations in rural areas, effort is needed in the understanding of rural poverty and the application of that understanding in the design of the Bank's interventions. More specifically, this will include development of methods for poverty analysis initiated under the preparation for *Reaching the Rural Poor*. More explicit integration of gender-sensitive **poverty analysis and diagnosis in operational strategies and project design**, and the introduction of a poverty-related Monitoring and Evaluation Framework in the project documentation will be sought. Poverty learning workshops, and at least two regional clinics or training sessions per year will be organized around enhancing the rural poverty focus, in cooperation with the WBI and Thematic Groups.

Improve the Sustainability and Institutional Development Impact
To improve the current low sustainability and institutional development impact ratings of completed projects, attention will be given to the identification of **improved procedures to enhance the long-term development impact** of Bank rural operations and **guidelines on how to assess and improve sustainability.** This will include an initial focus on financial and institutional sustainability, including institutional development (ID) as key determinants of lasting project impact. Beyond this, it will increasingly focus on how the Bank's rural development operations affect overall sustainability of livelihoods and poverty reduction in the rural space. Methodology for gender mainstreaming will be included in the sustainability analysis. The guidelines and standards now being used for sustainability analysis across the Bank will be improved. Issues of trade-offs between different aspects of sustainability (for example, between environmental and economic sustainability), will be addressed. It will also include the development of toolkits and staff training programs, in cooperation with WBI.

Continue to Improve Other Quality Indicators for Rural Development Operations

To continue to improve the key quality indicators for the strategy's objectives, such as the quality of Economic and Sector Work (ESW), Quality at Entry and Quality of Supervision, the Rural Sector Board will expand the program for Quality Enhancement Reviews (QERs) and clinics for ESW, Poverty Analyses, Public Expenditure Reviews, Gender and Social Analyses. At least twenty such events will be sponsored per year.

THRUST 4—IMPLEMENTING GLOBAL CORPORATE PRIORITIES AND ENHANCING PARTNERSHIPS

Increased Involvement in International Public Goods
High-quality, high-impact rural poverty reduction operations will require continued commitment and support to key global public goods in two critical

areas: first, ensuring that the interests of developing countries, and thus the rural poor, are safeguarded in an increasingly globalized world; and second, there needs to be ready access to new and appropriate technology, which in particular is suitable for poor farmers. Continued support for client countries in dealing with global trade issues is important in this regard. Support for the Consultative Group on International Agricultural Research is also an important component of support to **the global public goods dimension** of *Reaching the Rural Poor*. The Bank will also assist client countries in adjusting to the consequences of global climate change as it affects the rural space and work with colleagues in implementing the Bank's Environment Strategy.

Promote Trade Liberalization and WTO Process

Assisting developing countries in the WTO process and other international trade liberalization efforts is high priority in the implementation of this strategy. Specific actions envisaged in this area are discussed in Chapter 3.

International Agricultural Research

The Consultative Group on International Agricultural Research (CGIAR) researches technical and economic subjects vital to sustainable agriculture, food security, and poverty reduction. Through these activities, the CGIAR complements the Bank's efforts to enable developing countries to realize their full agricultural technology and production potential.

The Bank's current support for the CGIAR is being broadened to a multi-stakeholder initiative, including private industry, advanced research institutions, international research institutes, national agricultural research systems, and civil society, to harness global advances in science and technology for the benefit of poor farmers in developing countries. This will include:

- continued dialogue between the development partners and all other stakeholders, promoted by the Bank, in developing competitive instruments and achieving leverage of public sector funds for investments in science and technology for food security and poverty reduction;

- progressively allocating the Bank's contribution to up-stream research on global public goods, prioritized by share- and stake-holders, and carried out by consortia of the most competent institutions, under the leadership of the CGIAR. Considerable leverage of the Bank's current CGIAR funding could be achieved to increase cooperation and reduce competition between International Agricultural Research Centers and National Agricultural Research Systems;

- understanding and supporting policy adjustments in agricultural practices and technology as a consequence of anticipated impacts of global climate change; and,

- understanding women's role in agriculture to make agricultural research more relevant to women and other resource poor farmers.

Improving External Linkages

Partnerships can yield major benefits by harnessing the Bank's effectiveness in rural development. The Bank has a broad and intensive network of cooperation and partnerships in activities related to rural development. In addition to regular and well established institutional engagements with other international organizations and donors, the Bank has over 30 rural-related collaborative agreements and partnerships as of late 2001. Of these, 24 are global in nature and seven are concerned with specific regions. The Bank's Study on Partnership Selectivity and Oversight discussed by the Bank's Board in April 2000, and an OED review (2001), as well as the new ESSD partnership guidelines, provide a framework for improving partnerships in rural development.

The development of this strategy has provided an opportunity to refresh and improve these relations with the Bank's traditional rural partners, such as the FAO and IFAD; the bilateral partners including the Netherlands, USA, UK, Germany, France, Canada and Japan; various UN agencies; regional development banks especially with AfDB, ADB, IADB, and many others. The further development of relations with international partners was aimed at improving the distribution of labor among the various partners based on the Bank and the partners' specific comparative advantages. Coordinated support for the development of national rural development strategies, in conjunction with PRSPs and CASs, will be a major focus of the Bank's engagements with international partners. Through enhanced partnership arrangements and linkages with others, the Bank will also benefit from the experiences of best practice and innovation and from analytical and policy work. These partners can also strengthen the Bank's competence in addressing gender issues in rural development. Opportunities will be fostered to align Trust Fund allocations to the implementation plan of *Reaching the Rural Poor* and to seek means to establish multi-partner funding mechanisms to tackle key strategic issues.

Collaborative arrangements include formal agreements with partner organizations to address concrete issues in rural development, and/or are formed to implement a time-bound program. These arrangements, in which participating organizations allocate resources to achieve specific objectives, are considered to be essential components in implementing this strategy and further enhance Bank effectiveness in rural poverty reduction. New and revitalized collaborative programs will be institutionalized. These will include enhanced collaboration between the Bank and USAID focusing in the first instance on global public goods specifically agricultural trade and markets, environmental change including climate change, and science and technology; and with the European Commission on broad-based issues of rural poverty reduction in particular in support of the PRSP processes and key thematic programs including land reform and access, and community driven development.

Corporate Partnerships are either legal entities established to address high priority issues, or represent long-term programs between the Bank and a specific institution. They are the most visible components of the partnerships and high-level institutional commitments.

■ **FAO and World Bank Cooperative Program (FAO/CP).** The FAO is the Bank's oldest partner in rural development. The Bank entered into a cooperative agreement with the FAO in 1964,

---

An Outline for a Global Platform for Rural Development 8.4

Mission:
To contribute to the elimination of rural poverty and the enhanced economic development of rural areas through deepened global, regional and national cooperation and collaboration

Principles:

■ Direct participants — development agencies, donors and IFI

■ Fosters a range of interlinked formal and informal alliances and activities with stakeholder representatives

■ Places emphasis on action, flexibility and responsiveness

■ Light on overheads and bureaucracy

Outputs may include:

■ Raised awareness and advocacy

■ Sponsored policy and public debate

■ Increased levels of investment and development funding including increased co-financing

■ Joint analytical and policy work on challenging issues

■ Shared lesson learning in good practice and innovation

■ Authorizing and enabling environment for related alliances

■ Joint monitoring and evaluation

---

through which the FAO established and staffed a program to help countries design and prepare projects and help the Bank with sector work. The FAO/CP has almost 100 professionals who cover a full range of disciplines. The Bank provides 70% of the funding for the CP while the FAO provides the remainder (the Bank contributes about $10 million annually). The FAO/CP resources are allocated among the regions, and the respective sector units develop their programs with the FAO/CP directly. This cooperation is ongoing and both the FAO and the Bank are aiming for a higher degree of integration of the FAO/CP into core Bank activities and in particular in support of the implementation of *Reaching the Rural Poor*.

- **World Bank – IFAD Rural Partnership Initiative.** This new partnership aims to build on the complementary assets of the two institutions recognizing the shared commitment to rural poverty reduction. It will specifically focus on rural advocacy, knowledge management, scaling-up of good practice, and resource mobilization to address structural issues at both country and global levels. This initiative will work closely with the FAO.

New alliances to raise the platform and enhance global advocacy for rural poverty reduction—A Global Platform for Rural Development. There is growing consensus among international development partners including the Bank, FAO, IFAD, EC, regional development banks, and major bilateral agencies, that we will not be successful in meeting national and global poverty reduction targets unless we reduce poverty in rural areas. A global understanding of approaches to meet the needs of the rural poor has never been closer, as many of these agencies have recently taken stock of their past experiences and redefined their approaches and commitment to poverty reduction in rural areas. The Bank will work with others in a broad-based global coalition to make the reduction of rural poverty a major thrust for the coming decade. Efforts have recently begun to establish a **Global Platform for Rural Development** (Box 8.4). It is proposed that such an alliance be a flexible consortium of international donors, interested in cooperating on the challenges of rural poverty reduction, acting as advocates and champions for the rural poor and specifically in support to the strengthening of the rural focus in policy and investment decisions in our client countries. Moreover, it will serve as a platform for joint learning and identification of good practices.

Improved Links to the Civil Society and Private Sector. The Bank's links to citizens groups, producer organizations, and other civil society organizations

(CSOs) and non-governmental organizations (NGOs) have increased dramatically over the past ten years. Internet websites and information sharing now provide the opportunity for increased direct dialogue and interaction between the Bank and CSOs/NGOs. The consultation process on regional action plans and the new corporate framework for the rural strategy proved to be a valuable and productive means of enhancing relationships with both large numbers of NGOs as well as with the private sector across all regions. Improved linkages with the private sector in a country framework is among the top priority objectives for each region. In a rapidly globalizing world, links with multi-national companies active in agriculture and which have an impact on rural development are also important. As the process of scaling-up of good practice is further developed it is anticipated that the CSOs, NGOs and the private sector will play a key role both in the sharing of good practice and in support to scaling-up at the local level.

IMPROVING THE MIX OF INSTRUMENTS

In the past five years, the Bank has experienced a more significant change in lending instruments than at any previous period in its history. In addition to the traditional investment and adjustment operations, a wide variety of new, and often more flexible, instruments have emerged. Some of these instruments represent improved versions of investment lending such as Learning and Innovation Loans (LILs), Adaptable Program Loans and Credits (APLs); Community Based Rural Development (CBRD) and social funds. More recently, new instruments, such as PRSP-based programmatic lending and Poverty Reduction Support Credits (PRSCs) have emerged.

Addressing rural poverty in a comprehensive fashion requires that an evolving set of instruments are applied to Bank operations in rural space. This is challenge has also been reflected in the 2001 OED Annual Review of Development Effectiveness (ARDE) (World Bank, 2002a). There is clearly no one "golden rule" as to the optimal distribution between different Bank instruments. However, some general directions can be identified regarding Bank operations in rural space:

- the diversity of rural situations between regions, countries, and sub-country regions requires the use of a broad set of instruments with increased multi-sectoral character set within the CAS framework;

- traditional investment projects will continue to play an important role, however they should be blended with the new type of operations (i.e., LIL, APL, PRSC, etc) according to country requests and conditions; and

- the broader use of new instruments, such as programmatic lending, should be promoted only after careful study and assessment of the actual field experiences with these programs and assurance that there is adequate rural focus.

Ensuring an Adequate Rural Focus in Programmatic Lending. The recent internal changes within the Bank indicate that the increased use of programmatic lending tools, especially in the poorest countries (Box 8.5), may have a profound impact on the way that rural poverty can best be addressed. It is too early to evaluate the impact of programmatic lending in this respect, but there are both opportunities and risks in achieving rural poverty reduction objectives with this shift. Programmatic lending could help to set a framework for improved rural spatial analysis leading to improved cross-sectoral rural poverty design. It could also address overarching institutional and policy constraints, provide a channel for systematic gender inclusion, support better national poverty monitoring, and improve donor coordination. At the same time, the broader framework of programmatic lending might lead to the result that the rural aspects and features of rural livelihoods are less well covered than in smaller projects. The best way to guarantee that programmatic lending becomes an opportunity for rural beneficiaries is to provide the rural stakeholders in the countries with the assistance necessary to create high-quality national rural strategies and to undertake other well targeted analysis.

Expand Community Participation in Project Design and Implementation. In FY00 one quarter of projects in the rural space were implemented with community participation. The community-based approach is much welcomed and even

---

Programmatic Lending: Poverty Reduction Support Credits (PRSCs) 8.5

The first examples of Poverty Reduction Support Credits (PRSCs) involve a series of two or three programmatic operations that correspond to the time horizon of the PRSP and CAS. They typically have one tranche and are provided based on up-front completion of a set of priority reform measures and public actions that demonstrate satisfactory progress with the country's social and structural reform agenda. Some PRSCs will focus mainly on economy-wide policy or institutional issues, with limited rural content. Others will focus on sectoral policies, institutions, and regulatory actions. There is concern that rural space will not be fully incorporated in poverty reduction strategies or in programmatic lending. The rural family will monitor the use of these instruments to ensure an appropriate rural focus.

demanded by most of the Bank's client countries. While the concept of community-based development is appealing and compelling (Coirolo et al. 2001), the knowledge of how to do it properly and effectively, is still evolving. Recognizing this state of affairs would suggest that the expansion of community-based activities should be done with the flexibility to adjust and fine-tune designs as knowledge builds up. On the whole, however, it is desirable to increase the involvement of communities in program design and implementation to the maximum extent possible. It is equally important to assure that these processes are inclusive and take into consideration the specific time or cultural and social constraints of women.

MONITORING AND EVALUATION

This strategy presents a program to revitalize the Bank activities in the rural space, and increase the effectiveness in the Bank's work in rural poverty reduction. *Reaching the Rural Poor* will pay considerable attention to monitoring and evaluation of the strategy's implementation. A set of targets and benchmarks will be used as the baseline for evalu-

85

ating this progress over a five year period. These are presented within a framework of **results-based management** principles, i.e., inputs, outputs, outcomes, and impacts. The Bank's Agriculture and Rural Development Sector Board will work closely with senior management in the further alignment of the rural strategy implementation framework to emerging Bank work on results-based management. In conjunction with the implementation of the Strategy, an attempt will also be made, together with other international donors, to improve the monitoring of regional and global progress in rural development and rural poverty reduction. The Strategy has not proposed specific lending targets, as such targets no longer fit in the demand-driven nature of the Bank's operations. It is expected, however, that increased national demands and improved quality of the operations in rural areas should generate increased demands.

Implementation targets for rural operations will allow for continuous monitoring of strategy implementation. Additionally information will be provided for a selected group of key countries to gauge progress at the country level. The progress in implementing the strategy will be reviewed quarterly within the Bank, and annual reviews will be prepared for the Board of Executive Directors. In addition to presentation of progress against these indicators, the annual review will also provide an overall assessment of progress on strategy implementation and highlight any critical issues.

The impact of Bank operations by themselves on global rural poverty indicators, is difficult to attribute. Monitoring overall and regional trends, as well as country indicators in rural development and poverty reduction, however, results in very important information that can be useful in analyzing the implementation of the strategy in the evolving international context (Millennium Development Goals). General rural development indicators, and indicators for the food and agriculture sectors are not easily available, and improving the informational basis for rural poverty reductions requires international cooperation. The Bank has already established partnerships, such as the Africa initiative for enhancing the rural-related statistical database. This effort should be continued and broadened to

include other major international organizations such as the UN regional centers, and the FAO.

RISKS IN IMPLEMENTING THE REVISED STRATEGY

It is recognized that there are several risks inherent in implementing the strategy:

■ That *Reaching the Rural Poor* is not acknowledged within the Bank as a multi-sectoral strategy and that substantive multi-sectoral collaboration does not materialize. The effective implementation of the strategy necessitates that all sectors operating in rural space make appropriate efforts to embrace the opportunity offered (rise to the challenges of rural poverty reduction) and in particular engage actively with the establishment and operation of the regional implementation and coordination arrangements.

■ That the Bank will not maintain the momentum established through the preparation of the Strategy, in the implementation phase, and fail to address the necessary internal institutional arrangements, the incentive framework, funding resource allocation, and creation of an appropriate staff skills mix. One of the failures of the *From Vision to Action* was the lack of capacity to maintain commitment to the core principles and implementation processes.

■ That the emerging new lending instruments and trends in lending are not conducive to innovation and risk taking in the rural space. With increased interest in programmatic lending and large scale budget transfers, the incentive and opportunity to pay necessary attention to learning and innovation within the country context may be reduced. In light of the urgency of deepening the understating of risk and vulnerability of the rural poor and tackling key structural and institutional issues, space must be given for communities and countries to adapt and learn within an active investment framework.

■ That the Bank together with willing country partners and other stakeholders is not able to mobilize the voice of the poor rural women and men, and other rural stakeholders. The strategy recognizes the challenges of mobilizing national and international advocacy for the rural poor and has in place a number of approaches to address this. However the time frame for change in giving strength to such voices must be closely monitored and adjusted to meet the objectives. Every effort should be made to use the range of instruments available to meet this risk.

- **That overall long term growth is not achieved in client countries.** Long-term growth is a necessary but not sufficient condition for rural poverty reduction. This combined with continued progress towards maintaining a sound enabling environment including addressing long neglected issues such as those relating to enhanced and more equitable access to assets for example, land, are key factors contributing to desired outcomes for the strategy.

- That the Bank's willingness to open up to, and capacity to work with, a wide range of partners is inadequate to address the challenges. **The Bank cannot address rural poverty reduction alone.** Whilst there is broad consensus globally on approaches to rural development, this consensus must be fostered. The Bank should seek to work with others to develop its own comparative advantage and gain from working with others in those areas for which it is less institutionally or organizationally suited. The transaction costs of working with others is recognized. However, if well managed, the potential gains outweigh such costs.

The process of developing the new rural strategy from prioritized regional and country diagnoses, along with the proposed institutional arrangements (internal and global) should help mitigate these risks. The CDF, PRSPs and Millennium Development Goals provide the requisite framework within which poverty reduction is etched as a strategic objective.

BIBLIOGRAPHY

ACC/SCN (United Nations Administrative Committee on Coordination, Sub-Committee on Nutrition) in collaboration with IFPRI. 2000. "Fourth Report on the World Nutrition Situation." Geneva.

Alderman, H. 2001. *What Has Changed Regarding Rural Poverty Since Vision to Action?* Rural Development Strategy Background Paper 5. World Bank, Washington, D.C. Processed.

Alex, G., et al. 2001. *Agricultural Extension Investments: Future Options for Rural Development.* Rural Development Strategy Background Paper 10. World Bank, Washington, D.C. Processed.

Alexandratos, N., ed. 1995. *World Agriculture: Towards 2010: An FAO Study.* Rome, Italy: Food and Agriculture Organization of the United Nations.

Anderson, J. R. 2001. *Risk Management in Rural Development: A Review.* Rural Development Strategy Background Paper 7. World Bank, Washington, D.C. Processed.

Anderson K., Hoekman B., Strutt A. (1999). Agriculture and the WTO: Next Steps. CIES Discussion Paper 99/14, University of Adelaide.

Ashley, C. and D. Carney. 1999. *Sustainable Livelihoods: Lessons from Early Experience.* Department for International Development, UK.

Ashley, C; Maxell, S. 2001, Rethinking Rural Development. *Development Policy Review.* Vol. 19, Number 4, December 2001

Asian Development Bank. 2000. *Rural Asia: Beyond the Green Revolution.* Manila.

Barghouti, S.,. et al. 2001. *The Role of Public and Private Sectors in Science, Technology, and Rural Development for Rural Development.* Rural Development Strategy Background Paper 9. World Bank, Washington, D.C. Processed.

Barnett, A. and G. Rugalema. 2001. "HIV/AIDS". In Flores Rafael and Stuart Gillespie, eds. *Health and Nutrition: Emerging and Reemerging Issues in Developing Countries.* 2020 Focus 5. IFPRI (International Food Policy Research Institute). Washington, D.C.

Bathrick, D. 1998. *Fostering Global Well-Being: A New Paradigm to Revitalize Agriculture and Rural Development.* 2020 Vision Discussion Paper. Washington D.C.: International Food Policy Research Institute.

Bebbington, A. 1999. "Capitals and Capabilities: A Framework for Analyzing Peasant Viability, Rural Livelihoods and Poverty." *World Development,* 27 (12): 2021–2144.

Belshaw, D. 2000. *Strategic Options for the Reduction of Poverty in Sub-Saharan Africa: Welfarist Human Development versus Small-Scale Commodity Production.* UEA, Norwich, U.K. Processed.

Berdegue, J. and G. Escobar. 2001. *Agricultural Knowledge and Information Systems and Poverty Reduction.* AKIS/ART Discussion Paper. World Bank.

Beynon, J. 1996. *Financing of Agricultural Research and Extension for Smallholder Farmers in Sub-Saharan Africa.* ODI Natural Resources Perspective No. 15. ODI (Overseas Development Institute), UK.

Binswanger, H., K. Deininger, and G. Feder. 1995. "Power Distortions, Revolt and Reform in Agricultural Land Relationships." In Behrman, J. and T.N. Srinivasan, eds. *Handbook of Development Economics.* Vol. 3. Amsterdam: Elsevier.

Binswanger, H. and M. Elguin. 1989. "What are the Prospects for Land Reform?" In Maunder, Allan and Alberto Valdes, eds. *Agriculture and Governments in an Interdependent World.* Proceedings of the Twentieth International Conference of Agricultural Economists (IAAE), Buenos Aires. Aldershot, Dartmouth, UK.

Binswanger, H. and P. Landell-Mills. 1995. *The World Bank's Strategy for Reducing Poverty and Hunger: A Report to the Development Community.* Environmentally Sustainable Development Studies and Monograph Series No. 4. Washington, D.C.: The World Bank.

Brown, A., M. Foster, and F. Naschold. 2000. "What's Different About Agricultural SWAPs?" DFID Natural Resources Advisors Conference, July 10–14, London.

Brunetti, A., Kisunko, G. and Weder, B. (1998). Credibility of Rules and Economic Growth: Evidence From a Worldwide Survey of the Private Sector. *World Bank Economic Review,* 12(3): 353–84.

CGIAR (Consultative Group on International Agricultural Research). 2001. Working Paper of the CGIAR Inter-Center Working Group on Climate Change. Washington, D.C.

CGIAR (Consultative Group on International Agricultural Research). 2000. The Challenge of Climate Change: Poor Farmers at Risk. CGIAR Annual Report 2000. Washington, D.C.

Cleaver, K. M. and G. A. Schreiber. 1994. *Reversing the Spiral: The Population, Agriculture, and Environment Nexus in Sub-Saharan Africa.* Washington, D.C.: World Bank.

Coirolo, L. et al. 2001. *Community Based Rural Development: Reducing Poverty from the Ground Up.* Rural Development Strategy Background Paper 6. World Bank. Washington, D.C. Processed.

Committee on World Food Security. 2001. Mobilizing Resources to Fight Hunger. Twenty-seventh session, Rome, 28 May–1 June, 2001 (CFS:2001/Inf.7).

Cord, L. 2001a. Coverage of Rural Issues in PRSPs. The World Bank, Washington, D.C. Processed.

David, C, and K. Otsuka, eds. 1994, *Modern Rice Technology and Income Distribution in Asia*. Boulder, Co. Lynne Rienner.

——. 2001b. Rural Safety Nets: Lessons from Experience. Background Study for Updating Vision to Action. The World Bank, Washington, D.C. Processed.

de Haan, A. 1999. Livelihoods and poverty: the role of migration. A critical review of the migration literature. *Journal of Development Studies* 36, no. 2: 1–47

de Haan, A. and S. Maxwell. 1998. Poverty and Social Exclusion in North and South. *IDS Bulletin*, 29 (1): 1–9.

de Haan, C., *et al.* 2001. *Livestock Development: Implications on Rural Poverty, the Environment, and Global Food Security*. Directions in Development. Washington, D.C.: World Bank.

de Janvry, A. and E. Sadoulet. 1993. "Adjustment Policies, Agriculture and Rural Development in Latin America." In Singh, A. and H. Tabatabei, eds. *Economic Crisis and Third World Agriculture*. Cambridge: Cambridge University Press.

——. 1999. *Rural Poverty and the Design of Effective Rural Development Strategies*. Paper presented at the Junta Inter-Americana de Agricultura, Bahia, Brazil.

——. 2000. *Making Investment in the Rural Poor into Good Business: New Perspectives for Rural Development in Latin America*. Paper presented at the Annual Meetings of the Inter-American Development Bank, New Orleans, USA.

Deacon, B.; M. Hulse and P. Stubbs. 1997. *Global Social Policy: International Organizations and the Future of Welfare*. London: Sage.

Delgado, C., M. Rosegrant, H. Steinfeld, S. Ehui, and C. Courbois. 1999. *Livestock to 2020: The Next Food Revolution*. 2020 Food, Agriculture, and the Environment Discussion Paper #28. International Food Policy Research Institute.

Dixon, J., A. Gulliver and D. Gibbons. 2001. *Farming Systems and Poverty: Improving Farmers' Livelihoods in a Changing World*. FAO and The World Bank. FAO, Rome.

Dollar, D. and A. Kraay. 2000. *Growth is Good for the Poor*. Development Economics Research Group. The World Bank, Washington, D.C.

Dreze, J. and A. Sen. 1989. *Hunger and Public Action*. Oxford: Clarendon Press.

Echeverria, R. 1998. *Strategic Elements for the Reduction of Rural Poverty in Latin America and the Caribbean*. Inter-American Development Bank, Sustainable Development Department. Washington, D.C.

——. 2000. *Strategy for Agricultural Development in Latin America and the Caribbean*. Inter-American Development Bank, Sustainable Development Department. Washington, D.C.

Eicher, C.K. and J.M. Staatz. 1990. *Agricultural Development in the Third World*. 2nd edition. Baltimore: Johns Hopkins University Press.

Elbehri A., Ingco M.D., Hertel T.W., Pearson. K. (1999). Agriculture and WTO 2000: Quantitative assessment of Multilateral Liberalization of Agricultural Policy. Paper presented at the WTO/World Bank conference on 'Agriculture and the New Trade Agenda in the WTO 2000 Negotiations', October 1999, Geneva.

Elbehri A., Leetma S. (2002). How Significant are Export Subsidies to Agricultural Trade? Trade and Welfare Implications of Global Reforms. Paper presented at the 5th Annual Conference on Global Economic Analysis, June 2002, Taipei.

Ellis, F. 1998. "Household Strategies and Rural Livelihood Diversification." *Journal of Development Studies*, 35(1): 1–38.

——. 1999. *Rural Livelihood Diversity in Developing Countries: Evidence and Policy Implications*. ODI Natural Resource Perspective No. 40. London: Overseas Development Institute.

Evans, A. 2000. *Spatial Considerations in PRSP Processes*. The World Bank, Washington. D.C.

Falusi, A.O., and C.A. Afolami, 1999. *Effects of Technology Change and Commercialization on Income Equity in Nigeria: The Case of Improved Cassava*. http://www.ciat.org/poverty_workshop/papers.htm, International Centre for Tropical Agriculture, Cali, Colombia.

Fan, S., P. Hazell, and S. Thorat. 1999. *Linkages Between Government Spending, Growth, and Poverty in Rural India*. IFPRI Research Report 110. Washington, D.C.: International Food Policy Research Institute.

FAO (Food and Agricultural Organization of the United Nations). 1997. *The State of Food and Agriculture 1997*. Rome: FAO.

FAO (Food and Agricultural Organization of the United Nations). 2001. *The State of Food and Agriculture 2001*. Rome: FAO.

Gibson, P., Wainio, J., Whitley, D., Bohman M. (2001). *Profiles of Tariffs in Global Agricultural Markets*. USDA, ERS, Agricultural Economic Report No. 796. USDA, Washington D.C.

Hazell, P., Ramasamy, C. (1991). The Green Revolution Reconsidered: The Impact of High-Yielding Rice Varieties in South India. Johns Hopkins Press, Baltimore.

Holzmann, R. and S. Jørgensen. 2000. *Social Risk Management: A New Conceptual Framework for Social Protection and Beyond*. Social Protection Discussion Paper No. 6. Washington, D.C.: The World Bank.

IBSRAM. 2001. *Background Study on Land Degradation in Selected Regions and Some Consequences for Rural Development.* Rural Development Strategy Background Paper 11. World Bank. Washington, D.C. Processed.

IFAD (International Fund for Agricultural Development). 2001. *Rural Poverty Report 2001: The Challenge of Ending Rural Poverty.* Oxford: Oxford University Press.

Ingco M.D., Nash J., *et al.* (2003, forthcoming). Agriculture and the WTO: Creating a Trading System for Development.

IWMI (International Water Management Institute). 2001. Water for Rural Development. The World Bank. 2002. Processed.

Irz, X., L. Lin, C. Thirtle, and S. Wiggins. 2001. "Agricultural Productivity Growth And Poverty Alleviation." *Development Policy Review* 19(4): 449–466.

Izac, A-M. N. and P. Sanchez. 1999. *Towards A Natural Resource Management Paradigm For International Agriculture: Example Of Agroforestry Research.* Nairobi: ICRAF.

Johnston, B.F. and J.W. Mellor. 1961. "The Role of Agriculture in Economic Development." *American Economic Review* 51(4): 566–93.

Kabeer, N. 1997. Editorial: Tactics and Trade-offs, Revisiting the Links Between Gender and Poverty. *IDS Bulletin* 28(3): 1–13.

Kaosaat, M. and B. Rerkasem. 2000. *The Growth and Sustainability of Agriculture in Asia.* A Study of Rural Asia, Vol. 2. Asian Development Bank. Hong Kong: Oxford University Press.

Karmokolias, I. 1997. "Aquaculture de la Mahajamba." Private Sector and Development: Five Case Studies. Washington, D.C.: International Finance Corporation.

Kaufmann D., Kraay A., and Zoido-Lobatón, P. (2000). Governance matters, from measurement to action. *Finance And Development, A Quarterly Publication Of The International Monetary Fund (International),* 37, No. 2:10–13, June 2000.

Kaul, I., I. Grunberg and M.A. Stern, eds. 1999. *Global Public Goods: International Cooperation in the 21st Century.* Oxford: Oxford University Press for United Nations Development Program.

Killick, T., J. Kydd and C. Poulton. 2000. *The Rural Poor and the Wider Economy: The Problem of Market Access.* Paper in the Report on IFAD's Workshop on Rural Poverty, IFAD, Rome January 24–25, 2000. IFAD, Rome.

Komives, K., D. Whittington and X. Wu. 2000. *Infrastructure Coverage and the Poor: A Global Perspective.* Policy Research Working Paper 2551. Washington, D.C.: World Bank.

Krueger, A.O., Schiff, M., and Valdes, A. (1988), Agricultural incentives in developing countries: measuring the effects of sectorial and economy wide policies, *World Bank Economic Review,* Vol. 2, #3: 255–271.

Krueger, A.O. (1992). *The political economy of agricultural pricing policy Vol. 4. A Synthesis of the Economics in Developing Countries,* Baltimore: Johns Hopkins University Press.

Kydd, J., A. Dorward and C. Poulton. 2000. "Globalization and its Implications for the Natural Resources Sector: A Closer Look at the Role of Agriculture in the Global Economy." An issues paper for DFID Natural Resources Advisors Conference, July 10–14, 2000.

Lanjouw, P., J.A. Mistiaen and Ozier, B. 2000. *Micro-Level Estimation of Poverty and Inequality: Methods and Case Study Evidence.* Washington, DC. Processed.

Lanjouw, P. and G. Feder. 2001. *Rural Non-Farm Activities and Rural Development: From Experience Towards Strategy.* Rural Strategy Background Paper 4. World Bank. Washington, D.C. Processed.

Lewis, W.A. 1954. Economic Development with Unlimited Supplies of Labour. *Manchester School of Economic and Social Studies* 22(2): 139–91.

Lipton, M. and M. Ravallion. 1995. *Handbook of Development Economics.* Volume 3B. Handbooks in Economics Vol. 9. Amsterdam: Elsevier Science.

Malmberg-Calvo, C. and A. Ryan. 2001. *Rural Infrastructure, Development and Poverty Reduction—Challenges, Linkages and Actions.* Rural Strategy Background Paper 8. World Bank. Washington, D.C. Processed.

Markets and Agribusiness Thematic Group. 2001. *Promoting Agro-Enterprise and Agro-Food Systems Development in Developing and Transition Economies.* Rural Strategy Background Paper 12. World Bank. Washington, D.C. Processed.

Maxwell, S. 1999. *What Can We Do with a Rights-Based Approach to Development?* ODI Briefing Paper(3). London: Overseas Development Institute.

Maxwell, S. and R. Riddell. 1998. "Conditionality or Contract: Perspectives on Partnership for Development." *Journal of International Development* 10: 257–268.

McCulloch N., Winters A., Cirera X. (2001). *Trade Liberalization and Poverty: A Handbook.* DFID and CEPR, London.

Narayan, D., et al. 2000. *Can Anyone Hear Us? Voices of the Poor.* Washington, D.C.: World Bank.

OECD (2001a). *The Uruguay Round Agreement on Agriculture: The policy concerns of Emerging and Transition Economies.* OECD, Paris.

OECD (2001b). *OECD Observer,* Policy Brief, November 2001.

OECD (2002). *Agricultural Policies in OECD Countries: Monitoring and Evaluation.* OECD, Paris.

Okidegbe, N. 2001. *Rural Poverty: Trends and Measurement.* Rural Strategy Background Paper 3. World Bank. Washington, D.C. Processed.

Pinstrup-Andersen, P., R. Pandya-Lorch, R. and M.Rosegrant. 1997. *The World Food Situation: Recent Developments, Emerging Issues, and Long-Term Prospects.* IFPRI Food Policy Report 2020 Vision. Washington D.C.: International Food Policy Research Institute.

Pinstrup-Andersen, P.; Pandya-Lorch, R.; Rosegrant, M.W. 1999. *World Food Prospects: Critical Issues for the Early Twenty-First Century.* IFPRI Food Policy Report 2020 Vision, Washington, DC.

Task Force on Science and Technology for Food Security RDV. 2001. Investing in Science for Food Security in the 21st Century. The World Bank, Washington D.C.

Renkow, M. 1993. Differential Technology Adoption and Income Distribution in Pakistan: Implications for Research Resource Allocation. *American Journal of Agricultural Economics 75(1).* 33–43.

Riley, T. and W.F. Steen. 2000. Kenya Voucher Program for Training and Business Development Services. In Levitsky, J., ed. *Business Development Services: A Review of International Experience.* London: Intermediate Technology.

Rosegrant, M. and P. Hazell. 2000. *Transforming the Rural Asian Economy: the Unfinished Revolution.* Study of Rural Asia Vol. 1. Oxford: Oxford University Press for IFPRI and the Asian Development Bank.

Rosegrant, M., M.S. Paisner and Setal Meijer. 2001. *Long Term Prospects for Agriculture and the Resource Base.* Rural Strategy Background Paper 1. World Bank. Washington, D.C. Processed.

Sarris, A. 2001. *The Role of Agriculture in Economic Development and Poverty Reduction: An Empirical and Conceptual Foundation.* Rural Strategy Background Paper 2. World Bank. Washington, D.C. Processed.

Satterthwaite, D. 2000. "Location and Deprivation: Beyond Spatial Concepts of Poverty." IIED (International Institute for Environment and Development). London.

Schiff, M. and A. Valdes. 1998. *Agriculture and the Macroeconomy.* Policy Research Working Paper 1967. Washington, D.C.: The World Bank.

———. 1992. *The political Economy of Agricultural Pricing Policy Vol. 4.* A Synthesis of the Economics in Developing Countries, Baltimore: Johns Hopkins University Press.

Sen, A. 1981a. *Poverty and Famines: An Essay on Entitlement and Deprivation.* Oxford: Clarendon Press.

———. 1981b. "Ingredients of Famine Analysis: Availability and Entitlements." *Quarterly Journal of Economics* 96 (3) : 433–64.

———. 1985. *Commodities and Capabilities.* Amsterdam: North Holland.

Siamwala, A. and A.B. Brillantes. 2001. *The Evolving Roles of the State, Private, and Local Actors in Rural Asia.* Study of Rural Asia Vol. 5. Oxford: Oxford University Press for the Asian Development Bank.

Stamoulis, K.G., ed. 2001. *Food, Agriculture and Rural Development: Current and Emerging Issues for Economic Analysis and Policy Research.* Economic and Social Department. FAO. Rome.

Start, D. 2001. The Rise and Fall of the Rural Non-Farm Economy: Poverty Impacts and Policy Options. *Development Policy Review.* Vol. 19, Number 4, December 2001

Stern, N.H. 2001. "Strategy for Development." Annual Bank Conference on Development Economics Keynote Address. World Bank. Washington D.C.

Stiglitz, J. 1998a. *More Instruments and Broader Goals: Moving Towards the Post-Washington Consensus.* World Institute for Development Economics Research Annual Lecture, Helsinki, January 7, 1998.

———. 1998b. *Towards a New Paradigm for Development: Strategies, Policies and Processes.* 1998 Prebisch Lecture and UNCTAD, Geneva, October 19, 1998.

Timmer, C.P. 1997. *How Well do the Poor Connect to the Growth Process?* Consulting Assistance on Economic Reform Discussion Paper No. 178. Cambridge, MA.: Harvard Institute for International Development.

UNAIDS (Joint United Nations Programme on HIV/AIDS). 2001 "AIDS Epidemic Update: December 2000." [http://www.unaids.org/wac/2000/wad00/files/WAD_epidemic_report.PDF]. April.

Verissimo, P. 2001. *Promoting Knowledge and Learning for a Sustainable Rural Development: The Evolving Role of the WBI.* Rural Strategy Background Paper 14. World Bank. Washington, D.C. Processed.

93

Von Braun, J. and E. Kennedy, eds. 1994. *Agricultural Commercialization, Economic Development and Nutrition.* Baltimore: Johns Hopkins University Press.

White, H. and T. Anderson. 2000. *Growth versus Distribution: Does the Pattern of Growth Really Matter?* June. Draft. Institute of Development Studies, Sussex, UK.

Williamson, J. 1994. *The Political Economy of Reform.* Washington D.C.: Institute for International Economics.

Wolfensohn, J. D. 1999. *A Proposal for a Comprehensive Development Framework.* Discussion Draft. World Bank. Washington D.C. http://web.worldbank.org/WBSITE/EXTERNAL/PROJECTS/STRATEGIES/CDF

World Bank. 1997a. *Health, Nutrition, and Population. World Bank Sector Strategy.* Washington, D.C.: World Bank.

———. 1997b. *Rural Development: From Vision to Action.* Environmentally and Socially Sustainable Development Studies and Monograph Series 12. The World Bank, Washington D.C.

———. 1999a. Annual Report on Portfolio Performance (ARPP). Quality Assurance Group (QAG). The World Bank, Washington D.C. Internal.

———. 1999b. *Education Sector Strategy.* Washington, D.C.: World Bank.

———. 1999c. *Rural Development: From Vision to Action?* Operations Evaluation Department. The World Bank, Washington D.C. Processed.

———. 2000a. *Cities in Transition: A Strategic View of Urban and Local Government.* Washington, D.C.: World Bank.

———. 2000b. *Fuel for Thought: an Environmental Strategy for the Energy Sector.* Washington, D.C.: World Bank.

———. 2000c. *Population and the World Bank: Adapting to Change.* Revised edition. Human Development Network Health Nutrition and Population Series. Washington, D.C.: World Bank.

———. 2000d. *Reforming Public Institutions and Strengthening Governance: A World Bank Strategy.* Washington, D.C.: World Bank.

———. 2000e. *Rural Development From Vision to Action? Phase II.* Operations Evaluation Department Report No. 20628. The World Bank, Washington D.C.

———. 2000f. *Strategy for the Financial Sector.* Washington, D.C.: World Bank.

———. 2001a. *Engendering Development Through Gender Equity in Rights, Resources, and Voice.* World Bank Policy Research Report N. 21492. Oxford University Press, New York.

———. 2001b. *Global Economic Prospects and the Developing Countries 2001.* The World Bank, Washington D.C.

———. 2001c. *Globalization Policy Research Report,* DEC Draft.

———. 2001d. *Making Sustainable Commitments: an Environment Strategy for the World Bank.* Washington, D.C.: World Bank

———. 2001e. *Sharpening the Focus on Rural Poverty.* Operations Evaluation Department. The World Bank, Washington D.C

———. 2001f. *Social Protection Strategy: From Safety Net to Springboard.* Washington, D.C.: World Bank.

———. 2001g. *World Development Report 2000/2001: Attacking Poverty.* Oxford University Press, New York.

———. 2002a. *Implementing the New Rural Development Strategy in a Country Driven Process: Agriculture & Rural Development Project Profiles.* Agriculture & Rural Development Department, World Bank. Processed.

———. 2002b. *Integrating Gender into the World Bank's Work: a Strategy for Action.* Washington, D.C.: World Bank.

———. 2002c. *Private Sector Development Strategy: Directions for the World Bank Group.* Washington, D.C.: World Bank.

———. 2002d. *Sector Strategy Paper: Information and Communications Technologies.* A World Bank Sector Strategy. Washington, D.C.: World Bank.

———. 2002e. Annual Review of Development Effectiveness 2001. Operations Evaluation Department. World Bank. Washington D.C. Processed.

WRI (World Resources Institute). 1998. *World Resources 1998–99.* Oxford University Press, New York.

Yaron, J., P.B. McDonald and G.L. Piprek, G.L. 1997. *Rural Finance: Issues, Design, and Best Practices,* Environmentally and Socially Sustainable Development Studies and Monographs Series 14. Washington, D.C.: World Bank

ANNEXES

ANNEX 1: Lessons in Implementing *From Vision to Action for Reaching the Rural Poor*

Vision to Action Objectives	Outcomes	Comments	Lessons for Reaching the Rural Poor
APPROACH			
1. Shift from sub-sectoral to broad rural development focus and improve coordination between various actors.	With a strong increase in such areas as community driven development, and watershed development, the focus of operations has broadened.	Inadequately functioning inter-sectoral integrating mechanisms in the Bank still constrains multi-sectoral activities.	Strengthening the holistic approach by emphasis on non-agricultural, physical and human infra-structure while maintaining a strong commitment to agriculture. Develop internal institutional mechanisms to support multi-sectoral coordination and coherence.
2. Working with all stakeholders to integrate rural development in overall country development strategies.	Rural aspects increasingly treated in CASs and PRSPs.	Rural poverty reduction issues are satisfactorily treated in only 50% of CASs.	Increased support for broad based client driven processes for national rural development strategies to strengthen advocacy. Enhance internal and partner skills training.
PRIORITY ACTION			
1. Enhancing portfolio quality			
1.1 Increase ESW for the rural areas.	ESW budget remained stable at $9.5 m over FY 96-97 to $10.4 m over FY 99-00. Investment in sector work for agriculture as a share of total lending costs declined from pre-VtoA amounts by about 50%.	Rural portfolio review indicated need to increase both the quality and content of ESW for broad based pro-poor rural development.	Combine budgetary realignment with earmarked funds for increased ESW. Enhance pro-poor focus of future ESW and strengthen impact of ESW on strategy and design of investment lending.
1.2 Improve development outcome of rural projects to 80% satisfactory rating.	Development outcomes of rural projects declined from 66% in FY 94-95 to 60% over FY 99-00.	Sustainability and Institutional Development remain critical weaknesses of rural portfolio.	Maintain the goal of 80% satisfactory rating and strongly increase attention to Sustainability and Institutional Development, during project implementation.
1.3 Reverse decline in lending for rural development (without indicating specific goals).	Lending for agriculture, rural roads and water, and natural resources management declined over the period FY96-00.	Weak rural advocacy in client countries, and lack of incentives at country team level to focus on rural poverty.	Support to rural advocacy groups, link incentives for country teams to focus on poverty reduction.

Vision to Action Objectives	Outcomes	Comments	Lessons for Reaching the Rural Poor
		Lack of base-line against which to measure trends in wider rural lending.	Annual monitoring of lending against FY99-01 baseline for investment in rural space.
2. Enhancing knowledge management.	15 Rural Thematic Groups (TGs).	While shared learning clinics are felt to be effective in improving quality of project preparation, there remained a lack of a clear mechanism to assess impact and specific contribution to wider VtoA goals.	TGs need to be rationalized and aligned strategically with new strategic objectives to improve their effectiveness and to contribute to continuous learning and innovation within the Bank, with partners, and clients.
3. Strengthening alliances.	The Rural Family is engaged in over 30 rural partnerships and collaborative agreements.	The rapid increase in partnerships has raised some concerns about spreading resources too thin and diverting attention from Rural Family priorities.	Enhance partnerships with clear linkage to implementing the strategy.

MAJOR OUTCOMES

Vision to Action Objectives	Outcomes	Comments	Lessons for Reaching the Rural Poor
1. Bank seen as a leader in the fight to reduce rural poverty by fiscal 2000.	Bank remains a leader in rural development thinking and in providing development assistance to rural space.	Limited institutional capacity and lack of specific institutional arrangements to champion rural development has reduced potential for wider impact. Decline in agricultural lending.	More structured global initiatives with clearer responsibilities. Enhance role in advocacy at global and country levels.
2. Freer and fairer world agricultural trade.	The Bank has taken an active role in assisting client countries to prepare for the WTO.	Authorizing environment of the Bank in dealing with OECD countries and their subsidies and market access is limited.	Continued advocacy combined with focused support to developing countries to enable them to become beneficiaries of trade liberalization.
3. Reversing the low growth the trends of under-performing countries. Focus on 15 countries with support to their rural strategy.	Lending to focus countries increased from 54 % of total lending for agriculture over the FY 92-96 period (before they were selected) to 64% after the initiative (FY 97-01), and Quality at Entry was 100% for all Quality Reviews.	Longer term concentration on a limited number of countries, which are subject to political changes, led to variable results.	Focus on more specific objectives i.e., improving number of rural poor affected by the Bank operations and tie activities with the PRSP/CAS processes. Phase program of work on an annual basis with a larger overall number of countries and interventions.

ANNEX 2: Consultations in Strategy Preparation

More than 2,000 people (government officials, civil society, academics, private sector, and donor agencies) have been involved at some stage in the consultation process surrounding the rural strategy development. This has involved four major processes:

- Consultations on the regional strategies and the initial framework of the corporate strategy. Altogether there were nine regional consultations held in early 2001 (Nepal, Philippines, China, Lebanon, France, Kenya, Senegal, Russia, Panama, Belgium, and Japan).

- Consultations and seminars focused on the corporate strategy and its implementation. Three consultations specifically focused on implementation were held in 2002 (Vietnam, Nigeria, Ethiopia), and two more are scheduled (Jordan and Peru). Additionally, seminars were held at the Asian Development Bank in March 2001, African Development Bank in June 2002, and at an EBRD workshop in March 2002. Seminar presentations were also made in Australia (February 2002), Tokyo (March 2002).

- Presentations, seminars and panel discussions at major international gatherings with broad-based stakeholder participation. These venues include the IFPRI Conference – September 2001 (Bonn), FAO Conference – November 2001 (Rome), Conference on Financing for Development – March 2002 (Monterrey), UN PrepCo for World Summit on Sustainable Development – March 2002 (New York), European Sustainable Development Conference – March 2002 (Berlin), 35th World Farmer Congress – May 2002 (Cairo), World Food Summit – June 2002 (Rome), European Rural Development Forum – September 2002 (Montpellier).

- Rural strategy website and internet consultations on the final draft of the strategy. A website was created early in the strategy development process. All relevant material has been posted on this site for comment including background papers, seminar summaries, and early drafts of both corporate and regional strategies. From April to August 2002 the final stage pre – Executive Board draft was posted for public comment. A significant number of comments from academics, civil society groups, donors, governments, NGOs, and private individuals were received.

ANNEX 3: Regional Strategy Summaries

AFRICA

Sub-Saharan Africa's population remains predominantly rural (70%), and poverty is widespread. The international community's commitment to cutting the global incidence of absolute poverty in half by 2015 implies a massive effort in rural Africa.

Regional Context

Agriculture remains important in rural Africa, and indicators of rural well-being are closely correlated with agricultural performance. Aggregate growth rates in African agriculture overall improved during the 1990s. While Africa's agricultural growth lagged all developing regions in the 1980s, the gap narrowed in the 1990s due to improvement in Africa and deterioration elsewhere. Despite improved growth, African rural poverty remains deeper and more prevalent than in other regions.

General improvement in the 1990s masks wide disparities in the performance of countries throughout the region. The 48 countries of Sub-Saharan Africa are widely diverse in their resource and factor endowments and their abilities to commit politically to actions to increase growth and reduce poverty. During the 1990s 12 of the 48 countries of the region were able to maintain agricultural growth rates of 4% or better. This is a large improvement over the 1980s, when only five countries achieved agricultural growth rates of more than 4% (Benin, Comoros, Mozambique, Togo and Cape Verde).

Agricultural growth in a second group of countries has been positive, but less than 4% per year on average, and in many cases less than population growth. Rural poverty is gradually worsening in these countries, although again the measures are not complete. About half of African countries fall into this category.

A third group of countries is still immersed in civil or international conflict or unrest with sharply rising poverty and increasing desperation, particularly among rural people displaced by fighting. About 100 million Africans, a fifth of the region's total population live in these countries. About 4 million Africans are currently refugees, displaced from their homes and deprived of their livelihoods. The impact of conflict is clear from the statistics. Countries that enjoyed high rates of agricultural growth during the 1980s, including Burundi, Rwanda, Sierra Leone, Comoros and the Republic of Congo, all experienced low or negative agricultural growth when overwhelmed by conflict in the 1990s.

Growth of productivity has lagged that of agricultural output. Agricultural productivity per worker for the region as a whole has stagnated during the past ten years at an estimated $375 per worker (constant 1995 US$). This is 12% lower than in 1980, when value-added per worker was $424. Moreover, agricultural yields have been level or have fallen for many crops in many countries. Significantly, yields of most important food grains, tubers and legumes (maize, millet, sorghum, yams, cassava, groundnut) in most African countries are no higher today than in 1980.

Low productivity has seriously eroded the competitiveness of African agricultural products on world markets. Africa's share of total world agricultural trade fell from 8% in 1965 to 3% in 1996.

The Historical Legacy: How Relevant is it to Today's Agenda?

African rural areas are severely undercapitalized, as reflected in the low use of fertilizers, tractors and other agricultural technologies, limited infrastructure, inadequate education and health, and depletion of natural resources. Long secular persistence of poor policies and institutions explains the undercapitalization. Much of this can be attributed to the legacy of slavery and colonialism. Post-colonial policies did not reverse the decapitalization of rural areas, as governments pursued macroeconomic and agricultural policies that discouraged investment in rural areas, weakened local governments, and suppressed the development of civil society organizations (including voluntary producers' organizations).

The legacy of scarce capital, poverty, and dependence is thus very relevant to the agenda of today.

99

Rural areas still lack capital, including physical, human, infrastructure, natural resources, social and political (as in representation and influence) capital. Deep institutional and social changes are needed to remedy this multidimensional lack of capital. Changes cannot be ordained from the top, and must be derived from stronger participation of rural communities and greater voice of rural people.

The strategy emphasizes community participation, strengthening of voluntary producer organizations, primacy of the private sector in production and trade, a stronger role for markets, greater attention to the needs of women, enhanced activity of local governments in provision of public services, and transparency and accountability in the use of public funds.

The Strategy

Although specific elements of the strategy are unique to countries and regions, the strategic interventions fall into four broad categories:

- Making governments and institutions work better for the rural poor;
- Promoting widely-shared growth;
- Enhancing management of natural resources; and
- Reducing risk and vulnerability.

The strategic interventions apply differentially depending on circumstances of individual countries. Given the scarcity of resources, the fiduciary responsibilities of the World Bank, and lessons learned regarding the efficacy of aid, preference is accorded to countries that are performing well and demonstrate a strong commitment to reduce poverty. This preference is reflected in the allocation of resources among countries and in increased attention to systems of public procurement and management of public finance.

Other factors that affect the emphases of national strategies include:
- Stability and strength of local institutions (for example, presence or absence of conflict, and status of decentralization);
- Relative factor endowments (for example, abundance or scarcity of land and water);
- Potential for intensification through greater commercial integration of small-holders relative to

alternative farming systems for economically marginal areas;
- Prevalence of HIV/AIDS and other endemic diseases of people and livestock; and
- Cultural traditions affecting dietary preferences and livelihoods.

For example, in countries emerging from conflict, such as the Democratic Republic of the Congo, the rural strategy will focus on rebuilding livelihood systems at the community level through participatory diagnoses and micro-projects. In large and diverse countries, such as Zambia and Tanzania, different strategies are appropriate for different regions. In many places the potential for intensification through better linkages of producers' organizations to markets is substantial. In marginal areas far from markets, intensification based on purchased inputs is not appropriate, but improved rotations and cultivation practices can strengthen food security and stewardship of natural resources.

Making Government and Institutions Work Better for the Rural Poor

Issues of governance, including the general framework for security, the rule of law, and probity in public expenditure are particularly important for rural areas, since the least empowered within a political system suffer most from poor governance. These issues are high on the World Bank's corporate agenda.

In addition to supporting improved governance, the Africa rural strategy strengthens the institutional foundations for rural development by:

- **Supporting government's efforts to decentralize,** through technical assistance in design of decentralization, enhancing capacity of subnational governments, providing financing in support of decentralization, and assisting with design of systems of monitoring and evaluation.
- **Enhancing the participation of rural communities** in newly decentralized political and administrative systems, and providing resources to communities to use to pursue their own priorities for development.
- **Providing support for voluntary producers' organizations** by assisting governments to create

an enabling policy and legal environment within which producers' organizations can flourish, providing organizational support and technical assistance, and giving matching grants to producers' organizations that have demonstrated capacity to manage funds and activities on behalf of all their members.

- **Augmenting rural voice** in discussions of priorities for public expenditure and national development. Each of the interventions noted above also serves to enhance rural people's voice within the domestic arena. The donor community can help amplify rural voice in consultations and negotiations with partners and clients. The Poverty Reduction Strategy Paper (PRSP) process and its links to the Highly Indebted Poor Countries (HIPC) initiative provide important opportunities for the donor community to encourage participants in national policy dialogue to give appropriate weight to the interests of the rural poor.

Promoting Widely-Shared Growth

Agriculture remains high on the agenda for rural development in Africa—more so than in regions with greater food security and income levels supporting a more diversified economic base. While agriculture is not the only source of rural growth (tourism, mining, forestry, fishing and others are important in some places), in Africa today agriculture is the most important rural enterprise, contributing an average of 30% of total gross domestic product in the Sub-Saharan countries (excluding South Africa), and over 40% in one-third of those countries. Agribusinesses, which themselves depend on agricultural growth, are responsible for an additional 20% of GDP and about 25% of total rural incomes.

Agriculture and related rural enterprises are primarily private sector activities. Interventions to generate more income fall into five basic categories:

- **Continuing policy and regulatory reforms in OECD countries and within and among African countries to remove constraints to trade and business activities.** The faster growing African countries have made substantial progress on macroeconomic and sectoral reforms. Continued assistance may be needed to consolidate reforms and to support budgets of public entities fulfilling newly defined functions. An important part of the policy agenda lies outside the boundaries of African nations, in the evolving rules of the WTO and decisions regarding subsidies and market access of the OECD countries. The World Bank assists in the area of trade liberalization by providing analysis and advocacy for African countries, and by assisting their trade representatives to prepare for participation in trade negotiations.

- **Improving provision of agricultural services, including research and extension.** The technological lag in African agriculture is primarily a symptom of under-investment and lack of adoption, not low rates of return on research. In the future, African institutions of research and extension will need higher levels of support, stronger outreach to beneficiaries, and closer linkages with institutions working on the frontiers of scientific discovery.

- **Increasing investment in infrastructure and the quality of services in rural areas.** Access to infrastructure, education and health services declined during the 1990s, and indicators of well-being (life expectancy, infant and child mortality, literacy rates) worsened in most countries. Models of delivery of rural services are in a period of transition, away from centrally controlled provision by the public sector, and toward more decentralized, demand-driven, private sector approaches.

- **Expanding access to rural financial services.** A sustained process of income generation requires improved access to rural financial services, including credit, savings, insurance, collateralization of fixed and moveable property, transfer of funds, trade finance, and more complex financial instruments and transactions. A major focus of the rural financial strategy is to bring the commercial institutions closer to rural clients, and to make the clients more attractive to providers of service.

- **Improving water control systems.** Over 95% of cultivated land is rainfed. Many of these lands are in arid or semiarid areas where rainfall is unreliable and crop failures are common. Yet, providing water at critical stages of plant development (such as during the flowering stage of maize) can

101

dramatically reduce risks of crop shortfalls. Increasing yields on rainfed lands by just 10% would have far greater impact on total agricultural output than doubling area under irrigation. Moreover, such improvements would benefit mainly poor farmers living on marginal lands. Expanding irrigated agriculture also offers considerable potential in Africa.

Enhancing Management of Natural Resources

Africa is very diverse—ecologically, socially and politically—and countries are using a variety of approaches to improve management of natural resources. Important among these are efforts to:

- Avoid harm, through prior screening and use of environmental assessments;
- Mitigate adverse impacts through use of environmental assessments, environmental management plans and other measures;
- Empower communities and individuals to make a sustainable living using local natural resources and to take responsibility for managing them;
- Mainstream environmental issues into broader development programs through instruments such as national environmental action plans, environmental support programs and others;
- Address past damage and assist communities improve their management of natural resources through focused investments;
- Improve incentives for long-term environmental stewardship rather than short-term exploitation, such as through introducing charges for natural resources use; and
- Establish regulations and laws to protect the environment and build capacity to enforce them.

Reducing Risk and Vulnerability of the Rural Poor

Poor rural Africans face multiple risks everyday, and have few instruments for mitigation other than the traditional ones based on family relationships and livelihood strategies. The onslaught of HIV/AIDS has exacerbated preexisting risks and disrupted traditional coping mechanisms. Risks can be reduced through such measures as prudent macroeconomic management, basic public health programs, including widespread immunization, cost-effective nutrition

interventions, educational policies that guarantee poor children access, and actions to stop conflict and enhance security. Investment in infrastructure and measures to help farmers gain access to hardy crop varieties can assist rural people to reduce the variability of income. Improving access to rural financial services (savings accounts and credit) is also important. Other strategic approaches to manage risk include efforts to:

- **Find alternatives to the most harmful coping mechanisms.** Direct interventions to enable the poorest families keep their children well nourished and in school. Help poor families build the assets they need. Programs must be designed to ensure that they are well targeted and fiscally sustainable.
- **Give high priority to stopping the spread of HIV/AIDS and malaria and helping communities cope with its impacts.** Poor households facing HIV/AIDS are less able to cope with loss of labor and are more likely to dispose of assets to meet medical and funeral expenses than are more prosperous families. Governments and development partners should target assistance to the poorest households, especially in the period immediately following death, when families are struggling to reorganize their production systems.
- **Share risks and costs of adopting new technologies by offering matching grants to producers' organizations and other groups.** Early adopters demonstrate to others the benefits of new technologies, but they also bear high risks. The public sector can share risks through matching grants to encourage recipients to adopt new technologies, and initiate their wider acceptance by others.

Instruments and Actions

The program is varied and covers 48 countries. The pipeline for the next three years consists of about 80 new lending operations per year. As the program evolves, the Africa region's lending operations increasingly fall into three broad categories: budget support, community driven development and capacity building. Among the products in the work program, the following are most relevant to rural development:

- **Analytical and advisory services.** The Africa Region is increasing its commitment to analytical and advisory services, and a portion of the increase will focus on rural poverty.
- **Multi-sectoral poverty reduction support credits (PRSCs).** These are instruments to provide budgetary support to countries implementing well defined strategies to reduce poverty, as expressed in PRSP's.
- **Projects supporting decentralization.** These assist in developing the fiscal architecture for decentralization, provide technical assistance to build capacity of public entities facing new challenges, help put into place processes for participation and mechanisms to enhance accountability, and support design of systems of monitoring and evaluation.
- **Community driven development projects.** These are closely linked to decentralization, and focus on community participation in setting of priorities, creation of financial architecture to get resources to community groups, strengthening of local government, transfer of resources to the community level, and monitoring and evaluation.
- **Rural finance.** The newer generation of rural finance projects eschews lines of directed credit, and focuses on regulatory reform, capacity building, and reducing the transactions costs of linking providers and customers of financial services in rural areas.
- **HIV/AIDS.** Because of the catastrophic implications of HIV/AIDS for African development, prevention and mitigation of HIV/AIDS has been mainstreamed into most of the projects in the portfolio, either in the design stage or through retrofitting of components.
- **Agricultural research and extension.** Projects supporting agricultural services are increasingly responsive to the needs and requests of producers, and incorporate innovative features in finance, such as competitive grants, cost recovery, and matching grants.
- **Management of Natural Resources.** Africa's natural resources are valued at many levels, from the very local to the global.
- **Environment.** The Bank assists clients to mainstream environmental concerns into decisions on policy and investment, through advice on policy and regulatory issues, technical assistance to help ministries and departments of environment increase their capacity, investment projects, and grants for global environmental priorities. All projects are evaluated to ensure that relevant safeguards are met.
- **Basic education and health care services.** The Bank in the Africa region supports access to basic health care and primary education without user fees, in recognition that these contribute substantially to the public welfare and to poverty reduction.
- **Water management and irrigation.** Water management projects focus on simple designs that can be implemented and managed by communities as part of CDD operations. Given the increasing importance of water in the region, more will be done to help countries and communities manage shared water resources.
- **Infrastructure.** Infrastructure investments are needed in roads, electric power, and telecommunications. Cellular technology and new designs in off-grid power generation and non-traditional sources of energy, when coupled with basic regulatory reform, offer exciting new opportunities to reduce the shortage of rural infrastructure.
- **Land reform.** Land reform is an important issue in the region, and one underrepresented in our portfolio of assistance. Support for land reform addresses issues of the distribution of ownership, tenure security, and resolution of conflicting claims.

The Africa Region is taking a number of steps more sharply to focus its programs on poverty, which implies a shift toward rural priorities. Poverty reduction strategies designed by the countries are intended increasingly to be the foundation for country assistance strategies of the Bank. The process is still young, and not yet equally embraced throughout the region, but familiarity is growing and the quality of the strategies improving. The Region is using its commitment to increase economic and sector work to assure that the PRSP's of the future can draw on solid analytical foundations in the spatial dimensions and correlates of poverty and the implications for public expenditure.

The Africa Region is streamlining the portfolio in order to reduce the fragmentation of administrative budgets among many activities, a number of which may not ultimately lead to lending or other interventions with substantial impact. As the number of operations declines, the cost of supervision will also fall, allowing a shift toward more generous funding for supervision of remaining activities and an increase in resources for preparation.

The Africa Region has drawn on its experience in addressing the HIV/AIDS crisis, and is applying the lessons to other areas. In the early period, HIV/AIDS was perceived to be largely an issue for those in the health sector. As long as the approach was uni-sectoral, little progress was made. Health specialists did not have the expertise to address all of the dimensions of the HIV/AIDS crisis, and projects to address the pandemic competed with others in the Human Development portfolio for space in country lending programs. The region did not develop an effective approach to the crisis until Country Directors recognized HIV/AIDS as an overarching multi-sectoral problem of such high priority that it was incumbent upon them to seriously address it. Simultaneously, the region developed a new truly multi-sectoral instrument (the MAP) designed and implemented by experienced task team leaders from various sectoral units. MAP operations need not be designed from scratch for each country, since the basic elements can be adapted for country conditions. The MAP operations are multi-sectoral, quickly designed and approved, flexible to adapt as lessons are learned during implementation, and, correspondingly, intensive in supervision costs.

Elements of the MAP experience are relevant to rural development. The Country Directors must take the lead in seeking interventions and in holding themselves accountable for measured progress. In some fields, such as agricultural services and the CDD operations, basic elements of programs can be treated as modular units taken "off-the-shelf" and customized to suit country conditions. Our traditional models of project design have much in common with medieval artisanship—hand-crafted each time. Where circum-stances do not require such an approach, our resources can be more effectively used by incorporating existing designs, and allocating more attention to learning and revision while projects are under implementation.

In order to facilitate the work of multi-sectoral teams, the Region is orienting its training activities toward teams, rather than individuals. This is part of a Bank-wide move, but it is especially relevant in the Africa region due to the evolution of the lending portfolio.

The Africa region is decentralizing functions to the country offices, along with a limited number of additional staff formerly based in Washington. With decentralization of functions comes a substantial additional need for training and new definition of working relationships between staff based in Washington and in country offices.

Within the Africa Region's Rural Development and Environment Unit, a process of reconfiguration and renewal was launched in 2001. The process is intended to improve management of the units in order to better pursue multi-sectoral tasks, to integrate rural and environmental issues more fully in the PRSP processes, to facilitate more seamless interaction between the various units and staff in Washington and in the country offices, and to move forward with the regional commitment to decentralize functions.

The rural and environmental units work in partnership with other sectoral units within the Bank, with counterparts in government and civil society in client countries, and with other donors. The Bank contributes to the already established Multi-Donor Hub for Rural Development under Southern Africa Development Community located in Harare, Zimbabwe, and is working with other donors to establish a hub for food security in the Horn of Africa.

With strong partnerships, a streamlined portfolio, renewal within the rural, environment, and social family, and further decentralization, the Africa Region is well placed to make a significant contri-

Central and Western Africa: Dakar, Senegal 7–9 May 2001

The workshop was organized in collaboration with CODESRIA (The Council for the Development of Social Science Research in Africa). Participants included representatives of NGOs and civil society, the private sector, academia, consultants, parastatal agencies, governmental ministries, and international organisations and came from Cameroon, Nigeria, Gambia, Niger, Mali, Ivory Coast, Sierra Leone, Benin, Burkina Faso, Ghana, Guinea, Senegal. Participants noted that the plurality and diversity of Africa imply that no single strategy will be appropriate except at a very high level of generality. Participants underscored the importance of agriculture in Africa's rural development and the need to improve agricultural productivity, through improved technology, improved access to markets at all levels, including those of the OECD countries, and macroeconomic policies that do not overly tax agriculture. Issues related to water management need urgent and greater attention in programs to address rural poverty. Other important issues include:

- Conflict destroys present and future opportunities, and no rural strategy can show accomplishments until peace is secure.

- Gender equity is integral to agricultural improvement, since women are major economic agents in Africa's agricultural production and trade.

- Land issues and land reform merit increased emphasis.

- Rural-urban linkages and the role of small towns should be better understood.

- Workable mechanisms to mitigate economic risks should be explored, despite the well-known problems, since unmanaged risks can generate high social costs.

- More attention should be accorded to environmental issues.

- Rural constituencies need more accountable governments. The concept of public service is not well developed, and decentralization does not always bring improved public service.

- Rural development should be fully addressed in PRSPs (poverty reduction strategy papers) of individual countries.

Eastern and Southern Africa: Nairobi, Kenya 26–28 March 2001

The workshop was organized in partnership with the African Economic Research Council. Participants were invited from the public, private, and NGO sectors of Botswana, Burundi, Ethiopia, France, Guinea, Kenya, Madagascar, Malawi, Senegal, South Africa, Tanzania, Rwanda, Uganda, Zambia, Zimbabwe, and several international organizations.

Participants noted the importance of community-centered development, and argued in favor of emphasis on change at the community level accompanied by fiscal decentralization. Because African civil and political institutions are in many places weak, explicit measures are needed to constrain corruption. The role of the private sector should be explicitly recognized, and their input into formulation of specific strategies sought.

The supra-national organizations in Africa should devote more attention to rural development. Infrastructure is both a public and private mandate, and better methodologies are needed to guide decisions about investment in infrastructure. Environmental issues should be addressed in a context of sustainable utilization of natural resources.

The key issue of trade liberalization should be addressed; i.e., can African smallholders compete in a world of massive subsidies to producers in high-income countries and high marketing margins in their own? African producers could increase use the internet and other information technologies to overcome high costs of communication and the legacy of poor integration into trading networks. Conflicts and HIV/AIDS pose enormous challenges that will require external assistance as well as strong national and local leadership.

bution to reduction of poverty. Actual results, however, will require continued and strong leadership by the regional leadership team and a specific focus on rural poverty. Without this overarching focus, the current and projected lending program could fall short in efforts to reduce rural poverty. The existing lending program is one with high potential, but also considerable risk unless the regional leadership gives explicit priority to rural poverty in the design of the various sectoral operations.

Conclusions

Africa's rural people can contribute much more to their own prosperity and to global growth in the future than they have been able to in the past. The dynamics of rural growth and the factors that promote it are now better understood than before. Rural institutions are stronger in many places and democratic forms of government create opportunities for rural people to express their views and priorities. National governments have tamed fiscal deficits and opened economies in ways that improve incentives in rural areas. Increasingly, people at all levels understand how to manage natural resources so that they provide long-term benefits. New investments and developments in infrastructure link once remote areas more closely to their regional and national contexts.

Africans are acting on these opportunities despite formidable new obstacles. HIV/AIDS requires changes in behavior and investment of resources on a scale demanded of few societies or treasuries in more prosperous regions. The scourge of conflict creates new victims and destroys wealth. Natural resources are still subject to predation and degradation. Climate change is likely to hit Africa hard. And many OECD countries, despite rhetorical commitment to liberalization of trade, keep their own markets closed to Africa's most important exports. The commitment of Africans to reduce rural poverty despite these obstacles warrants dynamic and effective support from their partners. The Africa Region of the World Bank is committed to move on the actions noted above, and continually to seek new ways to assist.

EAST ASIA AND PACIFIC

Regional Context and Key Issues

Rural East Asia has undergone an unprecedented technological and economic transformation in recent decades that has dramatically improved food security, reduced poverty, and raised incomes. Despite the 1997 Asian crisis, the EAP region as a whole experienced the fastest rate of economic growth in the world over the past 25 years (Figure A3.1). This transformation was partly initiated by the application of Green Revolution methods to Asia's agricultural problems.

But serious problems remain. Despite substantial rural-to-urban migration, East Asia's rural population continues to grow, and the vast majority of people still depend on agriculture, forestry, or fishing for their livelihood. These activities place great stress on natural resources and result in degradation that diminishes the income-generating capacity of those resources. Agricultural growth in the nine major countries of East Asia lagged well behind growth in GDP during the 1990s. Nonetheless, the agricultural sector still employs about 70% of the working populations of these countries, and 80% of the region's poor dwell in the countryside and the mountains. Meanwhile, overall economic growth has not led to improved services, such as health, education, and infrastructure in rural areas, nor to a significant increase in non-agricultural rural jobs. More rapid economic growth in urban areas has resulted in most of the poor, and virtually all of the "poorest of the poor," being found in rural areas. The irony is that while rural East Asia provides the dominant share of employment and income, it is also the area with the most unemployment, underemployment, and poverty.

The rural-to-urban transition in East Asia is incomplete. The number of excess workers remaining in rural areas is in the millions in almost all the countries of East Asia. Rural areas need the benefit of policies, institutions, and infrastructure which encourage economic development and provide non-farm employment while urban areas must not be overwhelmed by rural migrants seeking job opportunities.

There have been some improvements in rural areas in terms of access to education, health care, transportation, and other public services. But it is also estimated, for instance, that as many as a billion East Asians in rural areas remain without access to safe water and sanitation. Imbalances like these in the provision of public services that favor urban areas are often accompanied by policy biases against agriculture, such as price controls on farm products and high tariffs on imported agricultural inputs.

The bias against the rural sector can also be found in national investment figures. Between 1994 and 1998, for example, public investment in the sector never exceeded 10% of all public investment in any of the nine major East Asian countries. In some, it is true, the percentage remained stable, but in others it drifted downward except in Indonesia. There, agricultural investment rose from a mere 3.1% of all national investment in 1995 to 5.9% in 1997-98. The increase occurred in a context of political instability in parts of rural Indonesia.

Yet despite the policy biases, low public investment, declining worldwide prices for agricultural products, and natural disasters such as floods and drought, cereal production in East Asia (mainly rice) has almost doubled since 1970.

Poverty in rural East Asia is also exacerbated by traditional hierarchical forms of government that have until recently largely resisted democratic reforms while failing to provide the kind of governance that is necessary to assure social harmony. In terms of commerce and trade, what is frequently absent are such things as transparent legal and judicial systems that guarantee both property rights and the fairness and sanctity of contracts for both rich and poor. Good governance also means the absence of corruption among those in authority, whether elected representatives or government bureaucrats. Corruption has been endemic in East Asia, but public outrage against it has swept through several countries since the financial crisis of 1997-98. It is often the rural poor who have been victimized most by corruption. Many steps—legal, judicial, institution—need to be taken in East Asia to assure honest government at every level.

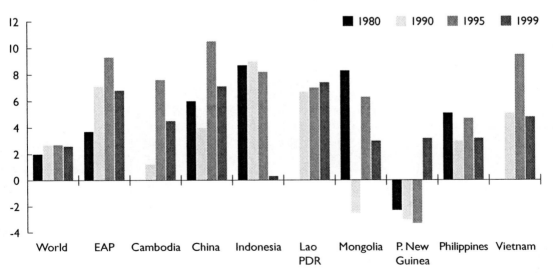

Figure A3.1: Annual GDP Growth (%) 1980-1999

■ 1980 ▨ 1990 ▤ 1995 ▩ 1999

Source: *Rural Development Indicators Handbook 2001*

Lessons Learned

Since the *From Vision to Action* report we have learned several important lessons that enhance the effectiveness of our interventions in client countries. Some lessons are to:

- Work at the community level for many projects rather than work at the central government level, thus giving rise to more projects modeled on community-driven development;
- Make more effort to consult with all interested stakeholders, including ministries beyond the sectoral ministry, during all stages of project preparation and implementation;
- Incorporate natural resource management issues into projects where feasible, and to pay strict attention to fulfilling the requirements of safeguard policies;
- Strengthen local implementation capacity and put good governance structures in place (especially important since the onset of the Asian Crisis in 1997);
- Convince our partners on the importance of viewing rural issues holistically, and using a holistic approach when selecting and designing projects;
- Have a rural strategy and sufficient economic policy analysis undertaken in order to maintain a coherent country dialog and lending program; and
- Place more emphasis on off-farm employment creation.

We have also learned that when the Bank places a special emphasis on a topic, our clients in country respond by making it a topic of special interest. Thus, the first vision to action paper and the compact resources that accompanied it spawned an increased level of interest and activity in rural development. This was especially true in Vietnam where the rural sector became the central focus of development.

Strategic Objectives

EASRD has developed four strategic objectives for its work that are relevant to a rural renaissance in East Asia. They are:

- Reducing rural poverty;
- Stimulating rural economic growth;

- Providing food security; and
- Supporting natural resource management.

Each is emphasized to a different degree in each country according to its particular circumstances. What follows are discussions of our four strategic objectives and the chief actions needed to achieve them:

Reducing Rural Poverty

In order to reduce rural poverty, EASRD is taking two approaches. One is the financing of projects that directly attack poverty through targeted, productivity-enhancing investments in very poor rural areas such as community development projects. The other is the financing of projects that enhance agricultural productivity and create non-farm rural employment—water management schemes, storage and processing facilities for agribusiness, research facilities.

Stimulating Rural Economic Growth

To stimulate rural economic growth, EASRD will continue to encourage governments to engage in projects and to carry out reforms that will create improved conditions for private companies that may be willing to locate in rural areas, especially those where poverty is widespread. In the broadest sense, we are encouraging East Asian governments to redress any anti-rural bias that may exist in ministries whose work affects both rural and urban areas. This means establishing or improving rural schools, healthcare facilities, electric power lines, telephone services, roads, and other facilities that are normally the government's responsibility.

Rural areas also need a local governance framework that establishes rules for the operation of economic enterprises—land-titling and registration, honest systems of weights and measures, laws for the resolution of commercial disputes, and standard regulations for permits and licenses. Instead of establishing such frameworks, many governments in East Asia continue to carry out commercial activities themselves through state-owned enterprises that provide fertilizer, seeds, agrochemicals, and other farm supplies, as well as financial services, including credit. Experience has shown that in most cases these goods and services can be delivered more effectively and efficiently by private firms.

Providing Food Security

Because of their experience with crop failures and hunger over the years, many East Asian countries have put in place policies designed to support domestic production and insulate it from the vagaries of the open market. Many have been reluctant to embrace the concept of free trade and have instead opted for subsidies for domestic food consumers. EASRD has placed increasing emphasis on exploring alternative and more efficient ways of providing food security to vulnerable populations. One example is the work done in Indonesia during the Asian crisis (which also coincided with a crop-reducing El-Nino event). On very short notice EASRD assisted the Indonesian government build a targeted food security program for Indonesia's urban poor. Establishing similar targeted social safety net programs in other East Asian nations as an affordable means of providing family food security is a goal.

Supporting Natural Resource Management

In many East Asian countries, the demand for food, fish, lumber, and other items obtained from natural resources continue to overshadow the desire to conserve and protect natural resources. Nonetheless, the Unit will continue to try to convince all our clients that intelligent management of land, forests, rivers, and oceans is essential to achieving sustainable economic growth, and we have begun placing much more emphasis on devising policies and programs to protect these resources. All countries in the region have natural resource management issues to address, and these issues are mainstreamed into Bank projects and the policy dialogue whether or not there are specific natural resource management or conservation projects in a particular country.

Some of the natural resource problems in East Asia are quite well-known: the continuing clear-cutting of forests in certain countries; the destruction of coral reefs in the South Pacific; overexploitation of coastal and inland fisheries in many countries; and the disappearance of coastal zones and mangrove areas. Other environmental problems, such as conflict over water resources between urban, industrial, and agricultural users are in the offing and must also be addressed.

In addition to funding traditional projects for land reclamation and flood control, EASRD has begun to promote conservation management of forests and biodiversity conservation projects in several of our client countries. We have also begun to make sustainability of natural resources a condition for approval of adjustment loans. We are adopting community-based approaches to natural resource management and we are processing a number of grants for projects to be carried out by such NGO partners of ours as the World Wildlife Fund, The Nature Conservancy, and the World Conservation Union.

Implementation Plans

EASRD is developing an active and ambitious action plan as a follow up to the consultation meetings on the East Asia Rural Development Strategy. The consultation meetings with governments, bilateral and multilateral donors, NGO's, and private sector representatives held in March 2001 were very successful and elicited considerable commitment to move forward with specific actions designed to advance rural development (Box A3.2, end of section). The action plan designed by EASRD builds on that momentum. In addition to a pipeline of projects founded on the individual country strategies, a series of specific activities and actions are planned for each country. Several clients have indicated that they wish to participate as "focus" countries in the region. EASRD plans a broader set of activities and actions for these countries and we will be seeking supplemental resources beyond regional Bank budget to support this effort.

In designing implementation plans for our country work, EASRD is making added efforts to ensure that the process is participatory, involving not only government counterparts but also NGOs, local government, communities, and other stakeholders, and is also placing added effort into engaging the private sector as a full partner. Since the lending program and pipeline is a matter of record and the general emphasis of that program has been outlined earlier in this summary, the implementation plans described here are those for the focus countries and for the region as a whole. The underlying concept is to work intensively with those countries wanting to move forward aggressively with additional activities in rural development and use them to inspire other countries in the region. The implementation begins with a country rural consultation patterned after the Consultative Group process where donors and government officials meet to decide on: a specific and time-bound action plan; which agencies will do what aspects; and who will fund which activities. It is to be followed perhaps six months later with a regional meeting (smaller than the original consultation meeting) to monitor and discuss progress, and showcase the work to other non-focus countries in the region.

Individual Country Action Plans

Strategic Objective/Country Action Plan	Cambodia	China	Indonesia	Lao PDR	Mongolia	Papua New Guinea	Philippines	Thailand	Vietnam
Reduce number of rural poor	●	●	●	●	●	○	○	○	●
Stimulating Rural Economic Growth	○	●	●	●	●	●	●	●	○
Providing Food Security	●	●	○	○	●	○	●	○	●
Supporting Natural Resource Management	○	●	●	●	●	●	●	●	●

CHINA

- Agricultural and water development projects will be targeted at the poor interior provinces in the Western region and designed to meet the needs of the poor in those areas.
- Remove any remaining barriers to rural migration; consolidate market information systems under a single agency; and invest more in rural infrastructure. Re-centralize taxation authority and establish reallocation mechanism that ensure resources are transferred to poor areas.
- Support continued commercialization and productivity increases through greater emphasis on research and extension, off-farm employment creation through villages and township enterprises and further liberalization of trade and marketing.
- In response to severe flooding and the subsequent decision to ban logging in the upper watershed of the Yangtze River, the Bank will support the government's new comprehensive framework for sustainable management of forest resources, soil conservation and biodiversity protection.

INDONESIA

- Delivering better public services for the poor through local government and community organizations.
- Encourage local revenue decisions that limit deterioration of the business environment. Establish a strategy that focuses on developing a market-based financial system and decreases reliance on subsidized credit programs.
- Implement pro-poor rice price policy. Maintain open rice trade, with moderate tariff protection and no domestic restriction. Shift from floor price to procurement price. Establish interdepartmental policy team. Prepare strategy for future rice policy.
- Implement CGI forestry commitments. Strengthen marine resource management and public participation in forest and protected area management. Establish policy framework for river basin management and irrigation management.

MONGOLIA

- ESW to deepen understanding poverty and livelihood dynamics, including urban-rural linkages and bring rural people's perspective to bear on national policy. Evaluation of lessons from experience under earlier National Poverty Alleviation Program through intensive learning ICR.
- Encourage fiscal decentralization whereby investments in community-level infrastructure are made with local participation. A coordinated and sustainable strategy for pastoral risk management established and functioning well throughout the country.
- Amendments to land policy legislation to strengthen implementation and facilitate transferability of land rights.

PAPUA NEW GUINEA

- Sustain support for NARI and better-funded role for provinces in supporting agricultural development.
- Continue dialogue for better credit delivery.
- Improve rural infrastructure by coordinating with other donors such as ADB and AusAID.
- Improve governance at ward, district and provincial levels. Dialogue on providing an enabling environment.
- Improve and expand community participation in forest management; strengthen regulatory apparatus and prevention of illegal logging.
- Engage communities and NGOs to clarify possibilities in fisheries and work toward a new national fisheries policy.

PHILIPPINES

- Promote community-driven agricultural and natural resources programs targeted to poor/marginalized provinces. Enhance smallholder productivity and diversification.
- Promote priority structural/policy reforms in rural development and natural resources.
- Expand access of rural people to productive assets.
- Strengthen institutional arrangements, coordination and capacities for planning and implementation with emphasis on devolution and community participation.

VIETNAM

- Intensify agricultural production by developing and transferring new technology. Continue to secure access to and develop market in, land-use rights.
- Diversify into higher value products and new markets.
- Promote off-farm employment. Reform rural SMEs, extend Enterprise Law to rural areas to promote rural SMEs.
- Target remote and upland areas by building rural infrastructure.
- Prevent and mitigate natural disasters by building on Central Provinces Initiative.

Three countries have indicated that they wish to be focus countries—Papua New Guinea (PNG), Philippines, and Vietnam. What follows is a brief description of additive activities that represent the rural action plan.

Papua New Guinea. The Bank has a history of unsatisfactory projects and programs in PNG. Since PNG is predominantly rural, most of the projects have been in rural space. Recently a broad rural-development strategy has been completed by AusAID and the Bank. This work sought to diagnose the sources of project failure in PNG and design an approach that might result in improved outcomes for the rural people of PNG. The document forms the basis for a new relationship in the rural sector with the government of PNG (GOPNG) and gives details on the action plan. The plan is to commence discussions with GOPNG and donors on the strategy at the CG meeting in late June. This will be followed with participatory consultations on rural

development and pre-identification of activities with local groups and stakeholders in PNG. It will result in an agreement on an institutional framework for taking the rural strategy forward and the modalities to implement the action plan. The next step will be to identify the operational instruments for donor support and the main components of a Bank operation. This will involve consultation with GOPNG, but more importantly, discussions with local and village leaders who will be responsible for implementing the plan. Finally, a monitoring and reporting system will be put in place that will allow cross-comparison of performance from village to village (or locality to locality) and cross-fertilization of successful approaches and ideas.

Philippines and Vietnam. The additional activities designed to respond to the rural action plan in the Philippines and Vietnam are oriented toward strengthening the ability of the relevant agencies to monitor and track rural development, which in turn

Box A3.2: Summary of Regional Consultations: East Asia

Two large consultation meetings with government, academic, NGO, international organizations (AusAID, ADB, DFID and FAO) and business stakeholders of the countries of East Asia and the Pacific were held in March 2001, in Beijing, China, and Cebu, Philippines. The objective was to gather feedback from the regional stakeholders on the Bank's draft corporate and regional rural action plans. The consultation also sought reactions on the strengths and weaknesses of the Bank's support programs and on how the Bank might improve the effectiveness of its services.

Main Comments from the consultation:

■ More focus on the rural poverty issue;

■ Strengthen policies that deal with rural poverty;

■ Improve access to social and economic infrastructure;

■ Facilitate agricultural growth and competitiveness;

■ Enhance the development of non-rural and private sector activities;

■ Improve natural resources and environmental management;

■ Pay more attention to gender and human resource development; and

■ Pay more attention to governance and institutions.

track changes in the rural development indicators over time and use the data to improve decision making both in terms of project design and location, and public policy. The third step, now being developed in the Philippines and to be introduced later in Vietnam, is a performance monitoring system for the public institutions serving rural space and relating performance of the institutions to performance of key employees in those institutions. The objective of this step is to develop structured accountability mechanisms in government agencies and to push this accountability down to senior staff in those agencies who would have performance-based employment agreements. The concept is simply to use these agencies as examples to the rest of government of modern public sector management approaches now in use in several industrial countries. This approach has been enthusiastically embraced by the Ministry of Agriculture in the Philippines and EASRD is working closely with them to develop and implement such a system. For some agencies, such as agriculture, data to implement this system is already available and performance indicators have been selected. For other agencies responsible for other aspects of service delivery in the rural sector, appropriate indicators will be developed as the third step in this process.

As part of our action agenda EASRD is also planning to identify and appraise a completely new rural project from our action plan and deliver it to the Board within a one-year period. This would be a pilot to test the feasibility of speeding up the rural lending program in the Region. It is probable that China would be our first pilot country and that the project would be one capable of being scaled-up. If successful, this would open the possibility of a large-scale expansion of our lending in China (and other countries where the model is applicable) in subsequent years.

Initial discussions have been held with the Asian Development Bank, AusAID, and JBIC regarding their interest and participation in a "Rural CG" meeting, seen as the focal point for coordination and monitoring of specific rural development activities. There is also a willingness among donors and agriculture agencies to design and allocate rural development activities in a CDF-type framework so

will allow greater precision in targeting interventions and improved policymaking ability. The first step is to strengthen the data-gathering and — analysis ability of the agencies responsible for rural data. Assistance will be provided to the rural statistics agency to set up a dedicated server on which a comprehensive rural database will be mounted. The database will use existing data on agriculture but will enrich it with broader socio-economic data from rural space and rural households. Specific "rural development indicators" will be identified. The data will be updated periodically and will be available on-line to other agencies and the public. Seed financing to commence this step has already been obtained. The second step is to monitor and

that problems of overlap, duplication, and competition, characteristic of previous interactions, can be minimized. Part of the function of successive "rural CG" meetings would be to formally monitor and evaluate progress based on agreed performance indicators and targets. The results of this exercise would be used to improve project and program design and drive performance. The outcome of the entire "rural CG" process would be shared with other clients in a joint consultation in order to demonstrate to them a successful approach to rural development.

EUROPE AND CENTRAL ASIA

Roughly 50% of the poor in ECA live in rural areas. This is a considerably lower share than in the rest of the world. ECA also has the lowest poverty rates of any of the Bank's Regions. However, poverty and inequality have increased faster in this Region than anywhere else over the past decade, and these average rates mask considerable differences across countries and within countries between rural and urban areas. In more than half of ECA countries, there are more poor in rural areas than in urban areas. Thus, making a dent on poverty in the Region will require continued work in rural areas.

Broadly, the share of ECA's lending program aimed at improving rural livelihoods has probably been commensurate with the share of poverty in rural areas (unlike in many Regions of the Bank), but this proportion needs to be sustained over time. In contrast, rural ESW is generally inadequate. PRSPs do not adequately reflect the rural dimensions of issues, and this will negatively affect our ability to ensure rural issues are appropriately integrated into Country Assistance Strategies.

We have a number of models that work well and which can be scaled up to national level programs or replicated in other countries. These include, among others, farm privatization and restructuring; micro-credit; development of community-based irrigation, institutions, forestry and watershed management; forest policy reform; land administration (registration and cadastre); and dam safety and flood protection. We are doing some innovative

work on food quality and safety and on off-farm rural infrastructure. We are still struggling with developing models for jump-starting the private sector (off-farm employment creation, agro-business and marketing) but these remain priorities of our clients and we are committed to helping them find solutions.

We will continue to do investment lending to support our program. We have found that our emphasis on community-based approaches and creating institutional capacity works best when supported by LILs, SILs and APLs. We have also found that we can support a number of policy reforms with these operations and that we gain more commitment from stakeholders when reforms are accompanied by investment. We will use SECALs sparingly, and only when there is a broad reform agenda and true ownership by the Borrower. We will try to integrate broad policy issues into PALs and SALs/SACs where leverage is greater.

Regional Context

Economy

The Eastern Europe and Central Asia Region has 415 million people (7% of the world's total) of whom 35% live in rural areas (compared with 54% worldwide). It has 20% of the world's arable land and 24% of its forests. The region is characterized by its diversity, with its countries differing widely in climate, natural resource base, income and progress with economic and social reforms. Incomes vary from nearly $10,000 (Slovenia), with 10 countries preparing to join the European Union, to $380 (Tajikistan and Moldova). The economies in the north and west are heavily industrialized, with agriculture contributing 10% or less to GDP, even though rural populations are 25-40% of total. Those further south and east are more rural, with agriculture contributing 30% or more of GDP in most Central Asian countries, but also in Albania and Armenia, and most people living in rural areas.

All countries have struggled with the transition to a market economy, and in all there were sharp drops in GDP after 1990. In all transition countries, the rural service economy was poorly developed; production and processing were closely integrated, and

113

there was a focus on increasing output rather than on responding to consumer preferences. While in Central Europe GDP levels are now well above those of 1990, in many CIS countries they remain below their pre-transition levels (e.g., in Moldova and Armenia they are less than one-third the levels of the late 1980s) despite reasonable progress with economic reform.

Social Issues

While the Region is highly diverse, there are some common features. All countries of the region except Turkey have experienced profound social changes over the last 10 years, following the break-up of the Soviet Union and the move to a market economy. There has been civil unrest and war in several countries (Croatia, Bosnia, Yugoslavia, Tajikistan, Azerbaijan, the North Caucasus). There has been a deterioration in law and order with widespread consequences, including protection rackets bribery and extortion. Although absolute poverty is lower in ECA than in other regions, poverty and inequality have increased faster than elsewhere, even in the most successful economies. On average, only 50% of the poor live in rural areas, but rural poverty incidence is higher than urban in almost every country, and there are more rural poor than urban poor in most countries.

Although poverty has increased, rural populations have gained greater power and influence over decisions that affect their lives through improved access to land, and freedom in how to use it, and by development of democratic local institutions.

ECA can be distinguished from other regions in a number of other ways as well. Except in Central Asia, population growth is stagnant or negative, literacy is almost universal and basic infrastructure is reasonable though deteriorating. Health indicators are quite good, although there have been sharp declines in male life expectancy especially in Russian and Ukraine, and infectious diseases such as tuberculosis are re-emerging as health systems have deteriorated.

Policy Issues

Prices and trade in most countries have been liberalized, industries have been privatized and land pri-

vatization is well advanced. It has been much more difficult to build up the institutions, governance framework and investment environment for businesses, banking systems and land, labor and capital markets to thrive. The "right" balance between public and private sector responsibilities is still emerging in most countries, and civil servants have seen large declines in real salaries.

The Central European countries, geographically and historically closer to Europe, have found it easier to reach consensus for economic reform than the countries further east, which are also further from western markets. For these Central European countries, policy is now dominated by issues related to EU accession. For the CIS, the key issue remains property rights, especially in land and the ability to engage in land transactions. In the Caucasus and especially in Central Asia water resource policy is a key focus.

Agriculture and Rural Economy

While the north and west has in general ample rainfall and plentiful forest resources, soils are only of moderate quality and growing seasons are short. Livestock contributes 30-40% of GDP and forests and forest industries are a major employer. The Central belt, stretching from Hungary through parts of Romania, Moldova, Ukraine, Southern Russia and Northern Kazakhstan, has some of the most fertile soils in the world. Together with the Southern Cone of Latin America, this area has the potential, if land is sustainably managed, to significantly increase production of basic food crops and to help meet the increase in world food demand projected over the next 25 years.

Agriculture has become an important social safety net as industry has contracted and people have returned to the land to survive. The share of agriculture in GDP has increased in many countries. Land has been privatized over most of the region, in some cases in small, fragmented plots, and administrative complexities with land titling have made it difficult for land to be used as collateral, and for transparent land markets to develop. A special feature of Russia, Belarus and Ukraine is garden plots (of 1 ha or less) cultivated by both rural and urban populations for subsistence, but also for small-scale commercial production. These produce the great majority of fruits, vegetables, potatoes and milk in these countries; they are dependent for cheap inputs on the large-scale former collective farms, which have mostly been privatized but still face soft budget constraints.

Lessons Learned in the ECA Rural Assistance Program

Our approach to helping our client countries with the transition has evolved. Regarding policy reform, the focus in the early 1990s was on liberalization and privatization of assets, on deregulation and reducing the role of government in the economy, with the main emphasis on growth and less direct intervention for poverty reduction. We argued that we should support investments only when policy reforms were well advanced. Since then, we have learned the following lessons:

- Fundamental reform takes time, sequencing is crucial, and privatization without a supporting institutional and regulatory framework does not necessarily lead to development of a market economy and prosperity. During regional consultations our stakeholders emphasized that our reform agenda has often been too ambitious in terms of pace. We have also learned that commitment to reform by technocrats and academics is insufficient; and that without support from elected representatives and civil society reforms are frequently not sustainable.
- Delaying investments until policies are right can hinder our ability to help large numbers of poor and can sometimes significantly increase the eventual costs of investments (e.g., for deterioration of irrigation and drainage infrastructure). Support for modest investments, combined with modest policy and institutional reform, is often a successful approach.
- Simple project design usually works best (and again our regional stakeholders made this point). Successful projects should be geographically focused if they support a complex agenda (e.g. community based watershed rehabilitation, rural infrastructure, land reform and farm restructuring with redesign of field irrigation systems) or should support only one area for intervention if they are nationally focused (e.g., community-based micro-credit). Complex, national-level projects have worked less well and this conclusion is supported by QAG and OED assessments of our projects.

- We have learned that the weakest dimension of our projects in the past has been development of institutional capacity and sustainability of project activities after withdrawal of Bank financing. We have learned that improvements in these areas can come through close work with local institutions and by supporting bottom up approaches such as community-driven project identification and implementation. We have also learned that institutional capacity building and community driven activities work best when supported by LILs, SILs and APLs; this type of development is difficult to nurture with SECALs and PALs.
- We have learned that there is little focus on rural energy, rural infrastructure (other than water supply and sanitation), rural health, rural education, rural private sector development by our colleagues in other sector departments and that it is difficult to create synergies between sector units, despite the existence of country teams.
- We have learned that we still do not have good models for supporting private sector development, whether it involves SME development generically or whether it is aimed at revitalizing or creating critical enterprises serving the rural sector, namely agro-businesses and marketing companies for delivering inputs and collecting outputs. Yet this bottleneck is a critical constraint on agricultural development and our clients are eager for assistance in this area.

Objectives and Strategies

Our overriding objective is to help our client countries pursue broad-based, sustainable growth of productivity and improved social well-being in the rural economy. We have five strategic objectives:

- Increased agricultural productivity and value-added;
- Off-farm rural enterprise growth;
- Development of physical and social infrastructure;
- Improved land, water and forest management; and
- Risk mitigation.

115

To achieve these objectives, we have individual sub-sectoral strategies. Overarching these strategies, we have certain themes that guide our work:

- In general, reform of prices and trade, and privatization of farms and enterprises remain prerequisites for sub-sectoral investments. However, where the economic rates of return for an investment are good, where the investment would help substantial numbers of rural poor, where delays would further increase the costs of that investment, and where the rural sector is "net-taxed," our strategy suggests that we support modest investments.
- Community driven investments will be the predominant approach to our work, but we recognize that there may be a tension between publicly funded investments selected in this manner and those selected using national efficiency criteria. We will try to integrate the better of the two approaches.
- There are trade-offs between equity and efficiency considerations. In selecting investments for support, we will accept that satisfactory, rather than optimal, economic returns to the economy may best reach poverty reduction objectives. Our strategy also takes into account political economy and social well-being and acknowledges that some reforms may have to be crafted differently or go more slowly than pure efficiency considerations would dictate.
- There are also trade-offs between short-term social well-being and longer-term economic benefits, and between short-term production maximization and sustainable natural resource management. Our strategy aims at balancing these considerations and not pursuing either extreme.
- Our borrowers have legitimate concerns that the move to a market economy from the previous socialist system brings considerable risks and uncertainty that require specific attention, particularly when many of the risk mitigation instruments of market economies are not yet available. We will explicitly address these considerations in our work.
- We will seek to emphasize institutional development, capacity building, the involvement of local participation and sound governance in all of our work.
- Action Plans.

Sub-regional Plans

Our assistance strategy by sub-region depends partly on the regional context and priorities. The level of emphasis given to each sub-region is determined by a combination of three factors: (a) need (a function of per capita income, geographical and social endowment, and economic performance); (b) interest and willingness on the part of our client countries to work as a partners, and to borrow; and (c) the capacity, including the institutional framework and governance, of the client country to use Bank support.

Table A3.1 below summarizes the proposed focus areas of our future assistance program by sub-region. In Romania, Bulgaria and Moldova we have an extensive program because there is a "congruence of need, willingness and capacity," as well as institutions which operate with a reasonable degree of transparency. In Central Europe, there is less demand for Bank assistance (with greater access to concessional funds from the EU), in the "core" CIS countries and in Central Asia the levels of "willingness" and or "capacity" are in some cases lower. Over time we would aim to increase our assistance to Central Asia, Ukraine, Russia and Belarus. Our IDA borrowers also have constraints on access to Bank financing, while even in the IBRD countries the overall country assistance envelope is determined by agreements reached through the Country Assistance Strategy process.

Thematic Plans

Our priority interventions are aimed at five general themes where our clients have indicated they want the most support from the Bank and where the Bank has a comparative advantage.

Increasing Agricultural Productivity and Value Added

In most ECA countries, particularly those in the CIS, agriculture remains a key sector of the economy and interventions to increase inclusive growth will require improvements in factor productivity in the sector itself. Areas for intervention include: supporting continued policy reforms, pursuing transfer of property rights through completion of land privatization and farm restructuring, creation of secure property rights and development of land markets, reversing the deterioration of irrigation and drainage systems and creation of community-based institutions to own and manage the systems, development of knowledge and information systems, and establishment of quality and safety standards.

Off-Farm Enterprise Development

The Bank historically been involved in agricultural credit. We have shifted our focus to development of sustainable rural financial services, including savings, leasing and risk reduction instruments, as well as micro-credit for all rural enterprises, not only farms. Aside from finance, we have done little to develop a vibrant private economy off the farm. The non-existent or poorly functioning markets for input supply and output marketing and agro-processing industries represent a major bottleneck for future agricultural growth. SME development in these and other manufacturing and services to support rural livelihoods are a necessary complement to a growing agricultural sector which should shed labor as it becomes more productive. Because of the critical importance of this issue to our clients, our strategy

involves a heavy emphasis on searching for successful models and reaching out more actively to our partners with expertise in this area (IFC, EBRD). We are testing some new approaches to off-farm employment creation in Poland and will monitor this experience closely for possible replication elsewhere.

Social and physical infrastructure

We are supporting improved water supply and sanitation in a variety of countries, focusing on community-based approaches. Increasingly we aim to support rural infrastructure projects which strengthen local government's implementation capacity and local democratic institutions. We do not have a clear strategy for either rural energy and telecommunications, or for rural road infrastructure. We support "lifeline" energy tariffs where poverty and rising energy prices have led to increased use of biomass and land degradation, and to support increased internet connectivity. With regard to health and education, our strategy is to improve delivery of services while increasing

Table A3.1: Priority Actions for Rural Development in the Region

Priority Actions	Central Europe, Baltics	Romania Bulgaria Moldova	Balkans	Turkey	Core CIS	Caucasus	Central Asia
Policy Reform	○	●	○	●	●	○	○
Land Reform	○	●	●	○	●	●	●
Irrigation and Drainage	○	●	●	●	○	●	●
Knowledge/info Systems	○	●	●	○	○	●	●
Quality and Safety	●	●	○	○	○	○	○
Agricultural Marketing	○	●	●	●	○	○	?
Rural Finance	○	●	●	○	○	●	●
Roads, Telecommunications, Energy	●	●	●	○	○	●	●
Water Supply & Sanitation	●	●	○	○	○	●	●
Health	○	○	○	○	○	○	○
Education	○	○	○	●	○	○	○
Land Management	○	●	●	●	●	●	●
Water Management	○	●	○	○	○	●	●
Forests	○	●	●	●	●	○	●
Regional Seas	○	●	○	○	○	○	●
Natural Disasters	●	●	○	●	○	●	●
Financial Risks	○	●	○	○	○	○	○

117

cost-effectiveness and rationalization of existing systems, where necessary. We are also supporting an emphasis on primary health and outpatient care and primary education, and improved supporting infrastructure (e.g., teachers' housing, electrification of schools, ect.) with community participation. We support creation of incentives for providers in rural areas and investments in basic equipment.

Land, Water and Forest Management (including landscape management and biodiversity conservation)

Land management. Our strategy involves increasing support for new technologies such as minimum tillage and support for better nutrient management and more environmentally friendly farming methods. We will replicate successful approaches in one country with appropriate adaptations to others, e.g., participatory natural resource management, where local communities work with local line ministry staff to select from and implement a "menu" of activities that improve soils and moisture retention and increase local incomes, which has been successful in Turkey. We will also aim to replicate elsewhere our successes with community range and forest management.

Water management. Our focus will continue to be on improved irrigation and drainage management, and we will also support dam maintenance. In Central Asia, our priority will be on support for investments that improve local incomes and management of the Aral Sea watershed. We will aim to support improved wetland management for ecosystems management and protection of fisheries' spawning grounds. Our strategy will be to support improved river-basin planning to help clients prioritize and balance water requirement investments at a country level. We will support the range of water resource investments where ERRs are adequate, the rural poor benefit and the environmental impacts are positive.

Forest management. Our strategy in the "forest-rich" countries is to improve public sector management, including fire and pest management, forest land-use planning, greater transparency in forest management, and support for sustainable approach-

es to land restitution, in order to increase the "value-added" to the economy and society from sustainably managed forests. In the "forest-poor" countries we will focus on community range, forest and watershed management for poverty reduction and sustainable livelihoods. We will also help our clients meet commitments to global environmental conventions regarding biodiversity conservation through supporting improved protected area management and landscape management in the production landscape.

Risk Mitigation

Improved security against man-made and natural disasters is one key element of human well-being. Our strategy, regarding natural disasters, has three main elements: (a) helping our countries to recover and reconstruct quickly following natural disasters; (b) helping them put in place disaster planning, preparedness and mitigation programs to reduce the impact of disasters when they do occur; and (c) through our regular lending, helping our countries restructure elements of their economies to be less vulnerable to disaster (e.g. through more supplementary irrigation in drought-prone areas, dam rehabilitation, and supporting better pest and forest fire management systems).

We will also seek to introduce financial risk mitigation instruments (e.g., new-style insurance programs and hedging) as part of our rural financial services.

Implementation

Internal World Bank Implementation Issues and Plans

In order to implement our strategy we need to work closely with other sectors, especially the Human Resources and Infrastructure Sector Units, but also Poverty Reduction and Economic Management, and Private and Financial Sector Development. Few projects outside ECSSD are aimed specifically at rural areas. We aim to put a particular emphasis on making sure that rural issues are well treated in CASs and PRSPs in the future. This means ensuring that the appropriate level of intervention is supported for the importance of the sector and the degree of rural poverty.

Donor Coordination Issues and Plans

We are committed to working with other partners, recognizing the enormous strengths and assets they contribute to our efforts. We have found, however, that this is not always easy and their priorities, procedures (especially procurement, but also many others) and time horizons can be quite different. In our strategy, we explicitly recognize that partnerships, even with IFC, are not cost-free or easy, and we adjust our expectations accordingly. We will strive to maximize synergies with our partners, carefully balancing the costs and benefits of these relationships for our clients. Partnership agreements reached at high levels often do not have adequate budget support at country level for effective implementation and we will seek to ensure that expectations are clear in light of fiscal realities.

Implementation Arrangements and Instruments

Our key instrument is lending but our ability to use this instrument is limited for a number of reasons. For Central European countries, with increasing access to EU funds and to commercial capital markets, our money is increasingly non-competitive. On the other hand, in the former CIS we are reluctant to lend to the slow reformers, and there are debt and IDA lending constraints on the poorest countries. On some occasions Bank procedures, particularly those regarding procurement, financial management and environmental safeguards, are regarded as cumbersome and expensive, and decrease borrower interest, even if overall they increase cost-effectiveness, transparency and project design. Our strategy is to continue to use lending instruments to the extent possible within these constraints, as we believe the development impact of this tool remains significant, but to expand our use of non-lending instruments as a complement where there is demand from the client.

Lending. We will continue to do investment lending to support our program. We have found that developing community-based approaches and creating institutional capacity works best in the form of LILs, SILs and APLs. We have also found that we can support a number of policy reforms with these operations and that we gain more commitment from stakeholders when reforms are accompanied

by investment. We will use SECALs sparingly, and only when there is a broad reform agenda and true ownership by the Borrower. We will try to integrate broad policy issues into PALs and SALs/SACs where there is more leverage. We find, however, that this type of adjustment lending needs to be complemented by investments to achieve lasting impact and to nurture the kind of local involvement, development of local institutions and capacity building that we believe are critical.

In general we will emphasize project lending that combines investment with support for sub-sector policy reform. Examples of success with this approach include: support to decentralization of water management and water users' associations through irrigation projects; involvement of local communities and local governments in design and implementation of natural resources and local infrastructure improvement projects; improved forest management policies through support to improved forest inventories, planning, financing and protection; land reform through support to farm restructuring; development of land markets through cadastre and land registration projects; and improved rural financial policy through FILs requiring market interest rates and elimination of subsidies. Locally driven development is frequently effective in overcoming the governance problems faced in many ECA countries and we will aim to use this approach as much as possible.

Non-Lending Services. We intend to continue to use IDFs to build institutional capacity. PHRD grants are an essential input into project preparation, and we will continue to use them to the maximum extent possible. We will aim to work with the Financial Complex to restore their operational flexibility.

GEF has financed pilot investments in improved ecosystems conservation and management of international waters. It has also often acted as a catalyst for Bank lending operations at a later date. Given the increasing financial and operational constraints with GEF, we aim to work more closely with our clients to persuade them to see the benefits of borrowing both for rural "public goods" (social services, better land and water management, research and extension) as well as for "global public goods."

We will put a high priority on doing country-specific economic and sector work which is country focused and operational, learning from project experience. We will aim to complete our ESW tasks more promptly, to have them carried out, to the extent possible, by the person who is responsible for lending in a particular country, and to have local ownership, to improve effectiveness. We will

A3.3   Summary of Regional Consultations: Europe and Central Asia Region

Consultation took place in Moscow (March, 2001) with over 80 participants from 22 countries. It provided valuable feedback and also an opportunity for members of the rural development community from so many countries of the region to meet one another. There were informal exchanges of views and a sharing of experience in several areas.

Overall approach:

- There was support for a broader approach to Rural Development, to go beyond agricultural productivity and include off-farm enterprises, physical & social infrastructure, natural resource management and risk mitigation.
- The strategy should address rural poverty especially the need for ECA to develop social safety nets to reduce growing rural poverty.
- Differences between countries were emphasized; there was a need for a strong sub-regional, country-specific and local focus in strategy development and implementation.
- The World Bank should be more sensitive to the political aspects of rural development
- The group expressed frustration with the tough policy requirements and conditions set by the Bank.

Thematic Areas:

- Western ECA region priorities emphasized EU accession, WTO, and market access, while eastern ECA region priorities emphasized land reform, institutional development, progressive pro-rural/farmer credit policies, and pursuing market reform.
- The Bank should support new emerging privatized farming structures and both small and big farms.
- Credit access is a priority, but there was concern at the lack of Bank support to the institutional development of private sector aside from credit.
- Development of agro-processing facilities as well as the private non-agriculture sector are critical to increased competitiveness of the region.
- The Central Asian region identified natural resource management as critical to rural development; especially irrigation, forestry and biodiversity.

Bank Instruments

- The World Bank should be flexible, quicker, and less bureaucratic, and use more local experts and expertise from the region.
- Bank lending should be combined with pilot grants for the projects.
- There should be more focus on simple, small grass-root projects rather than complex large-scale projects (APLs and SALs).

120

also put an increasing emphasis on providing "just-in-time" sub-sector notes that respond to specific issues raised by our clients, and we will draw more on international experience to provide our clients with options as they pursue reform. We support having country units hold a reserve for this type of ESW, for all sectors, not just rural.

Measuring the Success of our Work

Our individual investment operations generally include outcome indicators. Broader indicators, such as the decline in the number of rural poor or increase in off-farm employment in rural areas, can be measured but are difficult to link to our assistance strategy We will measure the success of our strategy implementation in the following ways:

- In the sub-regions summarized above, new lending and CAS objectives should reflect the priorities outlined in the strategy;
- The priorities and approaches followed in the new projects should reflect the sub-regional strategies; and
- New ESW should focus on the priority objectives of the strategy and should be operational.

A regional consultation was held during March 2001 to discuss this strategy. A summary of the major conclusions from that consultation are presented in Box A3.3.

LATIN AMERICA AND CARIBBEAN

Regional Context and Key Issues

The Latin America and the Caribbean Region (LCR) is a middle-income region well endowed in natural resources. LCR is the wealthiest of the developing regions with an average per capita GNP of $3,940 in 1998. At the regional level, it is also the least dependent on agriculture—an average of only 8% of GDP in 1998. However, this average ratio hides a great variation that ranges from 5% in Mexico, 8% in Brazil, 15% in Colombia, and 24% in Nicaragua. The region is also well endowed in natural resources. It has abundant tropical and temperate natural forests, with more than half the world's tropical forests, major biodiversity reserves, and around a third of the world's fresh water.

LCR is a highly urbanized region. Of its estimated 519 million inhabitants for the year 2000, 391 are urban, and 128 are rural. About one third of the population is poor, and about one sixth extremely poor. Poverty incidence in 1998 is lower than in 1992 but it is only back to the level of 1986. Projections for the year 2020 show that while the urbanization trend will continue and the share of the rural population will decline, the absolute numbers of people living in rural areas will remain roughly the same. Moreover, serious problems of equity exist and are particularly evident with respect to land distribution. LCR possesses the highest GINI (inequity) coefficients in the world. For example, it is over 0.9 in Peru, Paraguay and Venezuela and close to those levels in Colombia and Brazil.

During the 1990s, most countries in the region made a radical departure from heavy state intervention in prices and markets towards private sector-led models of development, reducing barriers to competition in domestic markets, and accelerating the process of trade integration with the global economy. Several countries, however, lagged in these reforms; e.g., Venezuela, Ecuador, Haiti, and Jamaica. The region as a whole benefited as evidenced by the return of macro economic stability, and the decline in the average public deficits. Growth resumed, but for many it was sluggish, not sustained and with recurrent crisis (Argentina, Brazil, Mexico). Growth of per capita GDP was below 1.5% per year in the 1990s and was accompanied by increasing inequality.

The high rate of urbanization notwithstanding, the strategic importance of agriculture and the rural sector remains for four major reasons.

- **Contribution to employment and to GDP.** Despite their modest contribution to GDP, primary agriculture accounts for a large share of the labor market: 20% in Mexico, 57% in Central America. However, when agriculture is broadly defined to include agro-industry, its share of GDP is much higher. For example, in Argentina, Chile, Brazil and Mexico (which together account for more than 70% of AGDP of LCR), agriculture accounts for around 40% of GDP

(1996). Opportunities offered by the sector are still large and untapped.

- **Impact on the environment.** Any growth at the cost of natural resource degradation is a short-lived victory. If nothing else, degradation weakens the resource base, exacerbates the destructive impact of natural calamities, and worsens the vulnerability of the poor. Agriculture is one of the sectors where the importance of integrating environmental and economic policies is most obvious.
- **The rural sector contributes to the development of the other sectors of the economy.** High-productivity agricultural transformation has fuelled the growth of most high-income industrialized countries. Urban demand for processed foods is rising and so is the demand for processed goods of higher quality. Also, the quality of urban development will be determined by a successful transformation of the rural sector.
- **Higher incidence of poverty in rural LCR.** Rural areas have the highest incidence of poverty (63%). Social and economic indicators in rural areas are low and much worse when compared to urban areas. Also, rural poverty disproportionately affects some groups.

Lessons Learned

Macro reforms were necessary but insufficient to remove the structural impediments constraining the rural poor. While the macro reforms helped put in place a policy framework more conducive to growth and private sector involvement, they were not complemented by "second generation" reforms. These are measures to improve the competitive functioning of factor and goods markets, reduce the high inequalities and the deep-seated structural problems that severely limited access of the rural poor to economic assets, markets, services, technology, and infrastructure. The macro reforms did not reverse the long history of un-egalitarian development. The rural sector remained relatively disconnected from the rest of the economy and many structural distortions and regional disparities were left untouched as the micro agenda was overlooked. In terms of its contribution to rural poverty, the structure of growth is as important as growth figures per se. In many cases agricultural growth was concentrated in the commercial sector and did not trickle down.

Sectoral policies and programs may skew incentives. Some countries implemented explicit or implicit taxation policies towards the sector, through overvalued exchange rates regimes, industrial protection or taxation of export commodities (with strong comparative advantage) and protection of import substituting food (with little comparative advantage). These protection and taxation patterns were highly inefficient. In a number of countries the incentive framework for agriculture remained relatively unfriendly with negative protection rates and negative real prices to producers for most crops, e.g., Mexico. Also, the use of subsidies to address poverty had perverse effects. Subsidized directed credit through parastatals was highly inefficient in terms of its fiscal cost, delinquency rates and outreach capacity. It also crowded out and inhibited the development of local self-sustained savings and loans initiatives. Subsidies for investment and equipment are difficult to target and risk accruing disproportionately to medium and large commercial farmers. This also drives up land prices, induces concentration of land, and makes access to land by the poor more difficult. Also, productivity improvements should be more closely associated to competitiveness as subsidies may skew the incentive structure of the various crops.

Need to find the right balance. This rural action plan argues that LCR cannot succeed in its poverty alleviation efforts without the contribution of the rural sector. However, finding the right balance is still a challenge. The development community has gone from one extreme to another, searching for the appropriate instruments and approaches to translate an holistic vision into effective actions. Too often, implementation capacity falls short of conceptual sophistication or poor policies impeded good projects to bear fruits.

Integration through a territorial, decentralized approach. While the integrated rural development projects of the 1970s were right about integration, they were wrong about the way they were carried out. These projects were implemented top-down, with no participation, no decentralization and in an adverse policy environment. There is a lot that can be recovered from the concept of integrated rural development in the new context of decentralization, differentiation, democratization and better policy framework which characterize most of LCR countries today. There is a compelling need to address equity issues in the context of a rural development strategy repositioned in the context of its "rural space." Under this approach, agriculture, off-farm activities, employment opportunities, social cohesiveness, municipal development, access to markets and services, are seen as equally important elements of a strategy that blurs traditional divides among sectors and among rural and urban approaches.

Need to build bridges beyond the community level. Community participation approaches helped build social capital and proved to be an effective mechanism for delivering micro-projects and productive investments. However, to ensure institutional sustainability, there is a need to link these community-driven projects to local governments. Such an approach should also build the bridges with the rest of the economy, promoting producers' organizations and providing the critical linkage to integrated supply chains, where the private sector would play an increasing role in the development of the family farms sector.

Need a culturally- and gender-sensitive approach. It is clear that the pervasiveness of poverty rates among ethnic minorities and the increasing role of women in rural society raises the issue of social inclusion and access to productive factors and assets. Government programs should devise approaches more adapted to cultural preferences and gender needs.

Objectives and Strategies
Main objectives. The overarching objective of the proposed regional action plan is to reduce rural poverty and promote broad-based growth in the context of the sustainable management of natural resources.

Strategic thrusts. The strategy revision process emphasizes the holistic nature of rural development, as opposed to focus on a single sector—agriculture, and the urgency to go beyond vision into action. The strategy is to build on successful experiences and scale up what is working well, strengthen

the missing links, and work better together across networks so as to better balance the different elements of a complex package and achieve synergism. A rural development strategy has to include several differentiated elements directed at different population groups while acknowledging that an adequate overall macro and policy framework is essential. In addition, the strategy wants to convey the message that while the rural sector confronts many challenges, it also presents many opportunities that makes it potentially attractive to investors and to rural dwellers, if the right mix of policies, institutions and support programs can be put in place.

Better addressing the rural-urban dynamics. While an important preoccupation of policy makers is to maintain rural-urban migration at manageable levels, this migration will continue. More training and education opportunities for the rural poor are important for facilitating their absorption into other sectors of the economy. However, outright promotion of migration as a rural poverty alleviation strategy is not viable, because it would exclude from a rural modernization process a large smallholder sector with growth and employment potential and convert it to slum dwellers. For the millions who continue to stay in rural areas, improving living conditions will depend on improvements on several fronts. These include intensifying small-holder agriculture and increasing productivity; providing infrastructure and services; improving access to assets such as land, education and financial services, and to markets; ensuring the sustainable management of the natural resource base on which they base their livelihoods; and providing better risk management tools.

Integration through regional development and a new "institutionality." A "rural space" approach based on regional development will provide the underlying vehicle to pursue sectoral integration. This requires improving the absorptive capacity of secondary towns in the context of increasing urban-rural integration and interaction. It also calls for investments in basic infrastructure, promotion of new off-farm opportunities, better integration with the labor markets, continued emphasis on community-driven development, municipal strengthening and the building of social and human capital. It also allows for better integration of environmental issues in an effort to build consensus around possible "win-win" opportunities. In this context a new "institutionality" will need to be built around the concept of increased participation of the local actors, farmers' organizations, civil society, local governments, and the private sector. This means a revision of roles where beneficiaries of Government programs become clients and take leadership of regional planning and priority setting, guide and negotiate local development processes, and create the conditions for more accountability and better governance.

Productivity, competitiveness and increased private sector involvement are key engines of growth. Agricultural productivity, competitiveness, access to technology and markets will remain critical for many producers independently of their size. However, in many cases the smallholder sector working for the domestic market should be subject to more attention and support in view of its potential and untapped contribution to growth and employment. Conditions for increased private sector involvement will need to be studied and barriers removed through private-public partnership.

Social safety nets for the severely marginalized. There is a group of rural poor who will remain marginally productive and will not be able to benefit from the rural non-farm economy or to migrate. Members of this group are typically older and female heads of households and farms in poorly endowed areas. For this group, social safety nets and risk management combined with the promotion of income generating activities, both off-farm and on-farm, are critical to assure basic decent living standards.

The Action Plan

The proposed action plan contemplates a series of priorities organized along a two-pronged approach. The enabling factors can be considered as critical underlying elements in the implementation effectiveness of the strategy in any country. The priority lines of actions describe the possible applications subject to country circumstances.

Enabling Factors

Maintain a supportive macro-economic and trade environment. This advocates a more pro-active role in the discussion of macro-economic and poli-cy issues that affect the rural sector. It also supports renewed engagement in economic and sector work to provide better underpinning and understanding of the factors that determine rural poverty, the incentive framework, the functioning of land, labor and financial markets, the decentralization process for the sector, etc.

Promote a new "institutionality" for the sector and good governance. The combination of increased decentralization and the development of local democracy are key elements to progressively create the conditions for greater participation and accountability at the local level. The main debate around the issue of how to better articulate the social demand for services with the institutional supply calls for a re-thinking of the respective roles of the public sector (both central and sub-national governments), civil society, interest groups, private sector, etc.

Develop a credible regulatory framework. This includes a number of elements conducive to more effective private sector participation and better functioning markets. It includes: a) establishing better-integrated price and market information systems; b) developing appropriate regulatory frameworks and enforcement capacity as critical factors for secure transactions, inventory-based financing, crop insurance, non-bank financial institutions, contract farming, and "collateralization" of assets; and c) facilitating the development of commodity quality standards based on industry participation and needs, and the development of food safety norms.

Lines of Action

Raise productivity and competitiveness as the engine of agricultural growth. This proposes to pursue public/private partnerships for the delivery of public goods and services (such as agricultural research and extension, animal and plant health control), facilitate access to adapted technology and equipment, while improving quality and cost-effectiveness. It also promotes more efficient cropping patterns and better vertical integration in the supply and marketing chain. It argues in favor of basing future irrigation projects on a decentralized integrated approach to sustainable management and use of water resources.

Pursue a systematic approach to improve the competitive functioning of markets. This addresses three essential markets. Land regularization and administration are to increase access to land and promote more efficient functioning of land markets. Rural financial services are in need of urgent revival and rethinking in terms of both the efficiency of existing public or semi-public credit delivery mechanisms and the importance of the non-bank sector through savings and loans "mutualistic" approaches. Product and storage markets should be made more competitive and efficient through the development of farmers' organization, higher value transformation activities, better information system and inventory financing mechanisms.

Foster a "rural space" approach and regional development. It proposes a more integrated approach that blurs the traditional urban-rural divide and repositions rural development in the framework of a territorial approach. This approach will foster better integration with the supply chain, labor and financial markets, the provision of basic infrastructure and services, sustainable natural resources management and will go a long way in rendering rural areas more attractive to migrants and to the private sector. Community-driven development would be scaled-up as an effective vehicle for building social capital, and delivering basic services and small infrastructure. However, the key links with local governments will be strengthened including more emphasis on building municipal capacities in the context of increasing decentralization.

Manage natural resources in a sustainable way. This is a key issue for the long-term sustainability of development programs but one that presents considerable trade-offs between short-term benefits and long-term social costs. A number of experiences exist in LCR that have developed win-win situations and instruments capable of better integrating productive, management, and conservation concerns. These initiatives are still relatively scattered and will need to be scaled-up so as to demonstrate their potential in ensuring a more sustainable use of the resource base. The Global Environment Facility should continue to play an instrumental role in facilitating better mainstreaming between conservation and development.

Build human and social capital. Expanding the delivery of basic education and health services are powerful tools for poverty reduction in a region with high rural-urban migration. Education should be seen as a priority for the rural population, and especially education for girls. It improves employment opportunities, prepares future migrants to access better jobs, and helps families to better plan their own future. Development programs need to promote social inclusion, build social capital and respect cultural diversity and preferences of minority and ethnic groups which shoulder a disproportionate burden of rural poverty.

Strengthen risk management and safety nets. Finally, a series of relatively new activities and instruments would be developed and expanded to reduce the vulnerability of poor people both to economic shocks and natural disasters. This covers a range of tools like early warning systems, prevention activities, price hedging tools, and crop insurance schemes. Also social security, safety nets and income support programs can be very effective instruments to reach the poor and they should be developed according to local circumstances.

Implementation

Internal WB Implementation Issues and Instruments

Cross-network participation. A major departure from the past is developing systematic partnerships between the rural network and other networks:

- The Environmentally and Socially Sustainable Development (ESSD) network and the Poverty Reduction and Economic Management (PREM) network would work jointly to ensure that the impact of the macro policies would be supportive of rural development. PREM would continue to focus on promoting macro stability, adequate trade policies, competitive exchange rate regime, more supportive public expenditure programs, the removal of distorting government policies in rural markets. In addition, they will develop decentralization strategies, and better understanding of the analytical underpinnings of poverty and of the incentive framework for the sector.

- ESSD and the Human Development (HD) networks would work jointly to elaborate more consistent programs in addressing social sector issues, participation of minorities and indigenous people development. They would also promote the inclusion of culturally consistent components in the health and education programs. They would work together to ensure consistency of implementation of Social Funds and Rural Investment Funds, and strengthening safety nets in rural areas.
- ESSD and the Finance and Private Sector and Infrastructure (FPSI) networks would develop joint strategies and programs on how best to help governments in the development of rural-urban linkages, deliver public goods and basic infrastructure services in rural areas, especially at the level of municipalities. They would also develop rural finance approaches that are consistent with the specificity of the rural sector and with the overall financial sector policies and regulatory frameworks.

A3.4 Summary of Regional Consultations: The Latin America and Caribbean Region

A regional consultation was organized in Panama City on April 3-4, 2001, under the auspices of the International Center for Rural Development (CIDER, the rural branch of the Inter-American Institute for Cooperation on Agriculture, IICA), to discuss the draft Strategy and Action Plan. The workshop brought together a wide array of countries and institutions including representatives from the Government, the National Congress, the Church, the private agro-business sector, producer organizations, academics, and all the donors active in the region. The participants hailed the Bank's initiative of reviving the discussion on rural development, a sector that has experienced an increasing neglect despite its importance. They recognized the remarkable convergence of opinion in the definition of the key strategic elements of a renewed action plan for the sector. Some themes prevailed in the discussion such as: the importance to "operationalize" an holistic approach for the sector and to redefine the institutional set-up through an effective participation of the key social and private actors in the decision making process; the necessity to maintain a strong link between the macro and micro agenda; the need to define differentiated policies with special reference to the youth, women and marginal or excluded groups; the promotion of regional development, urban-rural integration and off-farm rural employment; and how to pursue the concept of sustainable development. The consultation considerably enriched the final document and provided to the document an invaluable client perspective.

A holistic approach with a country focus. The Action Plan recognizes that only a multi-sectoral approach can work and offers the strategic directions and actions to be undertaken. However, it recommends a selective implementation at the country level in view of the Bank's added value, on-going dialogue and local circumstances. It is not a "one-size-fits-all" approach. Country Directors and Sector Leaders will be instrumental in ensuring adequacy and adaptation of the action plan so that it is consistent with the country policies and development agendas. The comparative strength of each network and family in each country context would determine leadership for the various initiatives and operations, but in most cases this will mean stronger inter-sectoral teams. This in turn requires the key involvement of Sector Directors and Sector Managers that would revisit the strategic skill-mix required for implementation of the action plan, guide the constitution of teams with adequate skills, and promote the review of the current budgetary process which hinders cross-network partnerships and support.

The high cost of safeguard policies may be a deterrent. While it is acknowledged that good compliance with safeguard policies is simply better quality business, it needs to be recognized that projects in the rural sector present a high level of compliance requirements which imply more resources and time to prepare. This may play as a disincentive if transaction costs become excessive. Also, it is important to recognize the higher level of risk that staff confronts and to remove possible biases against innovation and risk-taking.

Instruments for cross-network integration. Country Assistance Strategies (CAS), Poverty Reduction Strategy Papers (PRSP), and poverty assessments will be the ideal strategic instruments to ensure that rural issues are fully incorporated and internalized. With respect to lending instruments, investment projects will continue to play an important role especially for specific poverty targeted approaches and innovative interventions, which require strong implementation support and field supervision. More effective integration can be pursued through the use of lending instruments along thematic lines that require blurring the "silos" and sectoral frontiers. New instruments to explore are programmatic loans. By their nature (quick disbursing) they will require an adequate policy environment for the particular sub-sector to be financed, and solid institutions with sound procedures and implementation rules in place.

Donor Coordination

Promoting partnership is good business. It is generally felt that the strategic thrust of this rural development strategy for LCR countries is widely shared among donors. The Bank should continue to explore and develop regular channels for communication and consultations with other potential partners, to ensure consistency of strategies, and to explore co-financing possibilities. Partnerships should be sought on a country-basis with the objective of learning and transferring experiences and developing common ground in approaches among partners. Better consistency among donors will enhance the chances to leverage the establishment of a "rural constituency within Governments and pursue a coherent dialogue for increased effectiveness.

Implementation Approaches

Strengthening client ownership. Without client ownership this strategy and action plan are moot. Moreover, it has to be acknowledged that, in most situations, development efforts take the form of progressive quantum leaps that require considerable dialogue and buy-in from various constituencies in the country. In some countries there is already a high degree of convergence with the proposed action plan and most of it may already be under implementation; in others, agreement and interest may be only partial. This strategy and action plan should be seen as a contribution to the on-going discussion on LCR rural development issues and the way forward. Many of the elements of the proposed action plan are already under implementation in a country or another, and the document essentially tries to coalesce and build on what seem to be best practices and innovative successful approaches. Countries in LCR could seize this opportunity to provide momentum to their rural development agenda and, as a priority, look towards implementation with a sense of urgency. The Bank could contribute to a partnership that would offer renewed commitment and support for action on the ground. In addition, it could contribute with enhanced implementation capacity, and more accurate and specific analytical work to deepen the reciprocal understanding around rural development issues.

Performance Indicators and Monitoring

Monitoring and evaluation indicators need to be country-specific. In all operations and on a country base, the Bank will develop simple but effective monitoring and evaluation systems adapted from Millennium Development Goals (MDGs) on which international consensus already exists. While we should maintain flexibility in implementation and admit that trial and error will still be necessary as part of the learning process, a minimum set of robust indicators that are reliable, user-friendly, and cost-effective will be developed. Indicators should be built on the basis of the level of progress achieved by each country and the nature of the different programs being supported, so as to increase their relevance and realism.

MIDDLE EAST AND NORTH AFRICA

In 1997 the World Bank issued its rural development strategy, Rural Development: *From Vision to Action*. The purpose of this exercise is to update that strategy and to render it much more region specific and action oriented than the previous undertaking.

Our approach is to characterize the current situation in Middle East and North Africa (MNA) countries, examine the implementation of the Vision to Action strategy in MNA, develop a series of lessons learned from Bank activities in recent years—and then use all that material in developing the objectives, strategies, action plans and implementation approach for future rural development in MNA. This process is illustrated in Figure A3.2.

Current Situation in MNA Countries

Economy, Policy, and Agriculture
- Per capita income in MNA (excluding the Gulf countries) averages about $2000 and ranges from $350 in Yemen to $3700 in Lebanon.
- GDP growth has generally ranged between 2 and 5% per year, but for Morocco, Jordan, and West

Bank & Gaza, it has been zero or negative for the decade of the 1990s.

■ Variability in agricultural income from year to year is high in MNA, with the standard deviation of the agricultural GDP growth rate reaching 33% and 25% for Morocco and Jordan respectively. Thus countries with high variability have been experiencing negative growth or stagnation in agricultural value added over the decade.

■ Following are production systems typical of the MNA region:

  ■ Rainfed mixed;
  ■ Dryland mixed;
  ■ Pastoral;
  ■ Irrigated; and
  ■ Highland mixed

Although water availability is crucial to all agricultural systems in MNA, variability, and thus vulnerability, varies significantly across production systems.

Water policies are crucial in all MNA countries. Other important policy areas include natural resource degradation, land tenure issues, food subsidies, and rural infrastructure

For the development of the irrigated and humid mixed system, access to export markets is also essential. The largest trading partner for most MNA countries is the European Union (EU). The EU's policies are quite restrictive and limit export expansion by MNA countries.

Social

Illiteracy rates are high, especially for women. On average, half of women are literate in the region. In rural areas, literacy rates fall even from these levels. In Yemen and Morocco, only half of school-age children in rural areas are in school, as compared with 80-90% in urban areas.

Access to safe drinking water and sanitation for the rural population is quite low in many MNA countries and well below access in urban areas.

Public social safety nets are generally quite weak in rural areas, a problem which is accentuated by the high variability in rainfall and agricultural production,

and which leaves a large fraction of the rural population vulnerable.

Lessons Learned

The Bank has learned valuable lessons in its operations over the past few years. These lessons contribute significantly to the formulation of strategies for improving success in future rural development operations.

1. **More attention needs to be paid to political constraints and institutional capacities.** There is a need for Bank activities to accurately assess the political and institutional setting in planning and implementing rural development projects.

2. **Non-lending activities should have greater importance in some countries.** By emphasizing its comparative advantage in analytical and policy advice, the Bank can make strides in rural development. Lending activities should have built in flexibility, and analytical work should serve as support to that flexibility.

3. **Variability in climate and incomes has differential effects on policy decisions in the MNA region.** Many governments seek consumer and producer price stability as an objective, but the economic and agricultural policy frameworks may not match the climatic variability and production conditions in the country.

4. **Encourage private sector and mandate community participation.** A need for local participation for sustained success is not a new theme. However, unsatisfactory project results across varying rural development programs are often caused by a lack of community participation.

5. **A greater emphasis on small-scale projects in rural infrastructure and natural resource management is warranted.** Small-scale rural infrastructure projects have at least four desirable traits applicable to rural development in the MNA region:
   i) They often are more labor-intensive than large-scale projects;
   ii) They tend to involve the community more in the implementation;

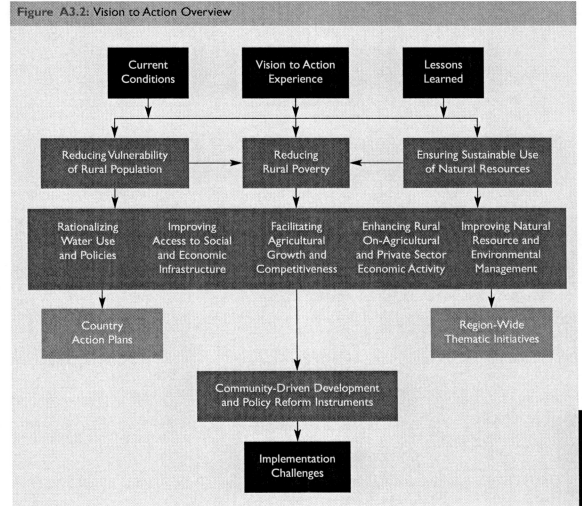

iii) They may be more sustainable in that rural asso-ciations may have the ability to carry out operations and maintenance; and

iv) From MNA experience, small-scale projects have the advantage of generally being able to target poorer quintiles of the population.

6. **The Bank needs to be sensitive to the negative implication of accepting a status-quo stance on issues requiring long-term, re-institutionalizing efforts.** Decades may be required in certain instances to implement policy change. Thus, the Bank should launch and continue dialogue on issues, even when it is only marginally effective in bringing about immediate change. This may particularly be the case for natural resource management, but is also true in MNA for regulatory and tariff reform. In the latter cases, the lesson may be that disbursements made that ignore compliance with an agreed reform agenda may send the same signal of a lack of concern by the Bank.

7. **The Bank's awareness of the need for integrated water management should be reflected in policy dialogue with governments and users.**

The Bank needs to ensure that all projects involved with supply creation or restoration are integrated with a participatory demand management element.

8. **A lack of indicators for rural development is inhibiting project planning and evaluation.** Often projects cannot be adequately planned or impacts measured because baseline data do not exist. The capacity to understand development needs and to address policies to raise income in rural areas and in particular in remote locations is hampered by such information deficiencies and mechanisms for on-going monitoring.

Objectives

Reducing rural poverty. Rural poverty reduction is our overall objective. This objective is the real guiding principle by which all other rural development objectives and policies are implemented.

Reducing vulnerability in rural areas. Income variability in rural areas is high, which means that the percentage of the population that is vulnerable to income swings is quite large. Reducing vulnerability is not synonymous with poverty reduction and goes beyond policies that endeavor to bring the poor to an acceptable minimum level of consumption. It also means putting in place a safety net to prevent the non-poor from falling below the poverty line, along with the creation of opportunities that will help improve living conditions for the poor and non-poor.

Ensuring the sustainable use of natural resources. There are four important components of the natural resource base of rural life to address – water, land, forests, and pastoral areas. These resources are scarce and fragile and our objective is to ensure the long term sustainable use of these natural resources.

Strategies

1. **Rationalizing water management and policies.** In MNA, efficient and effective water use is absolutely critical for success in rural development. Improving performance and productivity in water management requires institutional, policy,

and planning system reforms. This strategy calls for an examination and possible revision of legislative, policy, and institutional framework for water resources, along with actions to strengthen the role of rural communities, the public, and the private sector.

2. **Improving access to social and economic infrastructure.** Social infrastructure here encompasses especially health care and education for rural areas. Economic infrastructure includes rural roads, rural water supply, and rural electrification, and today also access to information technology. To increase rural agricultural and non-agricultural incomes, it is imperative to increase access to both social and economic infrastructure in rural areas. Particular attention needs to be paid to enhancing women's access to these services. Egypt, Morocco and Yemen provide encouraging examples where school enrollments in rural areas, and for girls, are increasing.

3. **Facilitating agricultural growth and competitiveness.** Reversing deteriorating agriculture performance and facilitating growth to increase rural income (farm and non-farm) is a fundamental means of realizing poverty reduction. Policy change, secure land tenure, creation of economically viable and efficient farms, facilitating the emergence of competitive and farmer-friendly processing and marketing infrastructures, and support of farmer-induced technological change in agriculture are critical for the promotion of competition in the region.

Increasing growth in agricultural exports, which requires the removal of anti export bias, namely high protection of importable agricultural or industrial goods and real exchange rates overvaluation. In MNA, increasing agricultural exports also will require changes in the protectionist policies of its primary trading partner, the European Union.

Formulating agricultural pricing and trade policies that consider reducing farm income variability as one of the strategic priorities (see lesson learned three). Agricultural policies must be better aligned with the climatic reality of the region, which is high rainfall variability and frequent drought.

130

Agricultural research and extension must be improved especially in adapting crop varieties to the drought-prone regions (and associated climatic variability) plus research on efficient use of irrigation water and irrigation techniques appropriate to each crop and region.

Land tenure reform. Land tenure issues in some MNA countries have become a major impediment to agricultural productivity growth. Rural development programs must address these issues.

Investments are needed in developing the public institutional capacity in policy analysis, particularly related to agriculture and natural resources.

4. Enhancing rural non-agricultural and private sector economic activities. A full integration of non-agricultural rural activities is one of the major challenges of this exercise. Following are some actions that can serve to effectively enhance the non-agricultural rural economy:

Agricultural policies can promote non-farm activities such as agro-processing and the other industrial, commercial and service sectors that characterize modern agriculture. Projects and policies aimed at promoting the non-farm economy should not just focus on improving the capacity of households to become involved in the non-farm economy, but should also stimulate the engines that pull rural households into the non-farm economy. Engines of non-farm growth that offer employment to women in particular should be emphasized.

Local government and institutional participation will have to be engaged in a whole variety of capacities, ranging from land-use planning, education provision, infrastructure investment, regulation, training and financing.

Facilitating the growth of small urban poles for regional development may be an attractive means of creating non-agricultural employment and incomes.

5. Improving natural resource and environmental management. Sustainable rural development is inextricably linked with sustainable natural resource management. Examining the impacts of projects on the sustainable use of natural resources must be a part of the design and implementation of all of our activities. Water is very scarce in MNA, and the productive agricultural areas, particularly pastoral zones, are increasingly threatened by human interventions.

Action Plans

Indicative action plans were produced for each country and major theme in MNA. The country plans are linked to the five strategies mentioned above and will serve to guide Bank actions linked to those strategies. The plans also include monitoring and performance indicators tied to the specific actions. In other words, the actions constitute the specific implementation measures for the five strategies, and the monitoring and performance indicators will help determine in what measure success has been achieved in future years. These action plans will be further elaborated in line with evolving issues, changing country priorities, and intervention by other donors.

The action plans are cross-sectoral; hence, successful implementation will depend upon strong support for cross-sectoral units in the Bank, technical ministries in client countries, non-governmental organizations and other agencies.

While these plans were developed by Bank staff to guide Bank actions, they also are presented to stimulate discussion and collaboration with governments and the development community as a whole. The Bank will need to look for synergies and partnerships with other lenders and donors to completely implement the plans.

Monitoring implementation of action plans will depend on having effective country teams within the Bank and client country support for acquisition of data on rural social and economic indicators.

Implementation

In implementing these plans, the Bank and other donors must recognize the diversity of situations in rural areas of MNA countries, both across countries and even within the same country. This diversity means that instruments must be tuned to the

131

specific region, with its unique economic, social, and cultural characteristics. Therefore, flexibility will be essential in developing programs tailored to each unique region.

The evolving experience in allowing communities to participate effectively in seizing opportunities to improve their well-being is an encouraging approach for rural development. Our approach will be to promote locally and spatially focused rural development (holistic approach to rural well-being) with strong community participation. Sectoral interventions would generate maximum development impact if they are appropriately coordinated and communities are part of the decision-making process (Figure A3.3). For example, for a given region of a country, we might have an education project operated by the education sector in the Bank in conjunction with the Ministry of Education and local authorities in the country. At the same time and in the same region, there might also be irrigation, health, or other projects. These projects will operate in parallel with collaboration across sectors and country departments in the Bank and similar collaboration among line agencies in client countries. Another approach is the

Rural Development Fund (RDF) being piloted in Morocco. Based on demand from the beneficiaries as expressed through a participatory planning process, the RDF would be used by the Governors of selected provinces, on the advice of a Provincial Rural Development Committee composed of relevant line ministry representatives, to complement or fill gaps in existing sectoral programs in a coordinated way, without any predetermination of funding by line ministry. These holistic, multi-sectoral approaches constitute a major component of the MNA implementation strategy for accomplishing our rural development objectives. It will also entail improving local institutional mechanisms for planning, coordinating, and implementing projects with greater community participation.

Another important issue for implementation is the implication for MNA staffing and resource allocation. We foresee a growing demand for MNA staff to work with government officials in strategic sectoral issues, economic policy analysis and knowledge sharing. For example, experience in other regions indicates that quick policy notes are increasingly proving very effective compared with the traditional sector

Figure A3.3: Parallel Project Orientation

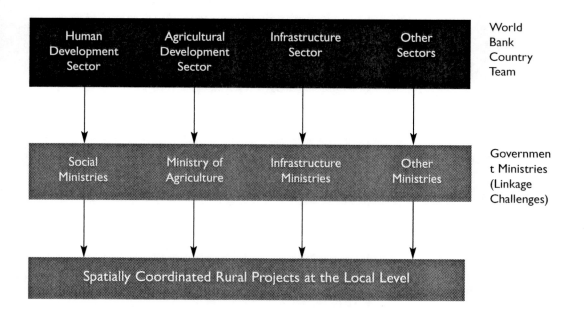

reports. We may not need to build full in-house capacity for all such services but to have the resources to be able to tap the best technical services on short notice. We also need to foster cross-sectoral task teams to address effectively our rural poverty reduction objective.

To enhance development assistance effectiveness, close collaboration among bilateral and international agencies is imperative. Interagency collaboration could take various forms. The most conventional method is participating in financing operations. Many MNA countries have access to grant and concessionary resources from bilateral and international agencies. The Bank is well positioned to avail its technical expertise for policy analysis and project formulation with a view to developing a multi-donor financing plan for an agreed rural development program. Collaboration among the international community could also be enhanced by improving the exchange of information on country strategies and programs.

A summary of the major conclusions of the regional consultation to discuss this strategy is presented in Box A3.5.

SOUTH ASIA

Introduction

The South Asia Region (SAR) consists of eight countries: Afghanistan, Bangladesh, Bhutan, India, Maldives, Nepal, Pakistan, and Sri Lanka. Rural South Asia is the home of over two-thirds of the population in the region, representing about one-third of the total rural population in world. The region is characterized by highly diverse agro-climatic conditions across and within countries, ranging from the atolls of the Maldives to the deserts in western India, the tropical fertile Gangetic Plain to the temperate hills and mountains of the Himalayas in Nepal, which in turn also pose diverse development potential and challenges. For the past decade, South Asia has been the second fastest growing region in the world, after East Asia, its GDP growing at an average annual growth rate of 5.3%. The region has made some progress in improving the social well-being of its population,

---

Summary of Regional Consultations: Middle East and North Africa Region A3.5

Consultations took place in Beirut, Lebanon and Montpellier, France (March 2001). A summary of the major conclusions follows:

- The scarcity and fragility of natural resources (mainly water) in MNA is the main characteristic of the Region and should constitute the basis for the design of rural development strategies in the Region. Agriculture should continue to be considered as the driving force of the rural economy, but given the rather low potential of natural resources in the Region, non-agricultural income generating activities should be introduced and developed at the local level which requires a competitive private sector.

- Conditions in the rural areas of MNA are highly diversified, both between countries and within the same country, a fact not adequately reflected in the regional development strategy document.

- In general, the proposed strategy was accepted, although certain participants underscored the difficulty of implementing such a multi-sectoral approach, both in the Bank and borrower countries.

- The need for participatory development was strongly endorsed, but many participants thought that the Bank's approach did not adequately take into account the complexity of the social and institutional processes involved and the profound change in the role of the State that it implied.

- Rural development is not receiving a level of support commensurate with its importance for poverty alleviation, which creates a "credibility gap" for the Bank and other donors in this area.

- In contrast to its declared emphasis on poverty alleviation, Bank projects in rural areas where most of the poor live have declined in recent years. This reinforced the perception that the Bank was more concerned with policy issues (e.g. removal of subsidies, fiscal reform, trade liberalization) than development operations targeted to the poor.

- There is a need for the Bank to strengthen coordination with other international and bilateral aid agencies to help developing countries to increase their bargaining power in world bodies like the WTO.

- National rural development strategies would help formulate specific and locally adapted solutions to a number of issues identified as common to the whole MNA Region.

- The participants expressed their deep appreciation for the opportunity given to them to share their experiences in dealing with rural development issues, and asked the Bank to consider the possibility of institutionalizing this kind of forum on an even broader scale.

133

especially as measured by the human development index (UNDP), although by world standards, they are still quite low. The agricultural sector remains an important sector in the economy of all countries, employing at least two-thirds of the labor force and contributing from 16% to 40% of the gross domestic product. Sustained food production growth in the 1980s and 1990s enabled SAR countries to achieve on average, food self-sufficiency in cereals.

Despite strong economic performance, South Asia remains among the most impoverished regions in the world. About 500 million people are still living in a state of severe deprivation, lacking sufficient access to adequate nutrition, health, housing, safe water, sanitation, and employment, the region is home to over 43% of the world's poor. Moreover, the UNDP Human Development Index (HDI) rates South Asia lower than all other regions (except for sub-Saharan Africa) in terms of average achievements in basic human development.

Rural poverty is sizable and significant throughout South Asia. Poverty in South Asia is largely a rural phenomenon. While all SAR countries have made progress in reducing the levels of poverty, it remains high in rural areas. About one third to almost one half of the rural population is poor in all SAR countries, except Maldives (22%). Based on national estimates, about 80% of the total 300 million poor in India reside in rural areas. In Nepal, the poverty rate in rural areas (44%) in 1995/96 is almost double the rate in urban areas (23%).

Rural poverty goes beyond inadequate incomes. Interviews of poor people in India for example, reveal their acute vulnerability to disease, crop failures, labor market fluctuations, domestic violence, natural disasters, floods and cyclones, which further exacerbate their sense of insecurity. Any one such event hits the poor particularly hard, causing them to fall, or fall deeper, into poverty. A sense of powerlessness, alienation, and inability to influence the environment in which they live, pervades being poor.

Faster progress in reducing rural poverty in South Asia, however, has been hampered by inadequate

government priority to ensuring a holistic and integrated approach to rural development. While governments have implemented a large number of programs in key sectors such as the social, agriculture, natural resource, infrastructure, and non-farm sectors over the last few decades, several factors undermined their effectiveness in fully achieving their objectives of fostering equitable rural growth and poverty reduction in rural areas. These included: (i) a predominantly centralized, top-down approach in the design and implementation of government programs, which undermined their longer term sustainability and also often bypassed vulnerable groups in society (women, tribal groups and the landless); (ii) the lack of coordination among various sectoral programs in rural areas that hindered greater synergies in their development impact; (iii) the creation of a highly restrictive policy and regulatory environment, which stifled private sector initiative, participation and investments in the farm and rural non-farm sectors that is instrumental for greater employment and income generation in rural areas; (iv) public expenditure patterns characterized by insufficient priority to social and human development in rural areas and an increasing share absorbed by highly distortive subsidies which took away resources for productivity-enhancing investments and in some cases (i.e. fertilizer, fuel, and water) are contributing to natural resource degradation; and (v) weak public sector institutional capacity which contribute to poor delivery of basic services in rural areas, especially to vulnerable groups. In recent years, the SAR countries have taken some positive steps to redress some of these constraints, but a lot remains to be done.

The development agenda for achieving the goal of fully eliminating rural poverty in South Asia and achieving social and economic well-being and broad-based rural development is enormous. It will require the strong and unrelenting commitment from our client governments, if this goal is to be achieved quickly this millennium. In support of this commitment, the South Asia Region of the World Bank, in close partnership with government and other local stakeholders, and in coordination with other donors and international agencies, has put together an assistance strategy and action plan for the short to medium term for moving this agenda forward.

Lessons

Several important lessons for achieving more rapid poverty reduction in rural areas could be drawn from the Bank's long involvement in the region. The most critical is supporting an integrated and holistic approach to rural development, bringing together efforts across critical sectors, including the social, agriculture, natural resource, infrastructure, and the rural non-farm sectors. This approach requires actions in several key areas, the most critical of which are:

- Defining and orienting the roles of Government (at all levels), communities, and private sector to build synergies among various sectoral development efforts, especially fostering community participation and rural decentralization to ensure greater government accountability and effectiveness;
- Creating an enabling policy and regulatory environment (i.e. land, inputs, credit, output markets) and developing appropriate institutions to encourage private investments in rural areas and ensure sustainable use of natural resources (water, marine, forests, land);
- Ensuring appropriate levels and composition of public expenditures towards productivity-enhancing investments for sustained human development and long term rural growth;
- Supporting research and technological innovations to improve and sustain agricultural productivity growth; and,
- Ensuring development initiatives are inclusive to also benefit vulnerable groups (e.g. women, tribals, landless).

Objective and Strategies

The overarching objective of the World Bank's Rural Strategy is to assist our client countries to eliminate rural poverty in South Asia. In view of the fact that the largest share of the poor in the world reside in the rural areas in the region, the development agenda for achieving the goal of eliminating rural poverty in South Asia and achieving social well-being and broad-based rural development is enormous. It will require the strong and unrelenting commitment from our client governments, if this goal is to be achieved quickly this millennium. In support of this commitment, the South Asia Region of the World

Bank, in close partnership with government and other local stakeholders, and in coordination with other donors and international agencies, has put together an assistance strategy and action plan for the short to medium term for moving this agenda forward. This agenda also contributes to achieving the Millennium Development Goals.

The World Bank aims to support an integrated, holistic strategy for rural development that would foster sustained rural growth and poverty reduction in all countries of the South Asia Region. This regional strategy for eliminating poverty has three major objectives:

1. fostering rural growth and opportunities for rural households, especially for the rural poor;
2. empowering communities and the rural poor to meet their priority economic and social needs and thus enhance their well-being; and
3. enhancing the capacity of rural households, especially the poor, to overcome and manage insecurity and risks.

Action Plans

To achieve the above objectives, while recognizing the wide diversity of development needs across our client countries in South Asia, the scope of, and priority areas for, development assistance varies significantly across countries. They also reflect the Bank's strengths and technical and financial capacity, relative to our other development partners. Thus in translating the rural development strategy into action, our program falls into four strategic priority areas. They are:

Enhancing human and social capital development in rural areas. These include our program of assistance to improve the delivery and quality of the health, nutrition and education services in rural areas, addressing the problem of HIV aids and other major diseases, and support for local government decentralization and community driven initiatives targeted to the rural poor and vulnerable groups.

Facilitating rural and non-farm growth and competitiveness. These would involve support for: (i) improving the effectiveness of government through fiscal and governance reform; (ii) the adoption of

135

decentralized, participatory, and beneficiary-driven approaches designed to improve the delivery of rural infrastructure and services (drinking water and sanitation, irrigation, extension, micro-credit); (iii) the rationalization of expenditures in rural areas to focus on investments that meet the social and economic needs of the poor, including improving access to other key infrastructure (rural roads, electricity and markets); (iv) the reform of the policy and regulatory environment to foster more efficient input (fertilizer, seeds, land, credit, etc) and output markets (trade, agro-processing, rural industries) and greater participation of the private sector in rural areas; and (v) re-orienting public institutions for more social inclusiveness across income, gender and ethnic groups and to enhance their effectiveness in delivering services in agriculture, water, forestry, energy, health, education, finance, and infrastructure sectors and through government safety nets. These activities will build on supporting analytical work to draw lessons from past and best practice experiences in India and other parts of the world.

Fostering efficient, sustainable and equitable use of water resources. We will continue our support to the water sector, with increased emphasis on the adoption of a comprehensive and integrated approach to planning and management of water resources (surface and groundwater) on a multi-sectoral and river-basin level; fostering greater participation of users in the development and management of systems and in financing operations (cost recovery) to ensure longer term financial (and fiscal) sustainability, particularly for surface irrigation systems; and shifting the orientation of water agencies towards greater client orientation and the delivery of high quality water services.

Improving natural resource and environmental management. We will continue to support joint government and community management of natural resources (joint forest management and watershed management, fisheries) to ensure their sustainable development, use and management. In forestry, the program aims to improve the livelihoods of the rural poor, while keeping as priorities forestry protection and the provision of environmental services (including conservation of biodiversity). In fisheries, we will support the development

of efficient fisheries management systems that would balance both economic and environmental priorities. This would also include assistance to reduce the risks from, and to assist rural households to cope with, the damages caused by natural catastrophes such as floods, droughts and cyclones.

Notably, the above measures will also contribute not only to promoting growth and human development in rural areas, but to reducing the vulnerability and risks faced by the rural poor. In addition to risks brought about by natural catastrophes, increased reliance on markets, hastened by increased globalization, exposes the rural poor to a broader range of risks of income and other shocks. The Bank's assistance program described above will contribute to reducing the vulnerability of the rural poor in several ways. Ensuring more reliable and sustainable delivery of surface irrigation and ground water, drainage management, improved watershed management, rural infrastructure and agricultural support services will strengthen the capacity for the rural poor to increase and/or diversify their income sources as well as mitigate the risks brought about by droughts, floods and other weather related catastrophes. Support for greater clarity of security of property rights would permit greater access by the landless and the rural poor to land through better functioning land sales and rental markets. The Bank's assistance program would also involve reducing the vulnerability of the rural poor by securing access to forest resources and by diversifying the community asset base and sources of income. It would also include improved access to health services, education, nutrition, and safe water and environmental sanitation services, which would reduce household shocks due of ill health or death due to disease.

India, by virtue of its large size, population, and number of poor, occupies one end of the development assistance continuum. To meet its sizeable development needs, our program of rural development assistance to India is the most extensive in scope and scale in the Region (Table A3.2). Adopting a focused approach to a number of reform-minded States, the Bank's assistance program brings together a coordinated, multi-sectoral package of assistance at the State level, that aims to address in an

Table A3.2: Summary of Short to Medium Term World Bank Action Plan for South Asian Client Countries

Actions	India	Bangladesh	Nepal	Pakistan	Sri Lanka	Maldives	Bhutan
Enhancing Social and Human Capital Development							
Improving delivery of health, population and nutrition services	●	●	●	●	●	○	○
Improving access to and quality of education	●	●	●	●	●	●	●
Supporting poverty targeted community driven programs rural water supply) (self-help groups, credit, watershed and forest management,	●	●	●	●	●	○	●
Supporting socially inclusive decentralization and local governance	●	●	●	●	●	○	○
Enhancing effectiveness of safety nets for the rural poor	●	●	●	○	○	○	○
Facilitating Rural Farm and Non-Farm							
Decentralization and improved fiscal management and governance	●	●	●	●	●	●	●
Liberalization of land, input and output markets	●	●	●	●	●	●	●
Rationalizing public expenditures in agricultural sector	●	●	●	●	●	●	●
Improving access to rural infrastructure: markets, roads, electricity/energy	●	●	●	●	●	○	○
Strengthening access to rural services: credit and telecommunications	●	●	●	●	○	○	○
Improving delivery of agricultural support services (research, extension, livestock services, etc)	●	●	●	●	●	○	○
Fostering Efficient, Sustainable, and Equitable Use of Water Resources							
Strategic inter-sectoral planning and allocation of resources, policy reform and institutional restructuring of government agencies and greater user participation in management of systems, following a river basin approach	●	●	●	●	●	○	○
Supporting community based rural water and sanitation programs	●	○	○	○	○	○	○
Improving Natural Resource and Environmental Management							
Sustainable development and management of fisheries resources	●	○	○	○	○	●	●
Sustainable development and management of forest resources, watersheds, biodiversity	●	○	●	●	○	○	○
Disaster management/Coastal Management	●	●	○	○	○	○	●

integrated fashion the critical constraints to rural growth, development and poverty reduction. This integrated program rests on a package of sector specific interventions, that links investments to key policy and institutional reform, in tandem with adjustment assistance for overall improved state fiscal management and governance to increase the development effectiveness of government where it is needed. The sectoral interventions are primarily targeted at the poorest sections in rural areas of the state and attempts to reach the most vulnerable groups (women, children and scheduled castes and tribes). Our rural development and poverty reduction program for India would include non-lending and lending assistance for water, natural resources management, rural infrastructure and energy, agricultural support services, social (health, education, nutrition) and focused poverty reduction programs. Our lending activities will involve individual projects and multi-sectoral adjustment and/or investment operations. A common feature of these operations is the emphasis on community/beneficiary empowerment to make decisions on design and implementation. The Bank will also support selective assistance in critical areas (e.g. drinking water) in other States.

At the other end of the continuum are the small countries of Maldives and Bhutan. In coordination with other development partners and through non-lending and lending assistance, the Bank will be supporting fiscal and macro-economic reform and more selective programs of the government in the rural sector, focusing on rural infrastructure, and human development (education and health) and the sustainable use of fragile natural resources (fisheries in Maldives, land and forests in Bhutan).

In between are the medium-sized countries of Bangladesh, Nepal, Pakistan and Sri-Lanka, where the strategy for rural development and poverty reduction covers a broad range of non-lending and lending activities. In these countries, the Bank's assistance program encompasses several sectors: health, education, nutrition, agriculture, forestry, water, and infrastructure sectors , while also supporting broad fiscal, governance and policy and regulatory reform. Assistance for disaster mitigation and coastal management will be key part of our

program for Bangladesh. For these countries, our program will include non-lending and lending activities. Our lending activities will involve individual projects and multi-sectoral adjustment and/or investment operations.

The Bank will focus support on three critical areas of major regional concern. These are trade and food security, riparian water issues, and disaster management. We will provide technical assistance and support forums for fostering joint initiatives among various stakeholders.

Implementation

Implementation of Action Plans
One of the critical factors that has hampered achievement of the desired development outcomes from Bank assistance is weak or lack of ownership of the programs by country counterparts and project beneficiaries. This is a critical issue as the region is politically volatile resulting in changes in government and which in turn often results in frequent changes amongst senior bureaucrats/ technocrats/practitioners. Future investments supported by the Bank will be preceded by joint Bank and client government analytical and advisory activities (AAA) to understand the issues and to explore options for addressing them, drawing on local and international best practice experience. A key aspect of the AAA work would be assisting government with, and facilitating consensus building among all concerned stakeholders on the sectoral development strategies. It will also involve developing communication strategies for our AAA and identifying and working with "champions for change" who would lead the change process. Our investment assistance will be guided by these sectoral strategies formulated and owned by our client countries. In the case of rural water supply in India, for example, the World Bank contributed significantly in facilitating the process of consensus building on a sustainable approach to rural water supply development. In 1999, such a consensus was achieved in what is now known as the "Cochin Declaration."

Building on lessons learned and best practice approaches developed, in past projects and innovative pilots, and mainstreaming these into new projects, are critical elements of the Bank's implementation plan. The Bank will continue not only to support innovative and best practice approaches, but also to assist clients in scaling up successful and effective programs. For example, two areas, where considerable knowledge and successful experience have been accumulated and where there is considerable scope for replication and scaling up are the watershed and rural water supply development initiatives in India.

Within the Bank, we will work closely with other SAR colleagues to ensure that the constraints to rural poverty reduction are addressed adequately and in an integrated fashion in the Bank's country programs. We will work closely with them in the preparation of the poverty reduction strategy papers (PRSPs), country assistance strategies (CAS) and other ESW activities linked to rural poverty reduction and participate in the conceptualization and preparation of multi-sectoral national and sub-national operations (adjustment operations, poverty reduction support credits, and investment projects). It will also involve more active participation in country teams and country management team activities (e.g. sectoral strategy and PCD/PAD

Summary of Regional Consultations: South Asia Region

A3.6

South Asia engaged in a broad process of consultations to help prepare the regional strategy and action plan. The approach focused first on dialogue between the rural staff and their counterparts in each country. These discussions led to the production of country-specific strategies and action plans for rural development. These country-specific documents were then synthesized into a draft regional strategy and action plan, which was presented and discussed at a two-day workshop (February 28-March 1, 2001) in Kathmandu, Nepal. The workshop was attended by 50 participants including officials from Government, academic institutions, NGOs, private industry, and other donors. A small delegation from the World Bank also participated and independent consultants were appointed to facilitate the workshop. The workshop consisted of presentations of the global and regional rural strategies and action plans, country-specific and thematic breakout sessions, and a panel discussion on regional issues affecting South Asia. Open discussions (questions and answers) on these issues were interspersed throughout the two days.

Detailed proceedings from the workshop were prepared by the independent facilitators with support from the Bank. The main recommendations emerging from the workshop are stronger emphasis on:

- Empowering community level institutions and local governments: The regional and country strategies should be tailored (even more strongly than is currently the case) around the themes of community-based development and rural decentralization. Participation, capacity building of local institutions, and issues surrounding sustainability are all areas that should receive high priority.
- Alternative service delivery mechanisms: Governments should focus on the delivery of public good and services and create an enabling environment for CBOs, private sector, and NGOs to deliver private goods and services. Efficiency and sustainability objectives would be better met with alternative forms of delivery.
- Stakeholder identification and negotiations for natural resource management: Sustainable management of land, water, and forest resources requires proper identification of local stakeholders and local capacity to make plans and negotiate between competing uses. The role of government, NGOs, and the private sector is to facilitate this process. The approach will vary based on biophysical and sociocultural conditions.
- River basin management and user participation in water resource development: A holistic approach to water resource development and user participation in planning, implementation, and system operation and maintenance should characterize Bank support. Policy and institutional reforms and strengthening would be central to this assistance.
- Capacity building: Strengthening the capacity of central, state, and local government institutions was highlighted as an important comparative advantage of the World Bank.
- Regional issues: The World Bank is also well positioned to help the region address cross-country issues (e.g. water basin management, trade, food security, etc.). The Bank's role as a convener and honest broker between countries should be leveraged more effectively.

The final strategy and action plan incorporated these important findings.

reviews) to insure that rural issues receive adequate attention, including funding. The South Asia Region has had good success in knowledge sharing through AAA activities and in cross-sectoral participation in project preparation and implementation. We will continue to build closer cross-sectoral linkages and collaboration with our other SAR colleagues. We will also build closer links to the Rural Anchor and Thematic Groups, to draw on the knowledge-base on the experiences in other countries and regions. This will also ensure that the design of projects and programs incorporate global best practices.

In implementing the country action plan, we recognize the importance of committing to a longer-term horizon in some sectors, where significant policy and institutional reform is involved. This would require adopting a phased program of assistance that will build towards achieving longer-term goals. For example, this is particularly relevant to the restructuring process occurring in the water and agricultural support services (e.g. research, extension, livestock services) sectors.

We will encourage our clients to make more use of the project preparation facility (PPF) and technical assistance in developing and implementing innovative pilot activities that could eventually be scaled-up. The use of PPF in SAR has been negligible in the past.

The ambitious action plans to deliver the country strategies would require close collaboration with our partners in development, i.e. UN agencies, Asian Development Bank (ADB), bilateral donors and international and national NGOs. We will build on our experience of successful models of interagency cooperation. While being selective in our assistance (e.g. Nepal, Bhutan, and Maldives), we will aim to complement efforts of other donors.

Performance Indicators and Monitoring
We will assess the progress in implementing the action plan by monitoring performance in the following areas:

- adequacy of treatment of rural issues in the CAS and sectoral strategies;

- composition of teams addressing multi-disciplinary issues (lending and non-lending);
- completion of activities for building ownership (conferences, workshops, published reports and pace at which policy and institutional reforms take place); and
- progress in meeting the performance outcomes and development objectives of our rural lending program.

A regional consultation was held in March 2001 to discuss the new rural strategy. The major conclusions of that consultation are presented in Box A3.6.

ANNEX 4: **Water**

Water is an essential input into the production of food as well as into the livelihoods of rural communities and into the health of the ecosystems on which those communities depend. This strategy encompasses all aspects of water as a resource: soil and land management, watershed management, irrigation, drainage, environmental flows, and the management of the water resource itself. However, the strategy's primary focus is the irrigation and drainage subsector, which accounts for well over half the Bank's investments in rural space.[1]

Re-Visioning Irrigation

Irrigation is one key basis for agricultural development, which continues to be the main engine for broad-based rural development.[2] Irrigation was instrumental in the success of the Green Revolution of the 1960s and 1970s when food security was the objective. In the outcome, the Green Revolution not only averted famine, but also stimulated real economic growth beyond the agriculture sector. Today, however, we face a different prospect: changing global environment, declining performance of the irrigation sector, challenges emerging from outside the sector, and pressing social and environmental issues demand a new vision and a new strategy for irrigation and drainage. With the benefit of hindsight and the perspective of foresight, our strategy embraces economic growth as the primary objective of future irrigation investments but with the equally important linked goals of: (1) poverty reduction; (2) food security; and (3) environmental protection.

Irrigation, Food Security, and Poverty Reduction

Over the last three decades, the world's net irrigated area[3] has increased by 73%, from 150 million ha in 1965 to 260 million ha in 1995.[4] In developing countries overall, the proportion of the total water supply that is utilized for agriculture exceeds 85% of total diversions.[5] Today irrigated agriculture represents only 17% of the cropped land but provides 40% of the world food supplies. In 50 years global food production will need to double, yet there will be (at most) only 10% additional land in which to grow this food.[6] An increasing proportion of developing country food supplies is likely to be imported as agricultural trade barriers are lifted in many countries. Yet the efficient production of food for local consumption and for export will become even more essential in safeguarding food security. Considering present constraints on available physical and financial resources, additional production has to come from improvement of existing irrigated agriculture.

In many regions, irrigated agriculture is the primary source of rural employment. It offers higher productivity than rainfed agriculture and provides an opportunity to introduce higher intensity technology at lower risk. There are several ways in which enhancing the productivity of irrigated agriculture can benefit the poor both directly and indirectly. Firstly, targeting poor regions and focusing on farming systems and technologies most critical to the poor offers ways of delivering irrigation's benefits to those who are currently shut out. Secondly, greater empowerment of the poor can result from participation in management. Thirdly, new economic opportunities can be gained through increased private sector investments.

What Does the Current Bank I&D Portfolio Look Like?

Trends in Irrigation and Drainage Lending. As of January 2001, there are 58 active irrigation and drainage projects (agricultural irrigation (AI) classification) with a total commitment of $5,736M. The number of projects has remained stable during the last three years, but at a level roughly half what it was in the 1980s to early 1990s (Figure A4.1). The portfolio, both in numbers of projects and in pre-project commitment is expected to decline even further as the number of approved projects and the per-project cost are declining. Irrigation components within projects outside the AI portfolio (e.g., social funds, area development, etc) represent a growing feature, one that partly offsets the reduction in AI investments. A total of seven non-AI projects include an irrigation or drainage component totaling $368 million. Between 1975 and 2000 the average number (5-year moving average) of drainage projects dropped from 16 to 6, and investment levels of new project approvals

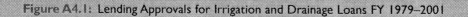

Figure A4.1: Lending Approvals for Irrigation and Drainage Loans FY 1979–2001

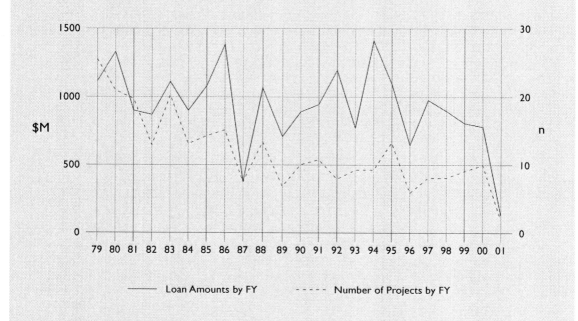

Figure A4.2: I&D in Active Portfolio, January 2001

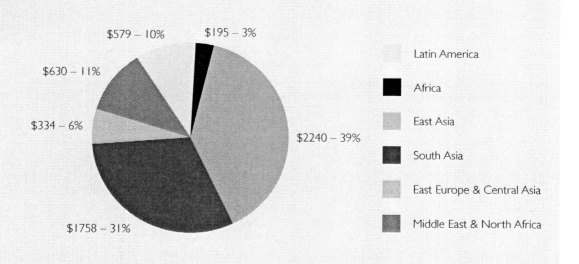

142

dropped from $1 billion (5 year average) to below $400 million.

The 1997 Irrigation Portfolio review indicated that Bank lending had shifted away from the development of new irrigated lands to rehabilitation and upgrading of existing systems. Many of the new projects emphasized sustainability and institutional issues in addition to infrastructure investments. The regional distribution of investment varies considerably, with EAP and SAR regions alone accounting for 70% of the total investment (Figure A4.2). Key findings from the active I&D portfolio review include the following.

Institutional Reform. The dominant reform which was introduced was federated water-user associations (WUAs), based partly on the Mexico model. This is particularly popular in South Asian and Latin American projects. Some transitional economies projects tend to emphasize financially autonomous utilities that sell bulk water to corporatized groups of water users. Relatively less has been done on restructuring of irrigation agencies and on private

sector participation within a context of broader national reforms.

Economic Incentives. The most commonly used incentives are water pricing (90% of projects) and user participation (59% of projects). However, in most cases 'water pricing' focuses mainly on various degrees of O&M cost recovery, instead of using it to signal the scarcity value of water. Relatively little has been done on recovery of investment cost. The OED report[7] acknowledged the role of water pricing (along with good management and appropriate fee collection) for ensuring efficient water service delivery by enabling system operation and maintenance—and thus meeting the Bank's poverty alleviation objectives. However, the Bank's water portfolio showed few pertinent examples, and most of those were outside the irrigation sector.

Poverty in the Irrigation Portfolio. Irrigation and drainage projects are increasingly focusing on poverty reduction as an explicit project objective. However, there is still a long way to go to integrate irrigation projects into the mainstream of the Bank's

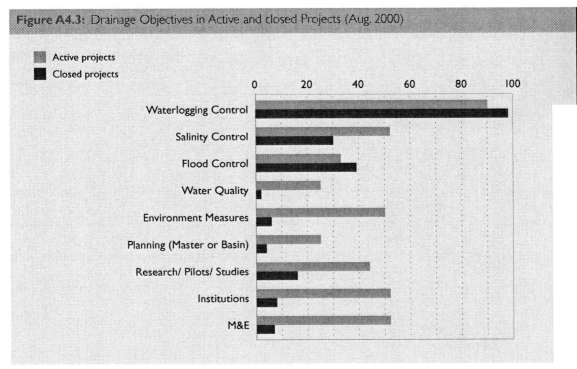

Figure A4.3: Drainage Objectives in Active and closed Projects (Aug. 2000)

- Active projects
- Closed projects

143

poverty reduction work. Of the 47 projects that became effective after 1997, less than half (47%) include any data on basic poverty issues.[8] Only 11% of the projects included special assistance components for the poor (usually in the form of matching grants for equipment purchases). Only 6% of the projects monitored the impact on small-farmer income, 23% included specific provisions to benefit women farmers. The OED report acknowledged that irrigation projects were effective in reaching the poor, however the perceived success was strongly affected by macroeconomic conditions.

Infrastructure Investment. Such investments did not address the changing needs of irrigation services within the basin framework. Rehabilitations of existing systems were mostly carried out to restore original project objectives rather than meeting current and future needs.[9] The declining investments in drainage can hardly be justified while many countries (e.g. India, Central Asia, East Asia's humid tropics and some countries of Latin America) have great potential to enhance their productivity through improved drainage.[10] On the other hand, projects in the active portfolio are becoming more environmentally strategic (Figure A4.3) with increased inclusion of salinity control, water quality improvements, environmental measures, planning, research, institutional aspects, monitoring and evaluation.

Challenges and Opportunities

Declining availability of renewable freshwater resources in terms of quantity and quality is the major problem facing development in the future. It is particularly so for irrigation, which consumes about 85% of the available water. Growing competition for the same resources from M&I and environment, combined with increasing trend of water pollution and impact of projected climate change, aggravates this problem. A WWF report[11] estimates that by 2025 countries in the Middle East, South Africa, parts of western India and northern China will not have sufficient water to meet all their irrigation needs.

Productivity and Irrigated Agriculture. In some expectations, irrigation water requirements will increase by 15% over the next 25 years.[12] The largest share of increased water supply for agricul-

ture must come from within the sector by increasing "use efficiency" through improved management practices and new investments. These include:

- **More crop per drop.** Water management on both farms and in delivery systems can be improved through the use of new technologies, reforms in management institutions, practices leading to real water gains,[13] greater attention to water rights, and the use of economic incentives. Improvements in crop genetics as well as in cropping patterns, cultivation methods, and soil-moisture management practices are also possible. Much of the increased production and increased value of production per unit of water consumption will come from these aspects. However, promoting deficit irrigation in water-scarce areas and improving yields in rainfed areas will also contribute substantially to the more crop per drop objective.

- **Pollution control.** Reducing waste loads in return flows from agricultural, municipal and industrial users can improve the availability of water for all uses, including agriculture (through reuse of treated effluent and agricultural drainage water).

- **Improving reliability of supplies.** Developing new storage to replace capacity lost to sedimentation and to save water lost during flood flows for use during times of scarcity, adopting a broader economic, social and environmental approach covering several sectoral uses and improving water supply infrastructure and services.

- **Utilizing the rainfed option.** Improving water management in rainfed agriculture (through flood control, drainage, water harvesting) can enhance productivity and in some cases obviate the need for conventional irrigation development.

Institutional Reform. Water management improvements entail significant adjustment in the institutional arrangements. Focus should be on identifying and characterizing institutional options that target:

- Managing irrigation within the context of integrated water resources management at the basin/sub-basin level. Priorities include the enabling policy environment, appropriate institutional structures, and land and water rights.

- Reforming public sector agencies that currently manage most of the world's large irrigation systems. This is arguably the number one priority for improving overall performance of the sector. They need to change into autonomous and self-financed agencies more directly accountable both to farmers and to civil society. In this context, benchmarking and related M&E, volumetric measurements, regulations, economic incentives, and water rights are key factors.

- Promoting private sector participation in service provision and irrigation investments guided by experiences from other sectors (water-supply and hydropower).

- Up-scaling user participation in irrigation management (notably through WUAs) and ensuring their professionalism and financial independence.

- Building capacity to reform policies and organizational structures is an important part of the reform process. The linkages between the institutional capacity to reform and the end result of the reform process are too important. In realizing this strategy the inputs of the World Bank Institute and other capacity-building partners (e.g., CAPNET) will be critical.

Environmental Sustainability. The future of irrigation development is tied in with the environmental problems related to irrigation management. Both the problems caused by irrigation and those that impact irrigation need to be addressed. Priority issues in this area include:

- Controlling waterlogging and salinity through improved water management and adequate drainage.

- Managing the disposal of drainage water to avoid mobilizing salts and agricultural chemicals, polluting downstream water bodies, and damaging wetlands.

- Regulating and monitoring abstraction of water for irrigation to ensure sufficient environmental stream flows and to avoid "mining" groundwater aquifers.

- Establishing appropriate rules and standards for managing the use/reuse of low quality water in irrigation.

- Creating a supporting environment and capacity for adaptation to climate change.

- Adopting environmental planning in the design of new irrigation and drainage schemes as well as in the modernization of existing ones.

Investments in Irrigation and Drainage Infrastructure. As a general rule, priority should be given to making better use of existing infrastructure. In this regard, the following issues should be addressed:

- Investing in modernization, rehabilitation and drainage to increase productivity and enhance growth without the need for additional land and water resources to extend irrigation to new areas. Such plans require characterization of the current systems to define the potential benefits due to improvement.

- Considering the high-need areas, particularly in Africa, and their urgent requirements for infrastructure development to provide access to water, as well as building the capacity to construct, maintain, operate and manage new and existing infrastructure. The challenge, particularly in Africa, is finding lower cost solutions that give greater emphasis to local technologies and participatory management.

- Using modern technologies that improve water productivity through more efficient conveyance systems, and most importantly, through better on-farm water applications and improved irrigation methods.

- Promoting technologies tailored for small holders. Affordable, small-scale technologies (e.g., treadle-powered and small-engine powered pumps and low-cost drip/sprinkler systems) have a particular role to play in the total effort to improve productivity and reduce rural poverty.

- Tapping the energy and dynamics of the private sector is a high priority for stimulating a demand for information and services that will lead to local investments and technology adoption.

Economic Viability and Social Sustainability of Irrigated Agriculture. This could involve the following:

- Crafting economic incentives (prices, subsidies, taxes) that recognize the opportunity cost of swater and water services as a key step in the overall reform process. Both the infrastructure (capital costs, operation, and maintenance) and the water itself require incentive systems to ensure sustainability.

- Giving greater attention to water rights that incorporate principles of equity within the context of customary rights; generate desirable economic, employment and environment effects; and provide a workable basis for water transfers among owners and uses.

- Ensuring that investments in irrigation are linked to the agricultural production systems in the client countries and associated with sufficient development of the rural infrastructure. Access to information and markets for agro-inputs and agro products, agricultural credits, farm roads, telecom services, etc. are basic requirements for realizing the full benefits of irrigation and drainage investments.

- Addressing the food prices and trade issues that prevent increases in productivity. Low global commodity prices depress the vibrant entrepreneurial energy that is needed to foster rural development. Implications of agricultural trade for water use need careful evaluation (virtual water). Trade arrangements should encourage water scarce regions to focus on production and export of high-value crops while importing water intensive lower value staple crops.

- Ensuring that marginalized segments of the farming population (including the poor, women, and ethnic minorities) stand to benefit from technologies tailored to very small land holdings, as well as from improving the performance and enhancing the productivity of large scale irrigation and through local decision-making arrangements (e.g., WUAs and participatory project design processes) that give greater voice to their interests.

- Using irrigation development as an opportunity to support the interests of rural women who use irrigation water directly (43% of the rural labor force is female) and indirectly (for household use and livestock).

Priorities for Bank Assistance

Given its comparative strengths, where can the Bank make a difference? Based on the experience gained and challenges facing the sector, as well as the demonstrated contribution of water users, NGOs, and the private sector to improving water management, there is a great need to pursue significant policy and institutional reforms. There is also an unprecedented opportunity for partnership in such a pursuit. In this regard, the Bank can:

1. Promote Productivity for Growth and Poverty Alleviation

- Facilitate the adoption of new technologies and water application practices that will improve irrigation efficiencies, sustain the resource base, save water, improve incomes, and enhance food security, keeping in mind the need to save "real" water and improve overall basin efficiencies. The Bank should also invest pro-actively, at the technical level in new approaches to irrigation and irrigated agriculture that will yield benefits disproportionately for the poor: small-scale drip and sprinkler systems and the knowledge for cultivating and marketing high value crops. Meanwhile, the Bank should continue to finance rehabilitation and modernization of irrigation and drainage infrastructure within a strategic framework of linked reforms that address the management failures symbolized by the faulty infrastructure and occurrence of waterlogging and salinization.

- Facilitate the adoption of new irrigation management techniques and practices. These include modernization of delivery and on-farm systems to meet current and future needs, rather than rehabilitation to restore the system to original

146

objectives. Support adoption of much-needed water measurement systems, benchmarking and performance standards. Given monopoly service providers in irrigation, measurement, M&E systems and user feedback are critical. New water management practices at the farm level include improved water application practices and installation of water measurement systems.

- Support drainage, flood control, and land remediation to improve output from low-productivity areas. Examples include lands that require drainage to permit double cropping of diversified crops, and lands damaged by salinity that require treatment to restore their productivity. Options and approaches that encourage the participation of local communities and farmers should be encouraged (e.g., Sodic Lands Project in Uttar Pradesh, India). Provide and disseminate best practices and lessons (e.g. from Australia, Egypt, Pakistan, Western United States) of drainage and salinity control from R&D for better design of strategies and programs; in particular, operating rules for water and salt management, drainage water disposal and reuse.

- Help meet the new challenges of using marginal water in irrigation through improving knowledge, institutional arrangements, building capacity, piloting and use of appropriate monitoring of economic and environmental effects.

2. Promote Irrigation Reforms Within a Basin/Sub-Basin Framework

- Help our clients address the competing interests of the multiple sectors involved in water resources development generally, and irrigation and drainage specifically. Improved management of irrigation and drainage must begin with this larger resource perspective. In this context, assist irrigation agencies to establish links with basin agencies, M&I and environmental interests to: a) jointly establish water allocation rules; b) prepare seasonal water management plans; c) negotiate agreed inter-sectoral re-allocation or water transfers. In relation to water allocation, some countries facing acute competition for water would require assistance in establishing water

rights and a forum for water users to negotiate management plans and potential water trades.

- Adopt a "demand-oriented" approach to helping our clients develop the capacity to introduce and sustain institutional and management reforms. The Bank can help engage our clients in a constructive policy dialogue to identify specific problems and possible solutions, and then provide expert assistance in formulating policies (e.g., water rights, water pricing, etc) or restructuring agencies (e.g., utility arrangements instead of departmental management). Through dedicated financing of capacity building activities (including strengthening university curricula on irrigation operations and management), or through technical assistance within larger project loans, the Bank can guide and accelerate the reform process.

- Provide specific support for innovative institutional reform pilots aimed at enhancing accountability of irrigation service provision, as well as the adoption of new institutional arrangements. The reorientation of irrigation agencies to focus on overall resource planning functions and the involvement of the private sector through management and service contracts, BOT or other appropriate arrangements (country specific) in irrigation operations management are important areas for study, piloting and sector-wide action.

- There has been some success with the promotion of the concept of user management in irrigation and drainage and thereby advancing operational and financial sustainability. The Bank can help actions towards empowering WUAs and up-scaling participation of farmers and communities in management and decision making. Further support can be extended through organized use of the wide network of consultants and international organizations with expertise in participatory irrigation management.

3. Stimulate the Reform Process Through:

- Linking irrigation reforms to broader issues of development and political economy. Irrigation and drainage reform efforts may have greater impact when linked to broader Bank (or other)-

147

financed investments in governance reform and decentralization. Internally this implies partnership with PREM, FPSI, and SDV (e.g., privatization and decentralization). In terms of clients, it implies greater interaction with ministries of finance, planning, environment, etc. Creating a national debate on search for options and adjustments in irrigated agriculture will provide the policy environment for specific interventions that bring irrigation reforms to the broader context of economic and political reforms in the country.

■ Linking irrigation strategy with agricultural strategy. In many countries, choice of agricultural strategy has serious implications for water use in irrigation. For instance, promotion of agricultural export strategies results in "virtual water" import or export. Systematic policy-oriented studies of impacts of agricultural policy choices on water consumption are critical for advising policymakers. Often much more "real" water savings can be achieved through focusing on crop genetics, cropping pattern and agricultural and irrigation practices that result in less evapotranspiration, than can be achieved through irrigation system efficiency improvements because much of the existing water losses in inefficient systems return to the surface or groundwater systems and therefore is not lost to the hydrologic system. The objective of achieving more crop per drop requires very close linkages between irrigation and agriculture strategies.

■ Knowledge and process. Designing reforms implies careful analysis and, most importantly, dialogue and capacity building among the relevant stakeholders. National dialogue on "water for food and rural development in the context of integrated water resources management" can be facilitated by the Bank, and organized by national agencies, institutes, or NGOs. The Bank's role could grow out of the approach we bring to such stakeholder consultation and sector work.

■ Sequencing and blending investments. The targets of irrigation and drainage investments include: a) policy adjustments; b) institutional reforms; and c) infrastructure and technologies. All three types of investments are needed simultaneously but at different intensities over time. Investments in infrastructure should be leveraged to advance institutional reforms over the short-term and be appropriately sequenced. Investments in policy need to continue. The Bank has the comparative advantage to help the client countries to design projects that are realistic in scope and objectives and programmatic in nature.

ENDNOTES

1 As used here, the terms "irrigation" or "irrigated agriculture" include the capture, use, disposal and/or re-use of water for agriculture.

2 Mellor, Keynote Address, Rural Week 2000.

3 The net irrigated area is defined as the area irrigated at least once during the calendar year (FAO 1999).

4 *The State of Food and Agriculture 1997* (FAO 1998).

5 *International Water Management Institute, Water for Rural Development,* (IWMI 2001).

6 L. Thompson, Keynote Address, Irrigation Institutions Workshop, December 11, 2000.

7 *Bridging Troubled Waters*. Assessing Water Resources Strategy since 1993, OED, December 2000.

8 The relevant "poverty issues" include data on land ownership, special project components targeting the poor, selection of poor regions for project benefits, monitoring income of the poor, focus on off-farm employment, a focus on livelihoods or well-being, and a particular focus on including women as project beneficiaries.

9 W. Easter, H. Plusquellec and A. Subramanian. 1998. Irrigation Improvement Strategy Review.

10 Vast tracks of once prime agricultural lands have been taken out of production over the past few decades, while only a small proportion of such lands have been treated and returned to agricultural use.

11 *Vision Report on Water for Food and Rural Development*. The Hague, 2000.

12 World Water Forum 2000, based on IFPRI and IWMI models.

13 For example, minimizing non-beneficial evapotranspiration in all water uses.

ANNEX 5: Physical and Social Infrastructure

The sustainable management of natural resources has traditionally been a basic pillar of the Bank's rural development strategy. This new strategy puts new emphasis on the importance of improved access to rural physical and human infrastructure.

Rural people of course have their own aspirations. It is important that assistance programs do not impose choices, but instead give rural people access to assets and the tools to manage those assets. It is also important to assist them in making informed choices for sustainable livelihoods. The more access rural people have to natural resources, infrastructure and human assets, the more livelihood choices they can make, thus reducing their risks and vulnerabilities.

Access to Rural Infrastructure

Despite widespread recognition of the potential impact of rural infrastructure investments, the rural areas' access to infrastructure remains low. A review of investments in 14 developing countries reveals wide disparities in infrastructure availability between rural and urban areas (Figure A5.1).[1] Average access to electricity in those countries is 46% in rural areas, compared with 89% in cities. In-house water taps are available to only 12% of rural households, compared with 59% of urban households. And only 8% of rural households have telephones, compared with 38% of urban households. The rural-urban disparity is true across all regions, except in the case of electricity in Eastern Europe and Central Asia.

There are three challenges to providing universal access to rural infrastructure.

- The first is how to ensure that infrastructure will be maintained. Because of the small number of beneficiaries normally served in rural areas, economic considerations dictate that infrastructure investments be designed to fairly low standards.
- The second is how to ensure that financing arrangements can be scaled up to universal coverage.
- The third is determining how to ensure the right balance between cost sharing and reaching poor communities.

The Bank and Rural Infrastructure. Rural infrastructure constitutes a substantial and growing component of Bank activities. Currently, over one-fifth of Bank lending in the rural sector is spent on infrastructure. That is substantially higher than the 1994 level of only 3% of total lending. Combined investments in rural transport and in rural water supply and sanitation account for 15% of rural sector projects and 20% of the funds approved for rural activities in FY 1999 and FY 2000. When other infrastructure sectors are considered—e.g., rural energy and rural telecommunications, as well as alternative multi-sector delivery arrangements (including, social funds and rural development funds)—the proportion is likely to be significantly larger—as much as 50 to 70% of total rural funding.[2]

That the actual value of investment is substantially higher than indicated by single-sector investment data is supported by a detailed analysis carried out by the Bank's Rural Development Group. This review of 500 projects approved Bank-wide in FY99 and FY00 found that more than two-thirds involved rural infrastructure or related activities, even though the majority of them were not identified as rural infrastructure projects. Notwithstanding this analysis, the Bank does not have a clear understanding of the size of the rural infrastructure portfolio. Most projects are not coded. As a result, the total amount of investment in rural infrastructure cannot be captured.

The focus and type of Bank lending for rural infrastructure have also changed. After the failure of centralized integrated approaches in the mid-1970s, the focus shifted to building infrastructure, with little or no attention paid to how infrastructure was to be operated and maintained in the long term. This resulted in short-lived projects. In response to the need to improve investment longevity, the concept of local participation was increasingly incorporated into rural infrastructure delivery, whereby communities became actively involved in project implementation. One study found that beneficiary execution of projects rose from nothing to 40% of rural infrastructure projects between the mid-1970s and the mid-1990s.[3]

Access to Rural Infrastructure: Percentage of Households in the Bottom Decile
with Infrastructure in the Home

Electricity (Percentage of Households)

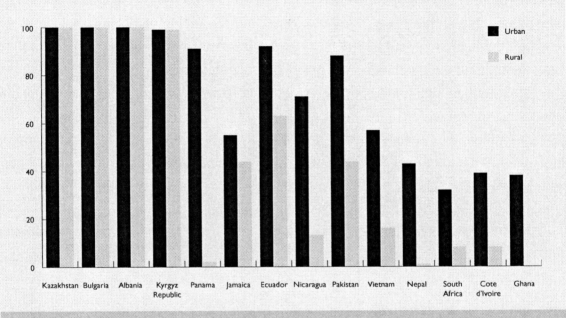

In-House Water (Percentage of Households)

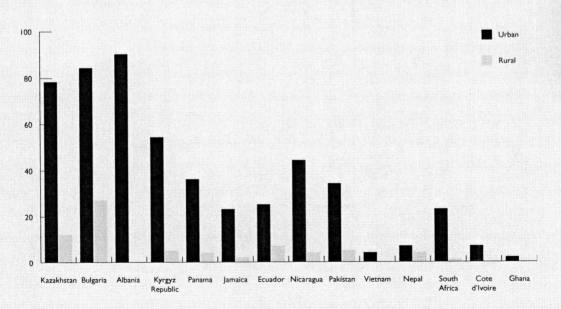

Notes: The Urban and rural households in each country were separately divided into deciles based on the per capita consumption of
each household. Albania does not include Tirana.
Source: World Bank LSMS surveys, as cited in Komives, footnote 1.

Increased emphasis on 'software' issues—i.e., training, capacity building, sustainability—has been accompanied by a shift to smaller subprojects, which increased from 20% to 60% of the portfolio during the same period. The consequence has been a focus on local-level actors and growing realization of the need to coordinate rural infrastructure projects with national decentralization strategies.

Actions for Developing Rural Infrastructure. Institutional and financing arrangements for rural infrastructure should be tailored according to: the nature of the service in terms of its public good versus private good characteristics (a rural road tends to be public in nature, an in-house electric connection a private good); and the scale of the service—whether the service helps a single community or many communities. As a rule, the potential for private sector interest in providing infrastructure increases as the activity shifts from public to private. A shift from smaller to more extensive coverage also tends to transcend community-based solutions.

Institutional Arrangements for Managing Rural Infrastructure. The dispersed nature of most rural infrastructure means that decentralized arrangements are a necessity; there is little sense in trying to manage the construction of village wells from the capital. But rural infrastructure services are also heterogeneous, ranging from energy grids to local health centers. Given this heterogeneity, decentralization cannot mean the same thing for all types of infrastructure. Similarly, the degree of decentralization may not be the same in all facets of the investment cycle (i.e., while planning and allocation should be highly decentralized, financing may need to be centrally driven).

To date, the involvement of the private sector in the provision of rural infrastructure has been limited, but growing evidence suggests that private sector partners can increase the efficiency and effectiveness of service delivery. Moreover, private sector management and financing of infrastructure services can relieve overburdened public resources and administrative capacity. Accountability is the key factor that argues for preferring the private over the public sector and local communities over regional

or national governments. But accountability cannot be taken for granted. Local communities are not less immune to corruption, incompetence and cronyism than central governments, and without competition and transparency the private sector is no guarantee of efficiency.

Financing Rural Infrastructure Services. Three broad principles should be applied in determining financing. First, adequate cost recovery is not only the simplest, but also often the only way to deal with lack of resources. Cost recovery is also critical to attracting 'profit-seeking' private sector investors. While subsidies to pay for operating and maintenance costs are often well-meaning attempts to address poverty, experience shows that they often do poor consumers more harm than good by forcing them to rely on alternatives that are more expensive than paying the full costs of adequate service. Achieving cost recovery for the delivery of some types of infrastructure services, such as rural electrification and feeder roads, can be a formidable challenge in rural areas with low populations densities and low income levels. Second, upfront contributions from beneficiary groups should be maximized, bearing in mind the affordability constraints of the poorest. Community contributions are an important component of any cost recovery strategy and increase the likelihood that decisions will be made in responsible fashion. There is little incentive for a community to turn down a cost-free investment, but if it has to make a significant contribution to the cost, it is more likely to think seriously about relative priorities. Third, promoting private sector provision of services must be complemented by simple and fair regulatory mechanisms, as well as effective financial intermediation.

Principles Behind Bank Actions in Rural Infrastructure. In the new strategy, Bank actions are envisaged as:

- promoting decentralized arrangements for providing infrastructure;
- facilitating private sector involvement;
- ensuring accountability in rural infrastructure projects; and
- ensuring adequate cost recovery and encouraging upfront contributions from beneficiary

groups to guarantee the sustainability of rural infrastructure investments.

Improved Education for Rural Populations

There are two educational needs in rural areas. The first is general education (primary and secondary schooling), while the second is education for agricultural and natural resource management. Empirical evidence shows that the social rate of return to primary schooling in most low-income countries is high (23%) and is substantially higher than the return on second and tertiary education (15 and 11%, respectively).[4]

Rural Primary Education. The divergence between the global goal of universal primary education and reality is especially stark in the rural areas of developing countries. There are also wide gaps in educational attainment between rural and urban children. In countries where cultural factors undervalue girls' education, male/female differentials in educational attainment create a further challenge. Girls in Central Africa, North Africa, and South Asia are at particular disadvantage.

Secondary Education. While universal primary education is of paramount importance, extending secondary school opportunities to rural areas is also critical and is likely to have high marginal returns. Secondary education is essential to maintaining a well-qualified supply of primary school teachers and also provides an incentive for children to complete primary school. But promoting secondary education in poor rural areas is hampered by the same supply and demand factors affecting primary schools. The opportunity cost of schooling increases as children get older and labor market opportunities increase. Since many rural communities cannot operate secondary schools efficiently, children have to travel long distances to get secondary schooling. Eliminating the gender gap in secondary education in rural areas is also difficult.

Agricultural Education and Training (AET). Education specifically for the management of farms and natural resources has played an important role in rural economic growth. AET systems range from those providing degrees in agricultural knowledge to extension services for farmers and extension staff in-service training. As agriculture grows, quality training is needed to maximize production efficiency and foster sustainable output. At the same time, it must be recognized that the value of extension services has diminished as farmers become more able to obtain information from the private sector.

The Bank and Rural Primary Education. The Bank has made appreciable contributions toward getting more children, both rural and urban, into school. Bank research has shown how to make better investments in schools, and the Bank's own investments have enlarged small-scale projects. It is difficult, however, to determine the volume of the Bank's educational investment. Project documents in the education sector seldom separate rural from urban data, and such analysis is further complicated because rural and urban environments are often not clearly distinguishable.

The Bank is committed to achieving free universal primary education. Rural development specialists need to ensure that the rural poor have access to a good primary education and better opportunities to get a secondary education. It is also important to ensure that governments distribute public funds for education in an equitable manner. There is also a need for closer collaboration between education specialists and rural development specialists. The CDF and the Poverty Reduction Strategy Papers generally focus on community-driven development, which is effective in providing access to public goods within the management capacity of community organizations.

Principles behind Bank actions in rural education. In the new strategy, Bank actions are envisaged as:

- placing great importance on achieving universal primary education;
- advocating gender equality in rural education;
- advocating quality improvements in rural schools;
- ensuring that public funds for education are distributed equitably;
- promoting closer collaboration between education specialists and rural development specialists;
- encouraging greater community participation in rural education;

- increasing investments in rural secondary education, particularly in countries close to attaining universal primary education;
- promoting literacy and training opportunities for unschooled rural adults; and
- ensuring that investments in agricultural training programs are in line with current needs.

Rural Nutrition and Health

Disease and illness are frequent consequences of living in poverty, while at the same time illness and disease are leading factors in pushing families into poverty. Communities routinely mention that poor health is a characteristic of the poorest.[5] Disease and illness also affect labor productivity and economic growth. The health and nutritional status of adults affect labor force participation and the intensity of work effort, while nutrition and health status affect the cognitive development of children.

A growing number of studies show the economic benefits of improving nutrition and health. Other studies reveal the significant negative impact of disease on economic growth. One study, for example, concluded that malaria reduces per capita GDP growth rates by at least 0.25% in the Sub-Saharan countries most affected by the disease.[6]

Trends in Rural Health and Nutrition. In developing countries the health and nutritional status of rural residents continues on average to be worse than that of urban populations (Figure A5.2).[7] Combining evidence on the global burden of disease with the fact that the majority of the poor still lives in rural areas indicates that communicable diseases and maternal, perinatal, and nutritional conditions are the primary causes of disability and death in rural areas. Non-communicable diseases, although on the rise, are less prevalent.

The prevalence of disease is closely related to socioeconomic status. Low family income, cramped living conditions, low maternal education, low occupational status, and unclean living conditions, for example, have all been associated with increased risk of diarrheal morbidity and mortality.[8] Malaria and tuberculosis are also closely linked to poverty.

HIV/AIDS is also a formidable challenge in rural areas. There are currently 36 million people with

154

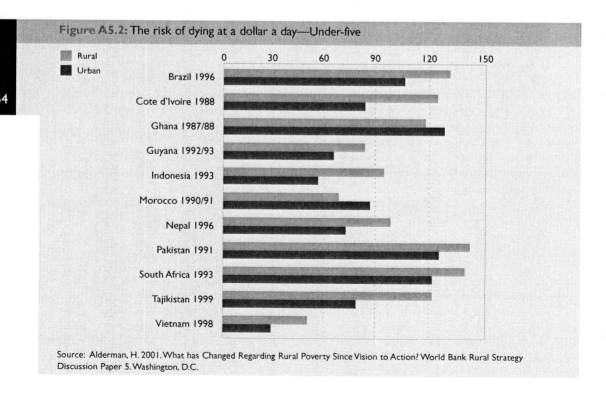

Figure A5.2: The risk of dying at a dollar a day—Under-five

Source: Alderman, H. 2001. What has Changed Regarding Rural Poverty Since Vision to Action? World Bank Rural Strategy Discussion Paper 5. Washington, D.C.

HIV/AIDS, of whom some 5.3 million became infected in 2000.[9] Currently, the region most affected is Sub-Saharan Africa, where approximately 9% of the adults carry the disease. However, it is estimated that by 2010 Asia will overtake Sub-Saharan Africa in absolute numbers.[10] Although HIV/AIDS has traditionally been regarded as an urban problem, it is gradually being recognized that rural communities are perhaps more vulnerable to the problem. In the 25 most-affected African countries, for example, more than two-thirds of the victims live in rural areas.[11] The costs of HIV/AIDS are largely borne by rural communities because many urban dwellers, at least in Africa, return to their village when they become ill.

Rural areas are also the scene of widespread malnutrition, which compromises natural immunity and contributes to the disease burden. In 1995, an estimated 36% of children under 5 years of age in developing countries were stunted. It is predicted that stunting will be reduced to 29% by 2005. This would represent a decline from 182 to 165 million children, which is still an unacceptable number, and there is mounting evidence that child malnutrition rates are stagnating or increasing in Sub-Saharan Africa. Childhood malnutrition rates are generally higher in rural than in urban areas.

Adult malnutrition in developing countries has serious repercussions since the health of working-age adults is an important determinant of household income. Recent evidence on fetal malnutrition and low birth-weight further stresses the importance of adult health and especially maternal nutrition status. Regionally, adult malnutrition appears to be particularly widespread in South Asia and Sub-Saharan Africa. Data from Bangladesh, for example, reveal that 54% of rural women were underweight. In Africa, the prevalence of adult malnutrition appears to be considerably less than in Asia, ranging from 21% of rural women in Madagascar to about 9% in Côte d'Ivoire.[12]

Challenges to Improving Rural Health. Rural residents in developing countries typically have less access to healthcare than urban populations. Data from a survey in Ghana, for instance, reveals that while the average distance to healthcare facilities in rural areas was 4.8 miles, it was 0.6 miles in urban areas.[13] Many children in rural areas do not get basic immunizations. Large percentages of women in rural areas do not receive antenatal care and are not attended by skilled personnel during childbirth.

Even when health services are accessible in rural space, they often offer low quality services and hence are underutilized. Income and time constraints pose additional barriers to healthcare for rural people. Rural facilities generally have difficulty attracting staff and often fail to have essential drugs and other supplies available. A study comparing geographic imbalances of physicians in 12 least developed countries found that only 3 of the 12 had a rural physician to population ratio that was better than 5% of the urban ratio. In 14 other developing countries included in the study, none had a rural physician to population ratio greater than 41% of the urban ratio.[14]

Poor rural infrastructure contributes to the burden of ill health in rural areas. Clean water and adequate sanitation are key to reducing the threat of waterborne diseases. Roads are critical in ensuring access. Electricity is essential for the operating of health centers and maintaining the cold chain for vaccines.

The World Bank and Rural Health. The Bank has long recognized that effective health services are critical links in the chain of events that allow developing countries to break out of poverty. The Bank's recent work in this area ranges from improving immunization and healthcare for children to improving access to clean water and sanitation. As the Bank increases the poverty focus of its projects, it is likely that the rural population will benefit proportionately more. The traditional prescriptions for improving nutrition and food security, such as increasing agricultural productivity and ensuring that national policies do not excessively tax,the agricultural sector, remain valid. However, the strategies recommended attempt to go beyond the traditional solutions to improve health and nutrition.

155

Principles behind Bank actions in rural health. In the new strategy, Bank actions are envisaged as:

- increasing collaboration with the health and nutrition sector as well as the education sector, so that rural development specialists can help to improve the health and nutrition of the rural poor;
- advocating the interests of the rural poor to ensure that government resources for health are not biased toward urban constituents;
- promoting community-driven cross-sectoral approaches to improving health and nutrition as these are likely to yield high returns;
- placing greater emphasis on food-based strategies to improve dietary quality and micronutrient status; and
- promoting the status of women in rural development to improve rural health and nutrition.

This last point is of special importance. As primary caregivers, women are key to improving health and nutrition, but their ability to invest in their own and their children's health and nutrition is hampered by their lack of control over household incomes, their poor education, and the health risks arising from their reproductive role. Currently, rural women produce between 60 and 80% of the food in most developing countries, but they continue to be disadvantaged in terms of access to land and non-labor inputs, such as fertilizer, credit, and extension services.

ENDNOTES

1   Komives, K., Whittington, D., and Wu, X. 2000. Infrastructure Coverage and the Poor: A Global Perspective. Infrastructure for Development: Private Solutions and the Poor. Conference Paper, 31 May–2 June 2000. London.

2   This value is extrapolated from a comprehensive study of the 1999 portfolio of rural water supply and sanitation projects. This study by the Bank's Infrastructure group showed that 25 Rural Water Supply and Sanitation projects worth a total value of $700 million were approved in 1999. However, only 4 (combined value $300 million) were focused single sector projects—the rest were under taken by a variety of sectors, predominantly as multi-sector social funds and rural development funds. This suggests that only 16% of the portfolio (by number of projects) and 43% of total funds (by project value) were single-sector projects, with the weight of the portfolio 'hidden' as multi-sectoral interventions. It is likely that the same scenario exists in the other infrastructure sectors, particularly in rural roads and to a lesser extent in rural energy and telecommunications.

3   Pouliquen, L. 2000. *Infrastructure and Poverty*. The World Bank. Washington, D.C.

4   Psacharopoulos, G. 1994. "Returns to Investment in Education: A Global Update." *World Development*. 22 (9): 1325–43

5   Narayan, D.; Patel, R.; Schafft, K.; Rademacher, A.; Koch-Schulte, S. 2000. *Voices of the Poor: Can Anyone Hear Us?* Published for the World Bank, Oxford University Press, New York, N.Y.

6   McCarthy, F.D.; Wolf, H.; Wu, Y. 2000. *Malaria and Growth*. World Bank Policy Research Working Paper 2303. World Bank, Policy Research Department, Washington, D.C.

7   One should, however, be aware that looking at aggregate statistics on rural versus urban health masks the fact that the health of the urban poor is often as bad or worse than that of rural populations.

8   Jamison, D.T.; Mosley, W.H.; Measham, A.R.; Bobadilla, J.L. (eds.) 1993. *Disease Control Priorities in Developing Countries: A Summary*. World Bank. Washington, D.C.

9   UNAIDS (Joint United Nations Programme on HIV/AIDS). *AIDS Epidemic Update: December 2000*. [http://www.unaids.org/wac/2000/wad00/files/WAD_epidemic_report.PDF]. April 2001.

10 Barnett, A.; Rugalema, G. 2001. *HIV/AIDS, Health and Nutrition: Emerging and Reemerging Issues in Developing Countries*. IFPRI 2020 Focus 5 Brief 3. IFPRI Washington, DC.

11 FAO. 2001. *AIDS a Threat to Rural Africa*. [http://www.fao.org/Focus/E/aids/aids1–e.htm.] March 26, 2001.

12 World Bank. 2001. *Country Reports on Health, Nutrition, Population and Poverty*. [http://www.worldbank.org/poverty/health/data/index.htm] March 2001.

13 Lavy, V.; Strauss, J.; Thomas, D.; de Vreyer, P. 1996. Quality of Health Care, Survival and Health Outcomes in Ghana, Journal of Health Economics 15: 333–357.

14 Blumenthal, D.S. 1994. Geographic Imbalances of Physician Supply: An International Comparison. *The Journal of Rural Health* 10(2): 109–118.

ANNEX 6: Natural Resources

Lessons learned from past Bank Natural Resource Management (NRM) activities confirm the strong relationship between resource degradation and poverty. For one thing, natural resource degradation significantly increases the level of poverty. For another, the lack of income sources for investments in natural resource management by the poor often leads to increased resource degradation. For the most part, though, these resource-degradation phenomena can be attributed to either market or government failures. The following are brief summaries of the extent of the degradation of four of the principal resources (land, water, forests and biodiversity). Also, included are projections relating to the effects of climate change.

Land

Most of the land available to meet current and future food requirements is already in production; any further expansion must necessarily involve fragile and marginal lands. This is particularly so in developing countries where population growth is high, poverty is endemic, and existing institutional capacities for land management are weak.

Only about one-third of the world's land is generally suitable for sustainable arable cropping, with perhaps another third suitable for sustainable rangeland use. Land that is not really suitable for agriculture requires intensive labor or maintenance (as on slopes), or is highly prone to erosion, (steeply sloping), or is not amenable to mechanization (too stony, too steep). On these lands, agriculture may be feasible for a few years by people lacking alternatives, after which the topsoil will be lost or exhausted and the land will be abandoned. For these reasons there is a severe limit to the expansion of the land area suitable for agriculture. At the same time, some suitable land is being lost in an irreversible manner by degradation.[1]

The sources of market failure involved in such degradation are several. Insecure property rights in the land resource is a major problem in many countries (such as Ethiopia), whereby the usual custodial roles of farmers are compromised by an obligation

to have exceedingly short planning horizons in their use of the land. In more arid areas where pastoralism may be a dominant land-use, and where regulatory controls are limited, similar situations contribute to processes of desertification. Failures to produce sufficient public goods in the form of better understanding of such processes is yet another source of market failure. Externalities associated with practices of farmers high in a catchment, with disregard for the downstream consequences of their actions for other farmers and other water users, is another important source of market (and sometimes too government) failure frequently encountered. Such diverse sources of market failure provide scope for cogent policy analysis and intervention, as is also noted for the other resource categories discussed below.

Overall current trends indicate that land has become a limited natural resource, and that it is being rapidly depleted. This depletion is still only moderate in AFR and LCR, strong in EAP, and severe in MNA and SAR. In three of the regions, land that is not suitable for sustainable agricultural production is currently being cropped, or will have to be cropped in the future. While AFR and LCR have still much land that could be brought into cultivation, major investments and socioeconomic changes would be required to convert those lands to arable farming, and due account must be taken of the environmental costs of any such conversion. Many such lands are forests or wetlands with significant option value for their biodiversity and other environmental (including global climate-related) values, and therefore they are candidates for conservation rather than conversion to agricultural land.

The review of regional land-use developments indicates that the situations in EAP, MNA and SAR call for major interventions to reduce further degradation, and that massive food imports are the only alternative to meet current and future demands.

In areas with marginal agriculture but where cropping could be sustainable, interventions are required to improve the prospects for economic returns to land management investments by farmers thus reducing land degradation. But on lands where agriculture will be unsustainable in the long run, non-farm employment and income generation programs will be required. At the same time, strong intensification of production in favorable areas is an effective way to increase food security and, in areas where most suitable land is already used, is the only real food-supply option, in addition to international food trade.

In AFR there is still adequate and suitable land for agriculture. However, there is the problem of inaccessibility, and constraints to human settlement due to climate and diseases. The situation in EAP indicates that the region as a whole is close to utilizing all suitable land for cultivation, and that since population distribution and activities are not homogeneous, increasingly, land is being cultivated in a manner that is ecologically unsustainable.

LCR is, of course, a highly heterogeneous region. it's the relative size of South America means that it rather dominates Central America in the regional picture, although the degradation problems in the latter are typically more severe.

Water

Water is the key ingredient for life, and its interaction with land and forests provides the refuge for all terrestrial species. Water use is often categorized as agricultural, domestic, or industrial. In recent years the environmental use of water for aquatic habitats has become important. Water is distributed across countries and regions very unevenly. At one extreme, LCR with only 8% of world's population is endowed with 34% of the world's total renewable water resources, while at the other extreme, SAR with over 20% of the world's population has only 5% of the renewable water resources. An increasing number of countries are suffering from water stress (insufficient water supplies for sustainable use) as populations rise and aquifers are exploited at faster rates than they are replenished. Water scarcity leads to increased competition between sectors and increases the potential risk of damage to ecosystems from which water is withdrawn and where return flows are discharged. This situation raises

alarming concerns about managing the competing demands of the different sectors in an integrated framework (Box A6.1).

Agriculture is the largest single user of water, accounting for 74% of the total amount withdrawn in 1995. Irrigation increases agricultural productivity and was a primary factor (along with high-yielding varieties and fertilizers) in the success of the Green Revolution from the 1960s to the 1980s. It is pertinent to pose the question, can today's rural development challenges be met through a second Green Revolution? The countries most in need of help no longer enjoy the surpluses of water that characterized the period of the initial Green Revolution. The opportunity cost of irrigation water is much higher today, not only because of scarcity within the agriculture sector, but because of much higher competition from other sectors vying for the use of the same water. Projections indicate that water withdrawal for agriculture will not exceed 67% of the total water supplies in 2025. The biggest challenge will be to increase agricultural productivity with less water available for irrigation.[2]

Environmental impacts of irrigation water are significant, and there are enormous potential payoffs from improved environmental management. Waterlogging and salinization are the most pervasive threats from irrigated agriculture; about 80 million hectares of the world's irrigated lands suffered from salinization by the late 1980s. Discharges of saline effluent from irrigated lands have caused serious downstream environmental problems (as in the case of the Aral Sea Basin and Indus Basin). As agriculture is forced by other sectors to reduce its use of freshwater supplies, reuse of treated wastewater and agricultural drainage water will continue to increase. In Jordan, 20% of the irrigation water is treated wastewater with a potential to increase to 60% by the year 2025. Egypt reuses about 7 billion cubic meters of agricultural drainage water in irrigation. This trend involves economic, environmental and health risks due to the high contents of salts, nutrients, sediments, agricultural chemicals and pathogens.[3]

Since water is critical for human survival, it can be characterized as a public good, and public authorities in most countries have assumed central responsibility for its overall management. Reliance on market forces alone will not yield satisfactory outcomes. At the same time, however, government actions often cause serious misallocations and waste of water resources. Three problems related to government activities are of particular concern: (a) fragmented public sector management that has neglected interdependencies among government agencies and jurisdictions; (b) reliance on overextended govern-

ment agencies that have neglected financial accountability, user participation, and pricing while not delivering services effectively to users and to the poor in the particular; and (c) public investments and regulations that have neglected water quality, health, and environmental consequences.

Problems related to scarcity of water resources continue to increase. Policies for development of water resources are also undergoing change. The current environment for water resources policy can be captured by the following key observations:

- the best sites for the construction of large dams and reservoirs have already been developed;

- the growing demands for fiscal austerity in most countries have stimulated interest in least-cost alternatives for meeting water needs;

- there is heightened public awareness and concern about the environmental impacts related to the construction of hydraulic infrastructure, particularly dams; and

- increasing competition by various sectors for scarce water resources adds further pressure to water development decisions.

These changes have caused a fundamental shift in the way that water resources development is considered—a shift from relying on construction, as a means for solving water needs to a reliance on improved policies and management as the solution. The strategy of achieving substantive improvements in water-use efficiency and water quality through better policies and management relies heavily on detailed knowledge on which management decisions can be based, and on a system of management, which can implement the decisions taken. Most developing countries are markedly deficient in both respects. Information needs for effective management include data on how water is presently used, interactions between water-use sectors and users along a watercourse, equity/poverty considerations, conditions of water supply, accurate and timely forecasts of meteorological events, alternative institutions for water management (e.g., basin planning organizations and water markets), and conditions requisite for their effective operation. Management needs include the institutional structures (policies, organizations) for implementing water management and also the governance resources for reforming the existing institutional structures.

Forests

Forests, woodlands, and scattered trees have provided humans with shelter, food, fuel, medicines, building materials, and clean water throughout recorded history. Forests have recently also become sources of new goods and service—including pharmaceuticals, industrial raw materials, recreation and tourism. Forests regulate water quality by slowing soil erosion, and filtering pollutants, and they help regulate the timing and quantity of water discharge. In addition, protection of forests, afforestation and reforestation also play very important roles in preventing and reducing land degradation.

Forests cover about 25% of the world's land surface, excluding Greenland, and Antarctica. Global forest cover has been reduced by at least 20% since pre-agricultural times and possibly by as much as 50%. Forest area has increased slightly since 1980 in industrial countries, but has declined by almost 10% in developing countries. Tropical deforestation probably exceeds 130,000 km2 per year, and perhaps the greatest threats to forests currently are conversions to other forms of land use. These include fragmentation by agriculture, logging, road construction and mining. Mining is notably responsible for opening up intact forests to pioneer settlements, and to increases in hunting, poaching, fires, and exposure of flora and fauna to pest outbreaks and invasive species.[4]

Although human actions have caused the world's forest cover to shrink significantly over the past several millennia, precise measurements of this shrinkage are difficult to make. FAO in its 1997 forest assessment, attributes the principal causes of forest loss in the various regions of the world as follows: a) Africa—the expansion of subsistence agriculture under pressure from rural population; b) Latin America—large scale cattle ranching, clearance for

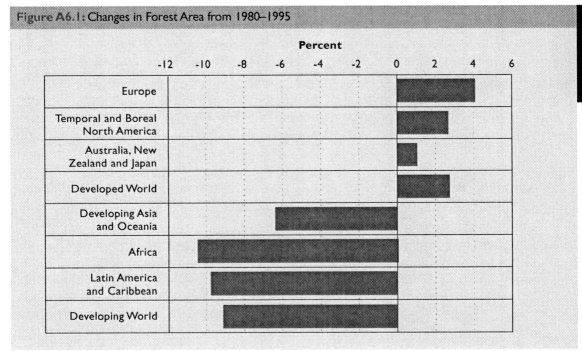

Figure A6.1: Changes in Forest Area from 1980–1995

161

■ Facilitating access to credit for beef cattle, mechanized agriculture, and large-scale forest and tree crop plantations in areas with substantial natural forests promotes forest conversion and provides limited long-term local employment.

■ Reducing poverty at the forest margin through improved market access, technology, and credit supply can potentially increase forest conversion by attracting migrants to the forest frontier.

■ Agricultural research and technology transfer will tend to encourage forest conversion when it promotes innovations that are: a) capital intensive, b) applicable to agricultural frontier situations, c) for export products, and d) used by farmers who face few labor or capital constraints.

■ Irrigation investments and infrastructure and support services for labor-intensive fruit, vegetable, dairy, and flower production outside frontier regions can offer alternative sources of employment and reduce migration to agricultural frontiers.

■ Policies favoring small-scale agriculture in areas with little natural forest can discourage migration to the agricultural frontier. Forest fragments and planted trees in these areas often provide substantial environmental services and forest products.

■ Eliminating fertilizer subsidies in regions where they influence farmers' decision whether to use more or less land-extensive cropping systems can lead to greater forest clearing.

■ Directed settlement not only leads to forest clearing but also rarely appears cost effective in the medium-term. In the longer-term, it may raise small farm incomes and regional production. Long-term effects on land concentration and the sustainability of local agriculture vary.

■ Uneven land distribution associated with production systems that provide limited employment may encourage poor rural families to migrate to forested areas. Under these circumstances, providing tenure security will only lock in existing inequalities.

■ Poorly designed agrarian reform policies can endanger forest remnants on large landholdings by either stimulating large landowners to remove forest or transferring land to smallholders under conditions that induce them to do so.

■ Tenure security promotes long-term investment. Whether this favors forests depends on what producers invest in. They may either invest in planting trees and managing natural forests or in converting forests to agricultural use. Making forest removal an explicit or implicit precondition to obtain ownership security promotes that activity.

■ Land taxes that favor reforestation, conservation, and intensive land uses over extensive agriculture can promote sustainable land use, but are difficult to implement and most countries exempt smallholders from payment.

■ Recognition of indigenous territorial rights reduces pressure on forests, at least in the short term. These groups lack the means to engage in highly destructive agricultural and forest activities and may refrain from doing so due to cultural factors and local regulatory norms. Nevertheless, timber sales to external purchasers can lead to forest degradation.

Source: David Kaimowitz and Arild Angelsen. 1999. The World Bank and Non-Forest Sector Policies that Affect Forests. Background Paper World Bank Forest Policy Implementation Review and Strategy. Center for International Forestry Research (CIFOR), Bogor Indonesia.

government-planned settlement schemes, and hydroelectric reservoirs; c) Asia—pressure from subsistence agriculture and economic development schemes, equally (Figure A6.1).

Growing road networks are a prime cause of forest fragmentation, resulting in two significant areas of impact: a) the direct effect on species biodiversity by diminishing the amount of natural habitat available, blocking migration routes, providing avenues for invasion by non-native species, and changing the microclimate along the remaining habitat edge; b) the indirect effect by providing access for hunting, timber harvest, land clearing and

other human disturbances that further change the characteristics of the local ecosystem.

In addition to outright conversion and fragmentation of forests, a third human-related pressure is fires. Wildfires are a natural and necessary phenomenon in many forest ecosystems, helping to shape landscape structure, improve the availability of soil nutrients, and initiate natural cycles of plant succession. In fact some plant species cannot reproduce without periodic fires. The human-related fires, however, greatly exceed naturally occurring fires in their frequency and intensity. Some are set intentionally for timber harvesting, land conservation, or shifting agriculture. Fires also result from disputes over property and land rights.

There is no single answer to the question as to what causes deforestation and forest degradation. Due to the complexity of the issues, the indirect nature of many of the causal relations involved and the wide diversity of situations, it is difficult to generalize. However, in many cases, inappropriate policies and market failures often lead to inappropriate forest clearing and degradation of forest resources as well as increased poverty. Often those who use the forest, or who cause negative impacts do not have to pay, or pay too little for the use of this resource or for the damage they cause. Governments have often not been effective in introducing economic and institutional (regulatory) measures to tackle market failures (Box A6.2).[5]

Despite significant resource flows, international concern, and political pressure, the potential of forests to reduce poverty, realize economic growth, and be valued for their contributions to the local and global environment has not been realized. A combination of market and institutional failures has led to forests failing to contribute as significantly to rural incomes, economic growth, or the local and global environment as would be possible under good economic and technical management. Instead, the forest sector often demonstrates the failure of markets and governance to capture the full value. Forests have often been disregarded in economic policy or considered a resource to be plundered for short-term gain and at the expense of rural people who depend on forest resources for their livelihoods. It is not surprising that forest policy has become one of the most controversial and heated issues in development.

Biodiversity

Biodiversity lies at the heart of sustainable agricultural systems. Agriculturists have created an impressive storehouse of knowledge through the development of landraces—genetically distinct varieties of crops—and complex techniques to select store and propagate valued species. The Tzetal Mayans of Mexico for example can recognize more than 1,200 species of plants that can be used for agricultural,

medicinal and spiritual requirements. In the soil, a wide range of organisms from fungi to beetles provide nutrient cycling and the fertility crops require, while flying insects, bats, and other species perform essential pollination services and help protect crops from increases in pest populations.

The findings of a study entitled the "Global Biodiversity Assessment" suggest that the earth contains some 14 million different species, the majority living in tropical forests and marine systems. Despite recent significant investments in biodiversity studies, it is believed, that decades, if not centuries, of further research will be required to provide anything more than the most rudimentary level of information regarding these species. Existing knowledge, however, provides some measure of appreciation of the extent of the diversity that exists, for example, roughly 3,000 bacteria have been scientifically described (although a recent study of one gram of forest soil in Norway uncovered 5,000 seemingly different species), and barely eight million species of insects even have a scientific name.

While our knowledge of nature's diversity is extremely meager, there is enough evidence that this heritage is being rapidly eliminated, with adverse consequences for natural products and sustainable use for economic activities. There is evidence of an "extinction momentum" in the earth's biodiversity with present rates of losses in the range of one to ten thousand times higher than historical rates. For example, 12% of all mammals and 11% of all bird species are threatened with extinction. Also, 52% of freshwater fish species are declining, while only 11% are increasing. With regard to habitat degradation, there is evidence that 58% of the coral reefs are degraded, and over 80% of the world's mangroves have disappeared, while 50% of all wetlands have been lost.[6]

It is important to recognize the root causes of biodiversity and habitat loss, and the relationship between specific socioeconomic factors and the environment. The consensus is that these root causes may fall into the following five categories: a) demographic changes; b) poverty and inequality; c) public policies, markets and politics; d) macroeconomic policies and structures; and e) social change and development.[7] It is important to emphasize that the losses, generally speaking, are occurring at the local level. They result from such things as farmers clearing trees for new land to plant crops, timber companies opening forests for logging, and hunters gathering game meat for urban markets. In various ways the factors listed above lead to loss of biodiversity essentially because the value of biodiversity, to the global society and the national society, is not recognized sufficiently by market forces. In other words, those who make decisions affecting biodiversity (farmers, logging companies, etc.) do not consider the loss as part of their cost. This market failure is not always fully resolved by government actions (e.g., conservation). In some cases, national government is reluctant to bear a high cost on behalf of the global community, or on behalf of future generations.

In the area of agricultural biodiversity, which is of primary importance for agricultural growth and productivity, the past century has seen an erosion of the genetic resources needed to sustain agricultural production, leaving the world's food supply more homogeneous and vulnerable to pests and diseases. Of the world's major food crops, just three—rice, wheat and maize—account for 60% of the world's caloric intake. The tremendous gains in yield since the Green Revolution have come at a cost of greater dependence on fertilizers and pesticides, reduced diversity, and reliance on a narrower gene pool.

Climate Change

With regard to agriculture and climate change, evidence shows that the past two decades have been the warmest in the past 100 years. Climate change caused by human activities (primarily burning of fossil fuels, deforestation, and agricultural activities) is already occurring, and further climate change is inevitable.

There is evidence that manmade greenhouse gases have probably already contributed most of the observed warming over the past 50 years. Unless concentrations of these gases are stabilized, the probable rise in their concentrations in the atmosphere could mean:

- severe water stress in the arid and semi-arid land areas in Southern Africa, the Middle East and Southern Europe;
- decreased agricultural production in many tropical and subtropical countries resulting from increases in temperature;
- higher worldwide food prices as supplies fail to keep up with the demand of an increasing population;
- increased vector-borne diseases, such as malaria, in tropical countries;
- major changes in the productivity and composition of critical ecological systems, particularly coral reefs, and forests; and
- increased risk of flooding and landslides due to rising sea levels and increases in rainfall intensity in coastal areas.

Predictions that climate change will mean severe flooding of coastal areas, an increase in storms and heavy rains in some regions, and more rapid desertification in others have enormous implications for agricultural productivity, water resources and natural ecosystems.[8]

Investments in programs for better management of these and other major climate change effects should be in three key areas: a) mitigation of green house gas emissions; b) reduction of vulnerability and adaptation to climate change; and c) capacity building to promote and implement these interventions.

ENDNOTES

1 The International Board for Soil Fertility Research and Management (IBSRAM). 2001. *Land Degradation in Selected Regions and Some Consequences for Rural Development.* Background Study, IBSRAM Bangkok, Thailand, p20.

2 The International Water Resources Management Institute (IWMI). 2001. *Water for Rural Development.* A Background Paper prepared for the World Bank. IWMI, Colombo, Sri Lanka, p94.

3 S. Abdel-Dayem. 1999. Sustainability of Low Quality Water Use in Agriculture. Keynote address, International Congress on Irrigation and Drainage, Granada, Spain, September 1999.

4 The World Bank. 2001. *Forest Policy Implementation Review and Strategy.* Draft Discussion Paper, The World Bank, Washington DC USA.

5 D. Kaimowitz and A. Angelsen. 1999. The World Bank. And *Non-Forest Sector Policies that Affect Forests.* Background Paper, World Bank Forest Policy Implementation Review and Strategy. Center for International Forestry Research (CIFOR), Bogor, Indonesia.

6 The World Resources Institute. 2000. *World Resources 2000–2001; People and Ecosystems.* World Resources Institute, Washington DC, USA, p389.

7 The World Wildlife Fund. 2000. *The Root Causes of Biodiversity Loss.* Wood, A. Stedman-Edwards, P. and Mang, J (Eds). Earthscan Publications Ltd. London and Sterling VA, p. 399.

8 CGIAR. 2000. *The Challenge of Climate Change: Poor Farmers at Risk.* CGIAR Annual Report, Washington DC, USA.

ANNEX 7: Successful World Bank Operations in Agriculture and Rural Development

Project	Project description	Impact on rural poverty
Fostering an enabling environment for broad-based and sustainable rural growth		
Turkey Agricultural Reform Implementation Project (ARIP) 2001	The ARIP is a hybrid operation with investment and adjustment components. Investment components are: to help set up the direct income support (DIS) system; to mitigate potential short-term adverse impacts of subsidy removal; to facilitate the transition to efficient production patterns; and, to build public support for the reforms. Components of the adjustment portion include: the establishment of the National Registry of Farmers; support for land registration; support for agricultural diversification; and, assistance in the implementation of the Law on Agricultural Sales Cooperatives.	A recent supervision report noted that the Government is on track in implementing the key elements of the Program supported by the ARIP as outlined in the Letter of Sector Strategy on Agriculture Sector, and all specific conditions of the tranche release have been met. With payments to over 2.18 million farmers, more than 50% of all farmers eligible for DIS payments have been paid, exceeding by four-fold the requirement that 12.5% of all farmers be paid. In 2001, direct and indirect agricultural subsidies are estimated to have totaled $2.02 billion, compared to $3.17 billion in 2000, and no new direct or indirect agricultural subsidies have been introduced.
Thailand Land Titling Projects 1984 – present	The major objective of the program is to issue to all eligible landholders secure real property rights supported by title deeds registered in decentralized public offices. It has also focused on strengthening the implementing agency, the Department of Lands. A secondary objective was to improve the real property valuation system mainly geared to boosting property tax revenues and facilitating compensation for expropriated properties.	As of 1998 about 5.5 million title deeds had been issued to about 2 million households. This was been achieved with massive community participation in an innovative systematic, village by village, parcel by parcel, approach involving local government and community leaders, the landholders and departmental staff. About 10 million people (16% of the national population) have directly benefited from the program mainly as a result of agricultural productivity increases and improved household incomes. The program has had a demonstration impact world-wide and served as an example for many of the 13 land titling projects under implementation (with Bank support) plus for 10 more now under preparation.
Bulgaria Agricultural Sector Adjustment Loan I&II (ASAL I&II) 1999 – 2002	The ASAL I&II sought to promote efficiency in the agricultural sector, contribute to rural employment generation, better living standards and more consumer choice through components including: promotion of a land market; development of a private grain market; privatizing agricultural enterprises; privatizing decentralizing irrigation system management; improving agricultural financing; and, liberalizing trade and market regulation in most agricultural products.	Under the loans, Bulgaria has transformed into one of the most open economies in the region. The loan has had significant institutional development impact through privatization in the areas of grain marketing, input marketing and farmer services. Grain crop production in 2002 was 4 million metric tons - the highest since the start of reforms following increased access of farmers to high quality seeds and fertilizer. These achievements are particularly significant given the potentially politically challenging nature of the reforms needed.

Project	Project description	Impact on rural poverty
Vietnam Rural Finance Project 1992 – 2001	The Rural Finance Project had several key components: 1. assisting in the transition to a market economy; 2. strengthening the rural finance system through finance targeted to agriculture and small and medium enterprises in rural areas, accompanied by technical assistance; and 3. reducing poverty by promoting growth and enabling the poor to respond to opportunities to improve their welfare. The project comprised the following components: a) a rural development fund; b) fund for the rural poor; c) equipment; d) vehicles; e) training; and f) technical assistance.	Since 1998, nearly 650,000 loans have been made to 250,000 households throughout rural Vietnam through seven participating banks. Thirty percent of borrowers were women. Most loans were small, averaging VND 5.4 million, equal to $360, and applied to expand farm production (crops, livestock and aquaculture), agricultural processing, services and trading. The repayment rate recorded to date is 98%. A study of the socio-economic impacts include: a) outreach to a large number of household borrowers; b) income of household borrowers has been increased remarkably; c) Small and Medium Enterprises helped create about 3,000 new jobs.

Encouraging non-farm economic growth

Colombia Agricultural Technology Development Project (PRONATTA) From 1995	The idea of the project was to bring applied research and extension closer to the priority problems of the target beneficiaries, who should henceforth participate in characterizing, prioritizing, and solving their problems. Main components: ■ A competitive fund in which resources are assigned to proposals responding to the technology needs of small rural producers. ■ An institutional development component to build capacity of municipal and regional institutional mechanisms in which a variety of stakeholders participate, especially small producers.	The competitive fund has expanded to all five regions of Colombia within two years, providing national coverage. In total over 600 projects have been funded with an average expenditure per project of about $50,000 of which nearly half is co-financed by beneficiaries and others. PRONATTA projects are demonstrating impacts in the field in terms of higher productivity, and adoption of sustainable management practices among small producers, especially through reduced use of agricultural chemicals and improved soil management practices. Projects based on similar principles have also been implemented in Peru, Ecuador, and Nicaragua, in different ways in Brazil, Mexico, and some countries in Eastern Europe and Central Asia.
Venezuela Agricultural Extension Project 1995 to 2003	Ensuring extension accountability to clients is a fundamental premise of the new institutional structure supported by the project. ■ Services are planned and implemented at the municipal level to ensure that activities address local problems and opportunities. ■ Extension agents are contracted through private firms and NGOs to provide flexibility and responsiveness to clients. ■ Client participation is encouraged through establishment of Civil Associations for Extension (ACEs). ■ Finally, co-financing by clients and local government ensures that recipients valued services being provided.	The new institutional structure has had a dramatic affect on extension services. Extension agents are now in the countryside, accessible to and in regular contact with clients. Countrywide, 488 extension agents deliver services to 43,000 farmers in 122 municipalities and have introduced over 4,000 innovations in different municipalities. Preliminary impact studies indicate that 73% of municipal projects have had good to excellent impacts on crops and livestock yields and 83% of participants have increased family incomes. ACEs are the most obvious example of increased social capital with 78 established ACEs and a total of over 10,000 members.

16

Project	Project description	Impact on rural poverty
Côte d'Ivoire Second National Agricultural Services Support Project 1998 – ongoing	The objectives of the project are to support sustainable agricultural growth through increases in farm-level productivity by improving the relevance and cost-effectiveness of the national research and extension system. By strengthening farmers' associations, the project fosters their capacity to be effective partners of rural development agents, including government, and provide services to their members and promote private investment in agriculture and related activities.	Workshops designed by farmers' organizations declared roaming herds as the primary issue for sustainable land management and agricultural productivity growth. In cooperation with scientists, the farmers' organizations developed a plan: the technology was not new, but the organization was. They decided to plant thorny hedges and shrubs around the crops to keep out herds. Within six months, they had planted an unprecedented 60 kilometers of hedges. A similar challenge had farmers' organizations establishing regional rules to prevent bush fires—applied and controlled by the farmers themselves.
China Mid-Yangtze Agricultural Development Project From 1991	This project aimed to increase production, productivity and marketability of fruit in the low income areas of Sichuan and Hubei provinces and Chongqing Municipality. The approach included: ■ developing new orchards on heretofore uncultivated hilly slopes and rehabilitating existing ones; ■ increasing abilities to identify, propagate and distribute healthy, disease-free planting material; ■ providing technical assistance for research and extension with staff training in fruit development and marketing; and ■ establishing new and strengthen existing commercially independent Fruit Development Corporations.	The project supported the establishment of almost 12,000 ha of new fruit orchards and rehabilitated a further 2,500 ha. New technologies for virus-free fruit stock production were created and successfully introduced, and profitable new management systems were set up for fruit production and marketing. 300,000 farm families in the project area have benefited from the project - incomes doubled from 1990 to 1995, including that of underemployed and landless farmers. Harvesting and post-harvest activities have, and will increasingly, provide job opportunities in both orchards and packing houses, where 30 percent of the workers are women. The project also reduced soil erosion by promoting the terracing of hilly land and by introducing vetiver grass to stabilize the soil.
Egypt National Drainage Project 1 & 2 1992 and 2000	The projects aimed to improve the technology and management of irrigation and drainage systems to improve agricultural productivity, reclaim land lost to water-logging and salinity, and increase the incomes of smallholder farmers in the country. Phase one targeted 309,600 ha for drainage improvement. The second phase will build on the successes and lessons of the first to target another 700,000 hectares of irrigated land for improved drainage. It will continue to build the capacity of the Egyptian Public Authority for Drainage Projects (EPADP) through a program of institutional support.	Over 5 million acres [hectares?] have been provided with subsurface drainage and 7 million acres are now served by the main drainage system. Crop yields increased by up to 20% for major crops on 7 million acres. Estimates show that the share of improved drainage accounts for 15-25% of the yield increase. Significant advances have been made in recovering the costs for investment and maintenance. Local users are also becoming more involved in operation & maintenance of subsurface schemes through Drainage User Groups/Collection User Groups.

Project	Project description	Impact on rural poverty
India Shrimp and Fish Culture Project 1992 – 2000	The project sought to alleviate rural poverty in five states in India by increasing shrimp and inland fish production and employment. The concept was to tap the potential of generally under-utilized inter-tidal resources for shrimp production and expand fish production from inland water bodies. Activities were targeted on the poorest segments of the rural populations in Bihar, West Bengal, Andhra Pradesh, Orissa and Uttar Pradesh states.	Fish catch has increased by up to 250% (up by 200% in Bihar, 200% in reservoirs and 400% in ox-bow lakes of Uttar Pradesh). In Bihar, Andhra Pradesh and Orissa, approximately 15,000 fisher members of the 118 project-assisted cooperatives are actively engaged in the fishing activity. The per capita income of fishermen has risen by Rs. 6,000 (Uttar Pradesh) to Rs. 13,250 (Bihar). Although the shrimp component was badly effected by an outbreak of White Spot Disease, in shrimp farms that did not develop the disease, the average production exceeded the appraisal target by 34%, with an output of 1.3 tons/hectare/crop.
Mexico Irrigation and Drainage Sector Project 1995 – 2000	The project aims to help the government move from a centralized, grant-based system of irrigation management to a decentralized system based on water user organizations, utilities, and bulk suppliers and a system of cost recovery. The project also sought to increase efficiency of the irrigation system by rehabilitating and upgrading existing schemes.	3.4 million hectares of irrigated land transferred to the management of farmers. Irrigated agricultural production increased from 0.4% (1982-1989) to 4.8% since the transfer program has been in operation (1992-1998). Payment of user fees increased from 20% to 90%. Water user organizations have federated and formed 10 new companies working in the irrigation sector. The government has passed a new Water Law allowing the sale of water use rights and addressing other changes needed for transition to a more commercial agricultural system
Albania Irrigation Rehabilitation Project 1995 – 1996	The project is an irrigation modernization program that deals with reforming institutions by changing the roles of governments, users and private sector: ■ communities operate and maintain the irrigation and drainage systems at the farm through secondary network level; ■ government invests mainly in headwork infrastructure, provide regulation and emergency assistance; and ■ the local private sector is contracted to do the work on most of the activities.	By 1998, the irrigation intensity had increased from 20% in 1993 to 60%. The scope of water user associations (WUA) responsibility far exceeded what was planned. More than 200 WUAs had been established over an area of 100,000 hectares involving 50,000 families, and 42 secondary irrigation canals covering about 98,000 hectares had been transferred to these WUAs. The WUAs collected funds from members for operation and maintenance of the secondary canals. Staff numbers in the public water enterprises were reduced within the project by 40% and 6 federation of WUAs had been established to manage irrigation canals.

Project	Project description	Impact on rural poverty
Mali Office du Niger Consolidation 1990 – 2000	The project sought to reduce poverty, increase agricultural production, and reduce government subsidies and support for agriculture by: ■ providing strong incentives to farmers to increase production, ■ improving the efficiency of irrigation management and ■ creating mechanisms for sustainable irrigation development. The method included reforming the irrigation agency Office du Niger (ON), rehabilitation and modernization of irrigation canals/structures, and agricultural policy reforms (rice price/market liberalization and land tenure).	The government has liberalized the rice trade and markets and sustained that reform and restructured the ON. Rice production increased from 98,000 to 271,000 tons and the production of non-rice crops, such as onions (71,000 tons), garlic (800 tons) and pepper (600 tons) increased. Real per capita income increased by $70/annum. 57 km of canals and main drains were rehabilitated and modernized, and meter fee collection rate increased from 60% to 97%.
Niger Pilot Private Irrigation Project 1995 – 2001	Niger potentially has 270,000 ha of land that can be irrigated, however, only 22% of the potential land is being fully or partially irrigated. To address the situation a private sector irrigation development strategy was launched. The project was implemented by a private irrigation association—the ANPIP—which tested and evaluated new, low-cost technology for small-scale private irrigation and built local capacity in the irrigation sector through private sector development and access to credit	The ANPIP grew gradually from a small group of ten people to 19 decentralized committees comprising 13,500. A follow-up of this campaign facilitated the formation of 1,521 economic interest groups (GIE), comprising 15,000 farmers. The increase in areas cultivated was 63% in the case of the manual technologies, and 24% in the case of the mechanized technologies. The increase in yields of the farms monitored was around 27% for onion and 32% for sweet pepper. These two crops cover 70% of the land areas farmed in the sites covered by the surveys.

Encouraging non-farm economic growth

Peru Rural Roads Rehabilitation and Maintenance Project 1996 – 2001	The overall objective of the project was to provide a well-integrated and reliable rural road system through rehabilitation and maintenance of rural roads and key links connecting to the primary road system. The specific objectives were to reduce transport costs and raise the reliability of vehicular access to expand markets for non-farm and agricultural products and to build up institutional capacity and generate employment for the rehabilitation and maintenance of rural roads.	The project reached 2.8 million people living in 390 villages, surpassing the target of 200 villages. Travel time have decreased markedly and transport tariffs have declined by 15% for freight on busses and 8.6% for trucks on project roads. Improvements of tracks/footpaths to facilitate non-motorized transport have brought the most isolated and the most impoverished communities to the mainstream of economic activity. The project generated 32,300 seasonal unskilled jobs through the rural roads rehabilitation program, and about 4,700 permanent jobs through the development of micro-enterprises that routinely maintain the rehabilitated roads.

Project	Project description	Impact on rural poverty
Latvia Rural Development Project 1998 – 2002	The project's objectives were to lay the groundwork for increasing incomes living standards of the rural population by promoting diversification and growth of economic activities by: ■ strengthening institutional capacity for formulating rural developing strategy and policy; ■ stimulating the flow of commercial bank financing to rural clients by improving the efficiency and self-sustainability of the financial institutions; and ■ facilitating rural business development and continuing support for land reform.	The Commercial Credit Line (CCL) has provided working capital and investment loans for rural enterprises with commercially viable and bankable projects with adequate collateral, financial rates of return, and demonstrated repayment capacity. The Special Credit Line (SCL) has provided small-size loans for diversified rural businesses at prevailing commercial interest rates to first-time borrowers. The government has modernized the Land Book, which has resulted in a boom in property and land markets. From 1997 to 2001, the number of properties registered increased by four-fold, the number of transactions increased five times, and the number of registered mortgages increasing more than eight times.
Bangladesh Third Rural Electrification Project 1990 – 2000	The goal of the Third Rural Electrification Project was to increase the use of electric power through expanding the distribution network and rehabilitating old systems, and to strengthen the institutional capacity for rural electricity delivery, including strengthening the performance of the Rural Electrification Board (REB) and the system of rural electricity cooperatives (RECs).	Consumer connections in the existing and the four new RECs were 60% higher than original estimates, with an excellent mix of households and businesses. Eight times more km of lines were taken over from parastatals (and rehabilitated) than originally planned. Network losses for these lines have fallen from the 30-50% range to 25-30% within 18 months of transition from the parastatal system. Institutionally, all the cooperatives met the financial covenants and management targets agreed and a system of performance targets was put in place in which each cooperative annually discusses and negotiates acceptable targets with the national Rural Electricity Board.

Improving social well-being, managing and mitigating risk, and reducing vulnerability

Tunisia Northwest Mountainous Areas Development Project 1993	The project aimed to alleviate poverty and improve natural resource management through the use of a participatory approach that emphasized community organization and training to increase local capacity to participate. Through these processes, communities would identify development priorities. It recognized the need to target special groups including women, unemployed youth and the landless because of the special challenges they represented in terms of illiteracy, unemployment and lack of access to basic infrastructure and social services.	Family incomes from agricultural production on small farms have recorded real annual growth rates of 6.3%. Increased agricultural production also raised on-farm employment opportunities. The proportion of target groups having difficulty with access to rural roads, potable water, and water for livestock was reduced from the baseline estimate of 48% to 18% by project completion. It is estimated that school building coupled with improvements in rural roads contributed to reducing average illiteracy rates from baseline estimates of 60% to approximately 44% among beneficiary populations.

17

Fostering an enabling environment for broad-based and sustainable rural growth

Project	Project description	Impact on rural poverty
Benin Borgou Region Pilot Rural Support Project 1999 – 2002	Targeting about 250 villages in the Borgou, the project sought to: ■ improve rural communities' capacity to better manage their socio-economic environment by supporting communities' implementation of sustainable development activities; ■ meet the Borgou's immediate needs in service delivery and productive and social investment; and ■ test new resource mobilization and implementation arrangements, as a prelude to Benin's 1999 Decentralization Law.	Two years after implementation 229 communities had completed 296 infrastructure subprojects, of consistently high quality, and made more than 30 natural resource management improvements. Over 14,000 Borgou residents had participated in capacity-building activities, from 5,638 people trained in basic literacy to the 22 women trained as midwives. The construction of new schools brought 5,400 new students to school, representing a five percent increase in the region's school enrollment. By shifting procurement responsibilities to communities, almost all of the sub-project works were contracted to local firms, providing work to 70 to 80 informal enterprises.
Indonesia Village Infrastructure Project I & II 1995 – 1999 1997 – 2001	The projects sought to reduce poverty in poor rural areas in new ways, and more specifically to: ■ promote village participation, empower villagers to decide priority uses of a grant and to implement infrastructure works; ■ provide public infrastructure needed in poor villages; ■ create jobs paid in cash for unemployed/underemployed villagers especially in the seasons of low agricultural activity.	The first project achieved, and in some cases surpassed, its objectives. A total of 1,230 villages compared to 1200 foreseen built a total of: 3,680 km of rural roads; 7,790 meters of bridges; 2,427 water systems; 1,230 communal sanitation units; and 2 piers totaling 61 meters. The benefits from the infrastructure are significant, in addition to the construction having provided employment for cash to villagers. The second project far exceeded its targets: Infrastructure was built in 7,044 villages compared to the intended 2,600. The construction of 15,069 km of roads and 42.5 km of bridges provided critical access to poor communities. With new access roads, transportation costs are estimated to have decreased by 40%. Also, a few villages received electricity connection. Clean drinking water available through construction of 8,722 communal water supply units not only improved health but also reduced the time spent on obtaining water.
Brazil North East Brazil Rural Development and Rural Poverty Alleviation Programs 1985 – present	The NRDP/RPAP programs support community-managed investment in about 100 different types of subprojects in three categories: (a) rural infrastructure (water supply, power); (b) productive activities (minor irrigation schemes, manioc and corn mills, small livestock raising, communal tractors); and (c) social services (for example, day care centers, community centers).	A total of 43,750 community subprojects have been financed at an average value of $26,000 in a total of 1,400 (of 1,665) municipalities, 30,000 community associations and some 1.9 million beneficiary families in Northeast Brazil. Sub-projects include 5,100 community water systems (600,000 families) and 8,000 rural electrification subprojects (320,000 households and 4,300 schools connected). It is estimated that 38% of poor rural families in the region have benefited with at least one subproject from the program.

Project	Project description	Impact on rural poverty
Ghana Community Water Supply & Sanitation Project 2000 – 2003	The program evolved out of a set of national workshops on improving water supply and sanitation in Ghana. It used the community-driven, demand responsive approach where rural communities identified their needs and the level of services they could manage and for which they were willing to pay. The new institutional arrangements included all levels of government, NGOs, communities, and the private sector to provide and co-manage services.	Now two years into implementation, the project has taken off and is working simultaneously in 1000 rural communities. In addition, it increased the capacity of NGOs, so that they could provide technical assistance for water supply and built capacity of small entrepreneurs to supply equipment for the infrastructure. The increased competition, created in response to increased demand from communities, led to a 50% reduction in the price of boreholes. The project also made specific achievements in gender representation with women comprising 50% of water and sanitation committees.

Enhancing the sustainability of natural resource management

Project	Project description	Impact on rural poverty
India Uttar Pradesh Sodic Lands Reclamation Project I 1993 – 2001	The objective of the project was to build upon Uttar Pradesh's programs by developing models for environmental protection and improved agricultural production through reclamation of sodic lands. Additional objectives were to reinforce local institutions to enable effective management of such programs and to improve the incomes of families managing sodic lands.	Project staff worked with farmers to divide the land into parcels and negotiate the complex process of ensuring clear title. Thousands of formerly landless farmers have obtained titles to land. Within six months of the beginning of reclamation activities, productivity and income began to increase: yields of rice and wheat doubled original project estimates, wage rates doubled, and land values quadrupled. Farmers have continued cultivating reclaimed lands even after the withdrawal of project assistance—a strong measure of project sustainability.
India Andhra Pradesh Forestry 1994 – 2000	Primary project objectives were to increase forest productivity and quality, protect the environment, alleviate rural poverty and strengthen/streamline sector policies to be consistent with these objectives. These were to be achieved by (a) introducing local participation in protection and management of public forests; (b) supporting forest regeneration and rehabilitation; (c) supporting biodiversity conservation; (d) increasing private participation in sector development; and (e) improving public forest management and development.	Under the project, 2,666 community groups (VSSs) have been established for protection and management of forest resources and 849,000 ha were brought under improved management and protection. Four new protected areas (PAs) were created; 11 PAs were brought under improved management and protection with positive effects on biodiversity conservation. There has been an improvement in family incomes (average increase in income within sampled VSSs was Rs. 5,600 per annum) and in the financial independence of women (1,699 women's thrift groups were formed).

173

Project	Project description	Impact on rural poverty
Turkey Eastern Anatolia Watershed Rehabilitation 1993 – 1994	The project sought to restore sustainable land-use management to degraded watersheds in three provinces of the Upper Euphrates River Basin, and increase the incomes of the local population living in these areas, which are among the poorest in Turkey. To do this it had to help restore sustainable range, forest and farming activities, reduce soil degradation, erosion and sedimentation in reservoirs.	The project has reached about 400,000 people living in over 50 watersheds (and will now be adopted in up to 20 more provinces in a follow-up operation). Integrated management plans were prepared including improved management and cultivation of fodder, reforestation, soil conservation, improved arable farming and fruit farming, construction of ponds for supplementary irrigation, bee-keeping, and gully protection. It improved opportunity and access to resources through targeted interventions, was cost-effective and could be maintained despite a difficult macro-economic environment.
China Loess Plateau Watershed Rehabilitation Project 1994 – present	Erosion causes 1.6 billion tons of sediment to flow every year from the Loess Plateau of northwest China into the Yellow River, creating tremendous downstream flood risk. The objectives of the project were to increase agricultural production and incomes through a more efficient and sustainable use of land and water resources in tributaries of the Yellow Plateau.	Farmers not only provided knowledge and planning, but also manual labor on their own lands. Today, the project has completed over 80,000 ha of terracing. Farmers have replanted 150,000 ha with forest trees and income-generating shrubs and trees. Crop yields have doubled and even tripled in some micro-catchments due to the terracing and conservation techniques. Half a million farmers have improved their standards of living as a result of this project.

174

Printed in the United Kingdom
by Lightning Source UK Ltd.
116589UKS00001B/10

9 780821 354599